30
BICYCLE TOURS
in Wisconsin

30

BICYCLE TOURS
in Wisconsin

*lakes, forests, and
glacier-carved countryside*

*Jane E. Hall
and Scott D. Hall*

photographs by the authors

Backcountry Publications
Woodstock · Vermont

An invitation to the reader

Although it is unlikely that the roads you cycle on these tours will change much with time, some road signs, landmarks, and other items may. If you find that such changes have occurred on these routes, please let the author and publisher know, so that corrections may be made in future editions. Other comments and suggestions are also welcome. Address all correspondence to:

Editor, 30 Bicycle Tours™ Series
Backcountry Publications
P.O. Box 175
Woodstock, Vermont 05091-0175

Library of Congress Cataloging-in-Publication Data

Hall, Jane E.
30 bicycle tours in Wisconsin : lakes, forests, and glacier-carved countryside / Jane E. Hall and Scott D. Hall.
     p.   cm.
ISBN 0-88150-286-3
1. Bicycle touring—Wisconsin—Guidebooks. 2. Wisconsin—Guidebooks. I. Hall, Scott D. II. Title. III. Title: Thirty bicycle tours in Wisconsin.
GV1045.5.W6H35   1994
796.6'4'09775—dc20   93-48061
      CIP

Quotation on page 9 from *Travels with Charley* by John Steinbeck, copyright © 1961, 1962 by The Curtis Publishing Co.; © 1962 by John Steinbeck; renewed © 1990 by Elaine Steinbeck, Thom Steinbeck, and John Stenbeck IV. Used by permission of Viking Penguin, a division of Penguin Books USA Inc.

10 9 8 7 6 5 4 3 2

Printed in the United States of America

Design by Sally Sherman
Cover photo by Jane Hall
Interior photographs by the authors
Maps by Dick Widhu, © 1994 The Countryman Press, Inc.

Published by Backcountry Publications
A division of The Countryman Press, Inc.
P.O. Box 175
Woodstock, VT 05091

Dedication

To Margaret Guthrie for encouraging us to get started on this project and for coaching us along the way. To Carl Taylor and the people at Countryman Press for making our first venture in publishing a joyful process. And to Eric Iverson, Bike Wisconsin/Encompass Cycling Vacations routing manager, intrepid cyclist, and lover of Wisconsin, whose spirit never flagged in pursuit of the perfect back road. And finally, to all of the other Bike Wisconsin/Encompass Cycling Vacations tour leaders, whose efforts through the years contributed to the development of the routes in this book.

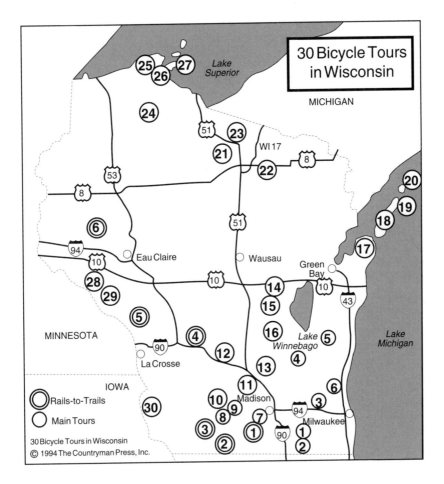

Contents

Introduction

Introduction

We moved quickly northward, heading for Wisconsin…a noble land of good fields and magnificent trees, a gentleman's countryside, neat and white-fenced…I had never been to Wisconsin, but all my life I had heard about it, and eaten its cheeses, some of them as good as any in the world. And I must have seen pictures. Everyone must have. Why then was I unprepared for the beauty of the region, for its variety of field and hill, forest and lake?

—John Steinbeck
Travels with Charley, In Search of America

Geography

Wisconsin's shape resembles a mitten—a fitting symbol since its inhabitants are often snowbound from November to March. The state measures about 450 miles from the most northerly to the most southerly point, and approximately 250 miles, east to west. The thumb of the mitten is the popular Door County peninsula, surrounded by the waters of Lake Michigan and Green Bay. This narrow strip of land, with its abundant orchards, artists' galleries, and working lighthouses, is one of the state's most popular cycling areas.

The tip of the glove extends its icy fingers into Lake Superior, the largest and most mysterious of the Great Lakes and the second largest inland body of water in the world. The northern third—above the knuckles—is blanketed by state and national forest land, where tall pines and pristine lakes lure hunters and anglers, as well as cyclists. In the palm sits rich, rolling farmland dotted with red barns, Lake Wobegon–like towns and winding farm-to-market roads. Along the western border lies the mighty Mississippi River, where high bluffs and hidden valleys challenge even the mountain-bred bicyclist.

There are few rides in this book where you won't come in contact with some body of water. With over 15,000 sparkling inland lakes, there's always one nearby for a refreshing plunge or impromptu lakeside picnic. The state borders on 860 miles of Great Lakes shoreline and boasts 190 miles of Mississippi River frontage. Hundreds of square miles of marsh and wetlands are resting places for migratory birds and home to myriad other creatures. Most famous of these is Horicon Marsh, where over 200,000 Canada geese stop annually in October for a brief respite en route to their wintering grounds.

Geology

Much of Wisconsin's landscape is a gift of the glaciers. When the last major ice mass covering the continent disappeared about 10,000 years ago, it so transformed the state that it is referred to as the Wisconsin Glacier. During the melting process, the glacier sprinkled its burden of unsorted boulders, rocks, and sand across the state. This glacial till, or drift, covers approximately two-thirds of Wisconsin, accounting for the state's fertile soil and gently rolling terrain. The most prominent glacial features are seen in the northern and southern units of the Kettle Moraine forest in southeastern Wisconsin.

In sharp contrast is Wisconsin's southwest corner, which stands untempered by glacial ice. Referred to as the driftless area, this part of the state is characterized by steep hills and narrow winding valleys, reminiscent of Vermont. The Door County peninsula also escaped glaciation. Its solid limestone bedrock, an extension of the Niagara escarpment, separated the advancing ice mass into two distinct paths or lobes that now make up the waters of Green Bay and Lake Michigan.

Early History

Wisconsin's original inhabitants were comprised of eight major Native American tribes—the Winnebago, Menominee, Chippewa, Potawatomi, Fox, Sauk, and Dakota. The culture remains strong today and several of this book's rides pass through reservation land, where customs are preserved through festivals and powwows. Other routes pass by impressive tribal burial mounds.

The first European to reach the area was Frenchman Jean Nicolet. Nicolet landed on the shores of Green Bay in 1634, dressed in a mandarin robe and convinced he had finally found the elusive passage to the Orient. He was welcomed as a god by the Winnebago tribe and while disappointed not to find the wealth and spices of China, he was impressed with the land's abundance of fish, fur, and timber.

Next came the fur traders, who were given rights to their bounty as an incentive for colonizing what had become known as New France. Trading posts were established in 1669 at LaPointe, on Madeline Island in Lake Superior, and at Green Bay, at the base of the Door County peninsula. Each party of fur traders was accompanied by several Jesuit missionaries, whose purpose was to convert the native population to Christianity. Many of the missionaries were explorers in their own right, including Father Jacques Marquette, who along with Louis Joliet discovered the Mississippi River in 1673.

Ethnic Heritage

A look at the Wisconsin map reveals a proud European heritage. Rhinelander, New Berlin, New Lisbon, Pulaski, Scandinavia, Rome, Hollandale, Germantown, Brussels, and Luxemburg are only a few of many Wisconsin towns settled during the nineteenth century's massive migration from Europe to the western Great Lakes states.

Lumber and mining industries recruited heavily in the Scandinavian countries, accounting for the predominance of Norwegian and Swedish surnames in Wisconsin today. Eventually saving enough to purchase small farms, Scandinavian settlers built the state's agricultural base. It was the Danes who introduced large-scale dairy farming to Wisconsin. Icelandic immigrants brought fishing expertise to the turbulent waters around Washington Island, which remains the country's largest Icelandic settlement. The Germans came with an aptitude for grain farming and a thirst for beer. Milwaukee soon became a brewing center dominated by immigrants named Pabst and Schlitz.

Road System

Thanks to a prosperous dairy industry and the need to get milk to market daily, Wisconsin is laced with an extensive network of smoothly paved secondary roads, most with little traffic other than a sputtering tractor or stray Holstein. State and national forest roads in the northern part of the state offer both paved and unpaved options through unspoiled wilderness. Wisconsin has a bicycle-friendly reputation and motorists generally give cyclists a welcoming wave and a wide berth.

Wisconsin roads are excellently maintained, though harsh winter weather necessitates continuous maintenance. Road repairs and detours are frequent during the summer season. Occasionally major highways are detoured onto smaller county roads, resulting in more traffic than usual. A listing of major highway construction projects is available from the state Department of Transportation and can be useful in predicting such detours.

The Wisconsin State Legislature has mandated that five-foot shoulders be added to all state highways carrying more than 1,000 cars and 25 cyclists per day. The improved shoulders are being added as these roads require resurfacing. The road labeling system in Wisconsin is simple and most intersections are well-marked. State highways in Wisconsin are designated with one- or two-digit numbers; county highways are designated with single, double or triple letters; and town roads are given descriptive names. Nearly any county or town road, chosen at random, will be suitable for cycling. State highways are appropriate only for short distances, except where paved shoulders have been added.

The state has also designated a number of Wisconsin's most scenic roads as Rustic Roads. To qualify, these roads must exhibit "rugged terrain, native vegetation, native wildlife, or open areas with agricultural vistas." The Rustic Road must also be "lightly traveled and not scheduled for improvements which would change its rustic characteristics." Speed limits are restricted to 45 miles per hour and roads are marked with a brown and yellow sign. (See *Resources.*)

Wisconsin is a leader in the national movement to turn abandoned railroad beds into bicycle trails. Completed in 1965, the state's Elroy–Sparta trail was one of the first rails-to-trails conversions in the country. The state has now developed eight such trails. The flat terrain (no more than 3 percent grade) and absence of vehicle traffic make the trails ideal for families with children, beginning bicyclists, and those looking for a leisurely ride.

The trail surface is a finely screened limestone that is suitable for hybrid and mountain bikes. Touring bikes should be equipped with 1⅛- or 1¼-inch tires. A daily or yearly trail pass must be purchased to use the trails. A booklet describing all of Wisconsin's state park trails is available from the Wisconsin Department of Transportation. (See *Resources.*) A Rails-to-Trails sampler of our favorite trail rides is included in this book.

Weather and Seasons

The cycling season in Wisconsin generally runs from early May through late October. The occasional warm, sunny day in April or November is appreciated and relished.

The spring cyclist gets a jump on the tourist traffic, a headstart on summer fitness plans, and the season's special rewards—a trillium blossom peeking out along a wooded roadside or a fawn scampering across the road. Farm fields are a patchwork panorama of green in every shade and the air smells of fertile, freshly tilled soil. Daytime temperatures average 55 to 75 degrees, with occasional rain showers.

June, July, and August are prime cycling months with daytime temperatures ranging in the 70s, 80s, and occasionally 90s, often with high humidity. These are great months to take advantage of Wisconsin's many clear swimming lakes and to indulge in its creamy, rich ice cream. In the summer you will happen upon small town festivals, auctions, flea markets, and band concerts. Bratwurst and sweet corn are always available for an impromptu lunch.

Autumn is both the most beautiful and most fleeting of seasons for cycling in Wisconsin. Labor Day leaves the bugs and tourists behind and small towns take on an added charm as they return to a slower, post-season pace. Roadside stands overflow with fresh produce at harvest time and you can spin your wheels to a serenade of southbound geese overhead.

The color calendar in Wisconsin spans from mid-September in the northern third of the state to a mid-October peak in the southern third. The leaves change later on the Bayfield and Door County peninsulas, because of the warming effect of surrounding water. Daytime temperatures range from 55 to 70 degrees in September and 45 to 60 degrees in October.

Selecting Your Bike

A bicycle properly fitted and tuned is the key to a positive cycling experience. The rides described here can best be enjoyed on either a touring bike or a hybrid bike. Though all of the rides are on paved roads, a mountain bike would also be appropriate for the shorter tours.

A touring bike looks like a racing bike, but has a longer frame, allowing you to stretch out and distribute your weight across the entire frame and both wheels. This provides stability if carrying panniers and camping equipment on longer tours. Touring bikes generally have dropped (ram's horn) handlebars, which allow you a choice of hand positions and let you keep a low profile when riding against a strong wind. We recommend that a touring bike be equipped with 1⅛- or 1¼-inch tires—these will see you through the occasional gravel stretch or cavernous pothole.

The hybrid or cross bicycle combines the comfort and durability of a mountain bike with the lighter weight and riding ease of a touring bike. The hybrid is usually equipped with upright handlebars and gear levers on or below the handlebar grips. With gear levers readily accessible, it's possible to shift without moving your hands. This can also be a drawback, as the lack of variations in hand position can result in sore hands, arms, and shoulders. Handlebar extensions, available as an optional accessory for most hybrids, help alleviate this problem.

Many people prefer the upright riding position because it provides a full view of the scenery, without straining the neck or back. However, it's important to note that a higher profile translates into more wind resistance. Hybrids are generally equipped with 1⅜-inch tires, adequate for any road surface including rough gravel.

While Wisconsin is not a mountainous state, most people are surprised at the hilliness of the terrain. Whether you choose a touring bicycle or hybrid bicycle, we recommend that you select a bike with a triple chain ring. The triple chain ring will be found on a bike with 18 or 21 gears. You'll find that the smallest of the three chain rings (also called the granny gear) is a lifesaver when climbing the short steep hills of the Kettle Moraine State Forest or the bluffs along the Mississippi River.

Other Equipment

Here are a few other items that will make your ride safer and more enjoyable.

A helmet is your most important piece of bicycling equipment. It has been proven repeatedly that helmets greatly reduce the risk of a fatal head injury resulting from a fall or collision. Many people mistakenly believe that if they are experienced riders, they do not need to wear a helmet. Another fallacy is that helmets need not be worn when cycling close to home or on off-road trails. The fact is that most accidents are not related to rider ability, but are "freak" occurrences that can't be predicted or controlled.

The good news is that helmets are becoming lighter and more comfortable every year. Whether you choose a styrofoam-type soft-shell helmet or a puncture-proof hard-shell helmet, be sure that it meets Snell and ANSI safety specifications. A helmet must fit well and be adjusted properly to be effective. It should rest evenly on your head above your eyebrows (some have a tendency to tilt back) and the straps should be secure. A good test is to open your mouth wide—if the helmet is properly adjusted you should feel a slight pressure on top of your head.

A good pair of sunglasses not only protects your eyes from the sun but from flying insects, dirt, and other airborne debris. If you look at the windshield of your auto in the summer, you will understand why glasses are important.

Padded cycling gloves will help alleviate sore palms, elbows, and shoulders. They will also cushion your hands in a fall.

A rearview mirror prevents you from looking over your shoulder for traffic, causing you to veer out into the road. Mirrors are available in many styles. Some models fit onto your brake hoods or handlebars; others attach to your helmet.

A handlebar bag is handy for carrying a camera, wallet, rain gear, snacks, and other incidental items. Most come with a transparent vinyl map case on top. This is a convenient way to carry your directions or map.

Bicycle computers record your mileage for a day trip, along with your average speed and the total distance covered over a longer journey. Because this book gives you the cumulative mileage for each turn and point of interest, a computer makes it easier to follow the written directions. One caution though—don't focus on your computer or you'll miss the passing scenery.

A pump, a spare inner tube, a patch kit, and a few basic tools are essential if your ride takes you out in the country, away from bicycle shops and gas stations. Be sure that your pump is compatible with the valve on the type of inner tube you use; there are two types—Schrader and Presta. A basic tool kit should include an Allen wrench set, tire levers, chain tool, adjustable wrench, Phillips screwdriver, and regular screwdriver.

A bicycle lock is important if you plan to stop for any length of time.

A first-aid kit that includes basic supplies such as Band-aids, gauze bandages, antiseptic, aspirin, and sunscreen is good insurance. Make up your own kit and keep it in your handlebar bag at all times, replenishing items as needed.

While no special clothing is required for cycling, there are a few items you may want to consider for reasons of comfort. Nearly every touring cyclist ends up riding in the rain at some time or another. Adequate rain gear makes cycling in wet weather bearable and, in many cases, even enjoyable. Raincoats consist of two types, breathable and nonbreathable. Breathable rainwear is preferable, since it keeps the rain out, and also lets your perspiration escape. Less expensive vinyl raincoats will do the job if you ride only periodically. Ponchos are usually not suitable for cycling, since they tear easily and tend to act as a sail in high winds.

Saddle soreness is a common problem for beginning cyclists and can be alleviated somewhat by using a gel bicycle saddle and/or by wearing padded cycling shorts.

Weather in Wisconsin often changes quickly. Always bring an extra layer of clothing along, just in case. Mornings can be quite cool, especially in the spring and fall. If you are planning a trip during the spring or fall, include tights or narrow warm-up pants, full-fingered gloves, and a headband or cap that can be worn under your helmet. Cyclists who experience soreness in the feet or ankles may choose to wear cycling shoes, which have an extra-firm sole.

Bicycle Safety

While bicycling is a fun and relaxing activity, it is important to be alert and attentive at all times. The following safety guidelines are worth reviewing periodically, even if you are an experienced cyclist.

Riding in control

Never ride at a speed faster than is comfortable for you. On downhill stretches, keep your weight to the back of the saddle and pump your brakes to prevent overheating. Watch for sand or loose gravel, especially on corners. This is especially important in the spring months in Wisconsin, when sand deposited by snowplows during the winter remains on the road.

Obstacles

Anticipate obstacles by looking well ahead of your bicycle. Scan the road for rough spots, debris, potholes, glass, and other items. Always check the traffic behind you, using your rearview mirror, before steering around these areas. Place your wheels perpendicular to railroad tracks and drainage grates.

Riding single file

Wisconsin state law requires that cyclists ride single file. Allow an ample distance between your bike and those ahead of you. When stopping to rest or chat, stay well off the road.

Hand and spoken signals

Let motorists and other cyclists know of your intention to turn, change lanes, pass, or stop by using hand and spoken warnings. It is customary to say "car up" and "car back" to warn people around you of oncoming traffic.

Dogs

Expect to come across dogs in Wisconsin's rural farm areas. If you are chased by a dog, remain calm, stop pedaling, and dismount your bicycle. Place the bicycle between you and the dog. Point at the animal and shout "stay" or "go home" in a commanding voice. Once the dog has quieted and retreated, walk slowly away without turning your back to it. Never attempt to outpedal a dog or to spray water or repellent from a moving bicycle. These actions are likely to cause a fall or to aggravate the dog into attacking cyclists riding with you.

Loose clothing

Watch out for loose clothing that can catch in moving parts. Shoelaces that wrap around pedals are particularly hazardous—they should be double-tied and tucked into your shoes.

Severe weather

Thunderstorms and tornadoes are common during Wisconsin's hot and humid summer weather. If you see severe weather approaching, or if you hear weather-warning sirens, seek shelter immediately. Don't hesitate to ask if you can wait out the storm in someone's barn or garage if you are in a remote area.

Slippery pavement

Brakes don't function well on wet roads that may be covered with a slippery layer of grease and oil. Test your brakes frequently for effectiveness and pump them lightly and continually, well in advance of your planned stop. In the fall, wet leaves can make road surfaces treacherous.

Food and water

Always carry a water bottle and some light snacks with you. A second water bottle is advisable if you're biking in an area with few services. You will maintain a higher energy level if you eat small amounts throughout the day and drink regularly, beginning well before you become thirsty.

How to Choose the Right Trip for You

When deciding which tour to embark on, you should consider both the distance and terrain. Remember that a 20-mile ride in hilly terrain may be more demanding than a 35-mile ride on level terrain. A strong wind also leads to faster fatigue and should be factored into your decision about how far to go.

A beginning rider or someone who exercises only occasionally will probably find a 20- to 25-mile ride to be quite satisfying. Novices may also find it useful to join organized tour groups that offer the "safety net" of tour leaders and a support van until they gain more confidence and endurance. An intermediate cyclist or a person who engages in aerobic exercise regularly will comfortably ride 30 to 40 miles a day, with enough time for lunch and sightseeing/shopping stops. While advanced cyclists frequently ride 50, 75, or even 100 miles in a day, these distances are goals to work up to gradually. Keeping a mileage log is a good way to track your progress throughout the season and to better determine your ability level.

Using the Directions and Maps

When using this book, we suggest that you read the descriptive information about each tour first. This will give you a feeling for the area and help you decide if the scenery and attractions are of interest to you. Then, look at the map for a general "lay of the land."

While cycling, we have found that it is easier to follow written directions than a map. Keep your map handy, however, in case you get turned around or confused, and want to refer to it.

Mileages may vary slightly depending on variations in calibrations of computers, whether or not you ride in a straight line (most of us don't), and how often you take detours or wrong turns. Occasionally road signs become twisted or become dorm room souvenirs. If what you see doesn't jive with your internal compass, ask the first person you meet for directions. You will get back on course quickly and probably have a pleasant conversation too.

Most computers can be switched off temporarily when you detour off the route and restarted when you return to the route. For tours that begin at Wisconsin state parks, mileage is calculated from the ranger station. Mileage for tours beginning at smaller parks is calculated from the park exit.

If you want to add to, or improvise on, the rides presented in this book, you may wish to carry a detailed map of the area in which you are cycling. Other map sources are listed in Resources.

Contact the local chambers of commerce for a complete list of lodging and dining options. The ones mentioned in the rides have special qualities and are ones we would recommend to a friend.

Resources

Wisconsin Bicycle Escape Guide

This four-map set details more than 10,000 miles of bicycle routes on lightly traveled secondary roads throughout the state. Contact the Wisconsin Division of Tourism Development, P.O. Box 7606, Madison, WI 53707, (800) 432-TRIP. Free.

Biking Wisconsin's State Park Trails

This 32-page booklet describes Wisconsin's eight off-road trails constructed on abandoned railroad beds. Contact the Wisconsin Department of Transportation, P.O. Box 7910, Madison, WI 53707, (608) 266-2181. Cost is $4.15, including tax and postage.

Wisconsin's Rustic Roads...

This 66-page booklet provides maps and descriptions of the state's 60 designated Rustic Roads. These roads were selected for their exceptional scenic and historic interest. Contact the Rustic Roads Board, Wisconsin Department of Transportation, P.O. Box 7913, Madison, WI 53707, (608) 266-0639.

The Wisconsin Atlas and Gazetteer

This comprehensive atlas provides a detailed rendering of national, state, county and town roads, as well as topographical information. It is of special value to the cyclist, because it indicates which roads are paved and which are not. Contact DeLorme Mapping, P.O. Box 298, Freeport, ME 04032, (207) 865-4171.

Wisconsin County Maps

Maps of Wisconsin's 72 counties are available from the Wisconsin Department of Transportation, Document Sales Office, 3617 Pierstorff Street, Madison, WI 53707, (608) 246-3265 or by contacting the county clerk at the courthouse in an individual county.

Milwaukee Map Service, Inc.

This company puts out a very detailed set of maps dividing the state into four quadrants—northeast, northwest, southeast and southwest. Contact Milwaukee Map Service, Inc., 4519 West North Avenue, Milwaukee, WI 53208, (414) 445-7361.

76 Bike Tour

This map shows the 76-mile bicentennial bicycle trail established by the Milwaukee County Parks Department. The trail utilizes off-road bicycle trails, park paths and municipal streets. Contact the Milwaukee County Department of Parks, Recreation and Culture, 9480 Watertown Plank Road, Milwaukee, WI 53226, (414) 257-6100.

Madison Daytrippers

This is a packet including lodging information, as well as maps and directions for approximately 10 day rides in the Madison area. They range from an eight-mile ride around the University of Wisconsin campus to a 70-plus-mile tour to Devil's Lake. Contact the Greater Madison Convention and Visitors Bureau, 615 East Washington Avenue, Madison, WI 53703, (800) 373-MDSN or (608) 255-2537.

SOUTHEASTERN
WISCONSIN

1
Southern Kettle Moraine State Forest

Distance: *31.1 miles*
Terrain: *Rolling*

Ice Age glaciers created the gentle undulations of the Kettle Moraine countryside, where you're nearly always climbing the ridge of an esker or coasting down a kame. In the springtime, the wooded roadsides are decorated with the soft pastels of columbines and pasqueflowers; later in the season, the color is intense and fiery as the hardwoods put on their autumn finery.

The forest is interspersed with fertile farmland and vast marshy areas. Springs that once drew visitors from around the world to "take the waters" at Waukesha County's fashionable health spas now trickle unattended into secluded trout streams.

Nearly all of this tour takes place within the boundaries of the state forest; acorn-shaped markers along the road point out portions of the popular Kettle Moraine Scenic Drive. If you ride a mountain bike, you might wish to combine this route with some off-road cycling at one of several popular mountain bike trails along the way. Directions are given if you wish to visit Old World Wisconsin, one of the country's premier outdoor living museums, while on on the tour. Set out early if you plan to do this—it takes a minimum of four hours to tour the entire complex.

The tour begins at Ottawa Lake State Park. From I-94, take WI 67 south for about 15 miles, to County Highway ZZ. Turn right onto County Highway ZZ, following signs to the the park. Good picnic facilities, a swimming beach, rest rooms, and water are available.

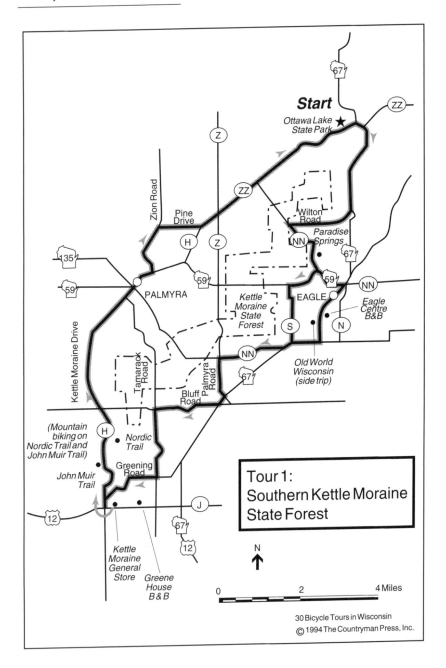

Start

Ottawa Lake
State Park ★

ZZ

67

Z

ZZ

Zion Road

Pine
Drive

Wilton
Road

*Paradise
Springs*

H   Z

NN

67

35

59

59

PALMYRA

*Kettle
Moraine
State
Forest*

EAGLE

59

NN

*Eagle
Centre
B&B*

S

N

Kettle Moraine Drive

NN

*Old World
Wisconsin
(side trip)*

Tamarack Road

Palmyra Road

67

Bluff
Road

*(Mountain
biking on
Nordic Trail and
John Muir Trail)*

H

Nordic
Trail

Greening
Road

*John Muir
Trail*

12

J

**Tour 1:
Southern Kettle Moraine
State Forest**

67

*Kettle
Moraine
General
Store*

12

*Greene
House
B & B*

N
↑

0   2   4 Miles

30 Bicycle Tours in Wisconsin
© 1994 The Countryman Press, Inc.

24

0.0   *Left from the park onto County Highway ZZ.*

0.2   *Right onto WI 67/County Highway AA.*

This is a busy road, but has a good shoulder.

1.5   *McClintock Springs Children's Fishing Area.*

1.9   *Wayside with water.*

2.7   *Pass Wilton Road, on your left.*

2.9   *Right onto Wilton Road.*

4.6   *Left onto County Highway NN where Wilton ends (no sign).*

5.8   *Paradise Springs Nature Area is to your left.*

This is a catch-and-release trout fishing area. Ages 16 to 64 need a trout stamp, available from the Department of Natural Resources; the season is January 1 to September 30. There is also a well-designed nature trail that illustrates how two types of stream vegetation, veronica and elodea, shelter smaller trout and provide food for insects eaten by fish.

The property was originally owned by Louis J. Petit, owner of Morton Salt Company. The clear pool of water known as Paradise Springs is four feet deep, 47 degrees in temperature, and pumps out 30,000 gallons of water per hour. The springs are formed when rainwater and melting snow seep into hills and ridges and build up an underground water table that is higher in elevation than the water table in the surrounding lowlands. Water from the elevated water table follows sand and gravel layers and seeps from the hill as a spring. There is a fieldstone spring house built by Petit in the 1930s, which originally had a wooden dome roof.

Photos show the area when it was a resort and popular honeymoon spot in the 1930s. In later years, a bottling plant for spring water, a horse track, and golf course were located on the property. Across the road is the hand-hewn Gotten Cabin, built by a Prussian immigrant in the 1850s.

Turn left from Paradise Springs, continuing on County Highway NN.

6.2   *Right onto WI 59.*

At this point, it's possible to make a side trip to Old World Wisconsin. See directions below.

7.1   *Left onto County Highway S.*

7.9   *Kettle Moraine Ranch offers horseback riding.*

8.6   *Right onto WI 67.*

8.9   *Right onto County Highway NN.*

10.6 *Left onto Palmyra Road where County Highway NN ends.*

County Highway Z goes right and Little Prairie Road goes straight here.

11.6 *Right onto WI 67 in Little Prairie.*

11.8 *Right onto Bluff Road.*

13.6 *Left onto Tamarack Road.*

15.4 *Right onto Greening Road.*

16.8 *Left onto County Highway H.*

17.0 *The Kettle Moraine General Store.*

This is a friendly store featuring health foods and natural beauty aids, run by Mike Bettinger, an avid bicyclist and bike advocate. Cyclists gravitate toward the smoothies and a sandwich called the "Mexican Smile." Mike can also provide a map of mountain bike trails in the Kettle Moraine forest, give you an update on trail conditions, and assist with bike repairs.

The Greene House Bed & Breakfast, (414) 495-8771, serves hearty home-cooked meals and has a "guitar gallery" featuring vintage instruments. It is located east of the General Store on WI 12.

To continue, backtrack from the store and head north on County Highway H.

The ups and downs of the Kettle Moraine countryside

18.6   *The John Muir and Nordic Trails are popular for mountain biking and cross-country skiing. There are rest rooms here.*

22.5   *County Highway H becomes West Main Street as you enter Palmyra.*

22.7   *Palmyra Village Park is to your right.*

23.0   *Downtown Palmyra (all two blocks of it!) has several small cafés and an ice cream parlor.*

23.8   *Left onto Zion Road.*

25.2   *Right onto Pine Drive.*

26.4   *Left where Pine Drive ends on County Highway H (no sign).*

27.0   *County Highway H becomes County Highway ZZ, where County Highway Z intersects. Continue straight on County Highway ZZ here.*

31.1   *Left into Ottawa Lake State Park.*

Old World Wisconsin Side Trip

Turn Left onto WI 59 and follow it into the town of Eagle, then turn right onto WI 67. You'll pass The Eagle Centre House, (414) 363-4700, a circa-1846 stagecoach inn that offers bed-and-breakfast lodging. Follow WI 67 south to the Old World Wisconsin entrance. Use caution on WI 59 and WI 67; both are busy roads.

This 560-acre outdoor living museum consists of about 50 historic buildings constructed by Wisconsin's immigrant settlers. The buildings have been moved from their original locations throughout Wisconsin and carefully reassembled at the Old World complex. Clusters of buildings represent 10 ethnic farmsteads and an 1870s crossroads village. Norwegian, Danish, Finnish, Polish, and German areas are among the nationalities included. Authentically costumed staff go about their daily chores—preparing meals, tending barns and livestock, and sowing and cultivating crops. Special events mark the changing of seasons. The Clausing Barn Restaurant serves cafeteria-style food with an ethnic twist.

To rejoin the route, turn right onto WI 67 at the exit and continue to County Highway NN. Refer to the 8.9 mile mark for the remaining directions. The detour will add about two miles to your total mileage.

Bicycle Repair Services

Bicycle Doctor
1089 Summit Avenue, Ocononowoc, WI
(414) 567-6656

Cooney Cycle Center
101 South Main Street, Oconomowoc, WI
(414) 567-7398

La Grange General Store
WI 12 and County Highway H, La Grange, WI
(414) 495-8600

2
Delavan/Lake Geneva

Distance: *50.5 Miles*
Terrain: *Flat to gently rolling*

Lake Geneva, a thriving summer resort community just over the Wisconsin border from Illinois, was launched as an aristocratic holiday spot in 1871 when wealthy Chicagoans set up households here in the aftermath of the Great Chicago Fire. The lakeshore is lined with opulent mansions that once belonged to the likes of Wrigley, Maytag, Marshall Field, Morton, Swift, Borden, and Calvin Coolidge, who made Lake Geneva the site of the summer White House. Illinois license plates still predominate—it's a convenient hour-and-a-half jaunt from Chicago.

The nearby village of Delavan, with its cobblestone main street, has a contrasting low-key demeanor. It is best known as the winter headquarters for over 25 circuses between 1847 and 1894 and the birthplace of P.T. Barnum's Greatest Show on Earth. Delavan was chosen by circus troupes for its abundant pasture land, pure lakes, and four-season climate, necessary for the well-being of both draft and performing horses. This route's level to slightly rolling terrain passes a number of horse farms and riding stables.

The ride begins at the Veteran's Memorial Park in Delavan, located on WI 11 (Walworth Street) just past the Wisconsin School for the Deaf. You will find ample parking, rest rooms, a picnic shelter, and a small swimming beach.

0.0 Left from the parking lot onto WI 11 (Walworth Street) and follow it through downtown Delavan.

> Signs of Delavan's circus heritage can be seen as you ride along Walworth Street where the pavement gives way to a

bumpy brick surface for several blocks. A statue of Romeo, a circus elephant, is in the town center. Romeo was 11 feet tall and weighed more than 10,000 pounds. He was one of the star attractions of the Mabie Brothers Circus in the early 1800s. His mate, Juliet, is buried at the bottom of Delavan Lake.

The Clown Hall of Fame and Research Center, (414) 728-9075, is just north of the corner of Walworth Street and Third Avenue. The center pays tribute to outstanding clown performers, operates a living museum of clowning with resident performers, and maintains a national archive of clown artifacts and history.

0.6   *Continue on WI 11 where WI 50 turns right. After this turn, WI 11 veers left and becomes Racine Street.*

1.3   *Right onto South Wright Street at the streetlight, where County O turns left. Follow for .7 mile to the outskirts of town.*

2.1   *Cross WI 50 and continue straight on Borg Road.*

The Geneva Lakes Kennel Club, (800) 477-4552 or (414) 728-8000, is on your left. Greyhound racing dates back to ancient Egypt. The track is open year-round, daily except for Monday, with post times at 1 and 7 P.M. Visit the adoption center for retired greyhounds; they are affectionate animals that make good pets.

3.2   *Left onto Linn Road just past the Kennel Club. Follow for .8 mile to the shore of Delavan Lake.*

4.0   *Right onto Shore Road by the Good Times Pub.*

Shore Road weaves around as it follows the north shoreline of Delavan Lake. You'll pass many large estates with idyllic names like Fair Knolls and Villa Clare. Some of the larger properties have been divided into lots for summer cottages.

4.5   *Left at the T intersection. Here Shore Drive becomes North Shore Drive, which weaves along the lakeshore.*

7.2   *Left onto County Highway O (unmarked), by the Wagon Wheel Supper Club.*

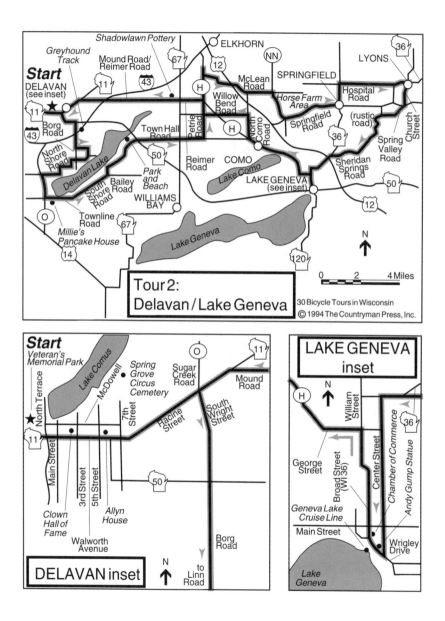

Southeastern Wisconsin

Shadowlawn Pottery
ELKHORN
NN
36
LYONS
Greyhound
Track
Mound Road/
Reimer Road
67
12
McLean
Road
SPRINGFIELD
Start
DELAVAN
(see inset)
11
43
H
Willow
Bend
Road
*Horse Farm
Area*
Hospital
Road
36
11
H
(rustic
road)
Church
Street
43
Borg
Road
Town Hall
Road
Petrie
Road
North
Como
Road
Springfield
Road
36
Spring
Valley
Road
North
Shore
Road
50
Reimer
Road
COMO
Lake Como
Sheridan
Springs
Road
50
Delavan Lake
*Park
and
Beach*
LAKE GENEVA
(see inset)
12
South
Shore
Road
Bailey
Road
WILLIAMS
BAY
N
O
Townline
Road
67
*Millie's
Pancake House*
Lake Geneva
120
14
0 2 4 Miles

**Tour 2:
Delavan / Lake Geneva**

30 Bicycle Tours in Wisconsin
© 1994 The Countryman Press, Inc.

Start
*Veteran's
Memorial Park*
Lake Comus
Spring
Grove
Circus
Cemetery
Sugar
Creek
Road
O
11
North Terrace
McDowell
7th
Street
Racine
Street
South
Wright
Street
Mound
Road
11
Main Street
3rd Street
5th Street
*Allyn
House*
50
50
*Clown
Hall of
Fame*
Walworth
Avenue
Borg
Road
DELAVAN inset
N
to
Linn
Road

**LAKE GENEVA
inset**
H
N
William
Street
36
George
Street
Broad Street
(WI 36)
Center Street
Chamber of Commerce
Andy Gump Statue
*Geneva Lake
Cruise Line*
Main Street
Wrigley
Drive
*Lake
Geneva*

8.2   Left onto South Shore Road at the Williamsburg Shopping Village.

Millie's Pancake House and Restaurant is a good spot to fuel up, if you didn't have a chance earlier. There are also shops featuring local crafts, antiques, and stitchery. Rest rooms are available.

11.1   South Shore Road takes a sharp left by the Delavan Fire Department. This is an easy turn to miss.

13.0   Town of Delavan Municipal Park.

Services include rest rooms, a swimming beach, and a concession stand.

13.1   Cross WI 50 and continue straight on Town Hall Road.

The white plank fences are a clue that you're in horse country. The Fantasy Hill Stables at 15.1 miles offers horseback riding.

16.2   Left onto Petrie Road.

17.9   Left onto County H where Petrie Road ends.

18.7   Right onto McLean Road.

19.7   Reindeer and llamas can be seen at the game farm here.

21.7   Right onto County NN just before the cemetery.

23.2   Left onto Springfield Road just past the Mary D. Arabian Horse Farm.

25.3   Left onto WI 120 North. You are now in the village of Springfield.

26.3   Right onto Hospital Road just before the cemetery.

28.7   Left onto WI 36 at the Johnnie Reynolds Supper Club, where Hospital Road ends, and follow for .5 mile to the village of Lyons.

29.2   Right onto Church Street, by the Rustic Road sign, and continue into downtown Lyons.

If you turn left on Railroad Street you pass the Olde Hotel Bar and Restaurant. This is a good lunch spot if you can't wait until Lake Geneva. The Village Store has snacks and the village park is a short walk or ride down Mill Street. There are rest rooms at the park.

30.1 Right onto Spring Valley Road.

30.2 Left onto Sheridan Springs Road.

31.4 Right on Sheridan Springs Road.

This is a pretty country road following the White River. You'll pass the Americana Lake Geneva Resort and Ski area on your left.

35.1 Left onto WI 36 for one block.

35.2 Left onto Center Street and follow into downtown Lake Geneva.

You'll cross Main Street; Center Street ends at the lake.

36.3 Right onto Wrigley Drive for .1 mile.

This road follows the lakeshore. You pass a charming gazebo in the park along with a statue of Andy Gump. Cartoonist Sidney Smith created the Andy Gump character, the first daily cartoon in the nation, published in *The Chicago Tribune* in 1917.

36.4 The Chamber of Commerce building is on the right and has an information center and rest rooms.

This is also a good place to park and lock your bike while you explore Lake Geneva. The village contains many shops, restaurants, and boutiques. There are also many tourists, especially during midsummer and fall foliage season.

The Geneva Lake Cruise Line, across from the Chamber of Commerce, provides one of the most worthwhile activities in the area. You can ride aboard one of the only remaining US Mail marine deliveries in the United States that still takes passengers. The Walworth II departs every morning (June 15– September 15) at 9:45 A.M. with a load of passengers, mail, and an agile letter carrier who must jump off the boat and onto each pier, deliver the mail, and then jump back onto the boat, which never stops moving! The cruise line also offers

Taking a break after lunch

steamboat and historical tours, ice cream socials, and dinner cruises. Call (414) 248-6206 or (800) 558-5911 for schedules. There is also a public swimming beach in downtown Lake Geneva where sailboats, sailboards, and jet skis can be rented. Right on Wrigley Drive from the Chamber of Commerce building for .1 mile.

36.5 *Right onto Broad Street. Follow through downtown. Be careful—this area can be congested with automobiles.*

37.2 *Left onto George Street (County Highway H).*

Follow County Highway H out of town.

40.4 *Right onto North Como Road just past the Sugar Shack, by the First Bank Southeast.*

41.3 *Left onto Willow Bend Road.*

43.1 *Right onto Petrie Road for .5 mile.*

43.6 *Left onto Reimer Road.*

44.6 *Cross WI 67. Continue straight where Reimer Road becomes Mound Road.*

Shadowlawn Pottery is on this corner in the former Shadow Lawn School building. Shadowlawn produces authentic reproductions of nineteenth-century salt-glaze stoneware. The process begins by hand mixing a special clay body, which is then hand thrown on the potter's wheel. Each piece is stamped with both the potter's personal mark and that of the factory. The pots are decorated with the same cobalt blue and patterns used more than a century ago. Rock salt, introduced into the kiln during firing at 2,300 degrees, vaporizes and forms a clear durable glaze on the pottery.

48.8 *Left onto Racine Street and follow it into Delavan. Continue straight on Racine Street as it joins County Highway O and becomes Walworth Street.*

49.8 *Cross Seventh Street at St. Andrew's Catholic Church and continue straight on Walworth Street.*

The Spring Grove cemetery is located .6 mile to the right on Seventh Street. Over 130 members of Delavan's nineteenth-century circus community are buried there. The graves are marked with a circus marker and numbers. Those who are particularly interested in circus history should contact Gordon Yadon, (414) 728-3025, president of the Delavan Historical Society and former postmaster. He lives nearby and gives a wonderful tour with many colorful tales about the animal trainers, trapeze artists, and grifters that once lived in Delavan.

To your right at 511 East Walworth Street is the Allyn House, (414) 728-9090, a 23-room Victorian mansion that has been lovingly restored and turned into a bed-and-breakfast inn by former teachers Joe Johnson and Ron Markwell. The inn is a treasure box of frescoed ceilings, parquet floors, and priceless Eastlake antique furniture.

50.5 Right into Veteran's Memorial Park.

Bicycle Repair Services

Quiet Hut
186 West Main Street, Whitewater, WI
(414) 473-2950

La Grange General Store
WI 12 and County Highway H, La Grange, WI
(414) 495-8600

3
Holy Hill

Distance: *44.1 miles*
Terrain: *Rolling to hilly*

The Gothic spires of the cathedral at Holy Hill reign supreme over the surrounding glacial countryside, reminiscent of a European castle. Holy Hill is a religious shrine that each year draws thousands of pilgrims in search of the healing powers that cured a French hermit here. In the autumn, people make a pilgrimage of another kind, to enjoy the breathtaking display of colored oaks and maples.

Located halfway between Milwaukee and Madison, this area is growing rapidly but still offers some pleasant back-roads riding, past prime fishing lakes and century-old country estates. To reach the start, take I-94 to County Highway C North, which becomes Genesee Street as you enter the village of Delafield. Turn left onto Main Street at the first stop sign and continue to Cushing Park Road (opposite The Frosted Mug). Turn right into this pleasant little park along the river, which has rest rooms, picnic tables, and parking.

0.0 *Left from the park onto Main Street.*

0.2 *Right onto Wells Street where the road forks.*

0.4 *Hawks Inn, (414) 544-4415, is to your right.*

> Built of hand-hewn timbers and handmade nails, the inn was built by Nelson Page Hawks, one of Delafield's founders, as a stagecoach stop on the Milwaukee to Madison plank road. Guided tours are available, May through October.

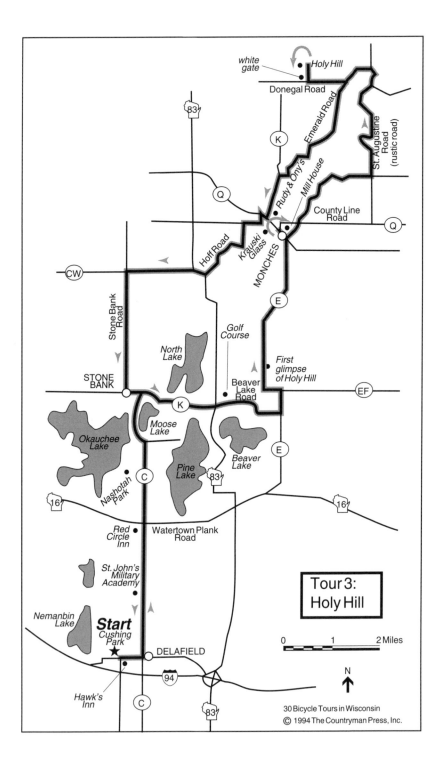

white gate

Holy Hill

Donegal Road

83

K

Emerald Road

Q

Rudy & Ony's

Mill House

County Line Road

St. Augustine Road (rustic road)

Q

Hoff Road

Krauski Glass

MONCHES

CW

E

Stone Bank Road

Golf Course

North Lake

First glimpse of Holy Hill

EF

STONE BANK

K

Beaver Lake Road

Moose Lake

Okauchee Lake

E

Pine Lake

Beaver Lake

83

C

16

Nashotah Park

16

Watertown Plank Road

Red Circle Inn

St. John's Military Academy

Nemanbin Lake

Start
Cushing Park

★ DELAFIELD

94

Hawk's Inn

C

83

Tour 3:
Holy Hill

0   1   2 Miles

N

30 Bicycle Tours in Wisconsin
© 1994 The Countryman Press, Inc.

0.5 *Left onto Genesee Street (County Highway C) through downtown Delafield.*

The Steeple Shops and Town Hall Shops both house antiques vendors.

0.9 *St. John's Military Academy is to your left.*

Delafield is well-known for this military prep school for boys, founded in 1884 by Sydney Smythe, a student at nearby Nashotah House Episcopal Seminary. The school's charter stresses quality, self-discipline, team spirit, and leadership. Enter the gates and take a spin through the campus to view the Old Gothic–style stone buildings with fortress-like towers, battlements, and serrated roofs. Especially beautiful is the Church of St. John Chrysostom, built in 1851.

3.3 *To your left at the junction with Watertown Plank Road is one of southern Wisconsin's finest restaurants, the Red Circle Inn.*

Watertown Plank Road was one of many such roads, also called corduroy roads, built in Wisconsin in the mid-1800s. It was used by fur traders and farmers hauling products to Milwaukee and supplies back over this route. Since timber was plentiful, plank roads were relatively cheap to construct, durable, practical, and safe. Built of aged oak, they lasted about eight years before requiring major repair. Horses could pull more weight on a plank road because of reduced friction, but they often became tired and sore on long journeys. The busier routes had two lanes, laid on separate beds of planks.

In 1847, Francis Schraudenbach received a territorial land grant to build a hotel with a tavern and dining room here. The inn catered to wealthy Milwaukee families vacationing in the area and in 1889 was purchased by Frederick Pabst, of the Pabst Brewing Company. He bestowed the name "Red Circle," which was part of the old Pabst brewing trademark. The original oak bar is still in use today. The Red Circle Inn offers elegant dining and specializes in Provimi veal.

4.2 *Nashotah Park, to your left, has rest rooms and picnic tables. The next stretch passes between Okauchee and Moose Lakes.*

6.5   Right onto County Highway K where County Highway C ends, in the village of Stone Bank.

6.7   Continue straight on County Highway K at the junction with West Shore, by the cemetery.

8.3   Cross WI 83 and go straight onto Beaver Lake Road, which passes through the golf course and provides some beautiful views of Beaver Lake to your right.

9.9   Left onto County Highway E.

10.4 Left onto County Highway E where County Highway EF turns right.

10.9 Continue on County Highway E where it makes a 90-degree right turn at the junction with Red Fox.

11.5 The silhouette of Holy Hill can be seen off in the distance as you come down this hill.

11.9 Cross County Highway VV.

14.5 Left onto Center Oak Street in Monches.

Settled predominantly by Irish Catholics in the early 1840s, Monches was originally called O'Connellsville, after the great Irish emancipator, Daniel O'Connell. You will notice many road names with an Irish theme and many Irish flags flying along this route. John Hartley, the town's first postmaster, renamed the town Monches, after a Native American leader.

14.7 The Monches Mill House, (414) 966-7546, a cozy bed-and-breakfast inn, sits reflectively on the banks of the village mill pond.

Innkeepers Elaine and Harvey Taylor purchased this historic gem at auction in 1975 and its eclectic decor features art acquired on their frequent travels to France and the Caribbean. The Taylors live in a solar home behind the Mill House and raise vegetables, fruits, and eggs used in luncheons offered on Wednesdays and Fridays.

14.9 Krauski Glass is a stained glass workshop where commissioned work is done and classes are offered. Visitors are welcome.

15.0 *Rudy and Ony's Tavern is now the only canteen in town; in the 1890s, Monches supported three saloons and more than a dozen shops.*

> Backtrack through Monches on Center Oak, past the Monches Mill House.

15.6 *Left onto Hartley Road.*

> The first home on your right (also the dog pound) has several llamas and a camel in the backyard.

16.1 *Cross County Highway Q and jog slightly to the right onto Monches Road.*

18.6 *Left onto St. Augustine Road by St. Paul's Church.*

> This wonderful, winding Rustic Road conjures up images of leprechauns lurking in the ground fog that gathers in the hollows. There is one steep downhill, with switchbacks. Ride in control!

21.0 *Stay left at the junction, still on St. Augustine Road (no sign here).*

21.5 *Left onto Emerald Road.*

22.3 *Right onto Donegal Road.*

23.3 *Right into the back entrance of Holy Hill. There is no identifying sign here—look carefully for the white metal gate and the No Hunting signs.*

23.9 *Right at the junction and continue to the top of the hill.*

24.3 *Parking lot.*

> The cathedral sits atop the area's largest kame—a glacial feature you won't soon forget after pedaling up it! The word kame comes from the Scottish, "coomb," meaning steep hill. Kames were created when water swirled in gigantic eddies through holes that resembled reverse funnels in the glacial ice sheet.
>
> The origin of this magnificent Catholic shrine centers around a story about a young Frenchman named François

Soubrio. As a young man studying for the priesthood in France, Soubrio fell in love with a pretty young maiden. They decided to marry, and despite vehement opposition from his family and the church, Soubrio renounced his priestly vows. While Soubrio was away on a trip, his fiancée married another suitor. When he found he had been forsaken by his betrothed, he killed her in a fit of anger. He then fled to Quebec, where he became a recluse in a monastery in the old city.

He remained there for years, tortured by remorse. While studying old French manuscripts in the monastery library, Soubrio read of the voyages of Marquette and Joliet through the Great Lakes waterways. He was particularly interested in a reference by Marquette to a lofty, cone-shaped hill that the explorer had climbed, raising a cross and dedicating it to his patron saint, Mary. Soubrio set out to rediscover this "holy hill," to re-erect the now-decayed cross, and to seek his atonement.

Along the way he was stricken with a partial paralysis of his legs, and was forced to complete the final stage of his journey on his knees. When he finally crawled through the dense woods to the summit, he spent the night praying to St. Mary. At dawn he rose from his knees to find his paralysis gone. News of the miracle spread and people began to come seeking relief from their own ailments. Their crutches are displayed in a small glass case. One day Soubrio disappeared and it's said that his ghost is still seen kneeling before a cross.

In 1855, the Reverend Francis Paulhuber bought the land and later built a log chapel. The original building has been replaced by the brick structures that now stand on the summit of Holy Hill. These include a Romanesque church with balconies overlooking the glacial countryside, a religious gift shop, a cafeteria, and lodging for pilgrims who visit the shrine. Holy Hill is staffed by the Discalced Carmelite Friars, (414) 628-1838.

Exit Holy Hill the same way you came. Left at the T intersection by the parking lot, opposite of the car traffic.

The cathedral at Holy Hill

25.3 Left onto Donegal Road at the white entrance gate.

26.3 Right onto Emerald Road.

29.1 Left onto County Highway K at the cemetery.

There's a small spring, just before the road sign for County Highway Q. Look for water bubbling out of a small pipe.

26.3 Right onto County Highway Q and up the hill.

30.5 Left onto County Line Road (the sign to the right differs).

31.2 Left onto Hoff Road.

31.9 Continue on Hoff Road where it bends to the right.

32.8 Right onto WI 83 where Hoff Road ends.

32.9 Straight onto County Highway CW where WI 83 veers right.

34.6 Left onto Stone Bank Road.

36.5 Stone Bank Community Park offers rest rooms and a picnic area.

37.3 *Left onto County Highway K.*

37.6 *Right onto County Highway C.*

39.9 *Nashotah County Park.*

43.6 *Right onto Main Street in Delafield.*

44.1 *Right onto Cushing Park Road to your starting point. But first quench your thirst at The Frosty Mug—a modern-day stagecoach stop.*

Bicycle Repair Services

Bicycle Doctor
1089 Summit Avenue, Oconomowoc, WI
(414) 567-6656

Cooney Cycle Center
101 South Main Street, Oconomowoc, WI
(414) 567-7398

4
Horicon Marsh

Distance: *51.0 miles (including 8 miles on unpaved Wild Goose Trail) or 41.8 miles (road route)*
Terrain: *Gently rolling to rolling*

Be sure to bring your binoculars on this tour, which circles Horicon Marsh, where 200,000-plus Canada geese descend each October for a brief respite en route to wintering grounds in southern Illinois and western Kentucky. At the peak of the migration, the skies above the marsh are laced with complex landing patterns that resemble Heathrow or O'Hare airports.

The 850- to 1,000-mile journey begins in Hudson Bay and takes these skilled avian aviators 12 to 16 hours. They are known to ascend to 9,000 feet in search of a good tailwind and reach speeds of 70 miles per hour. A drafting technique, similar to that used by bicycle racers, minimizes air resistance and turbulence and accounts for the familiar chevron formation.

In addition to the Canada goose, about 250 species of birds have been officially sited at the marsh. It is the largest nesting area for redhead ducks east of the Mississippi River and the Four Mile Island Rookery (accessible only by boat) is home to black-crowned night herons, double-crested cormorants, great blue herons, and egrets.

The scenery alternates between cattail-marsh views, rolling farmland, and prairie remnants. Included is an eight-mile stretch on the Wild Goose State Trail, an off-road trail with a crushed limestone surface, constructed on an abandoned railroad bed. An alternate road route is included for those who don't wish to ride the trail.

October is a prime time to visit the marsh; autumn colors and the waterfowl migration will be at peak levels. You should be aware that fall is also hunting season for ducks and geese, and while hunting is not permitted in the marsh itself, you may hear gunshots in the distance. Avoid this trip during July and August because of high humidity and lack of shade along the route.

To get to Horicon Marsh, take WI 33 to Horicon, Wisconsin. As you enter town, WI 33 becomes Barstow Street. At the Kwik Trip store, turn left onto Larabee Street and follow it to Clausen Park, where the tour begins. The park is located along the Rock River in downtown Horicon and has a picnic area and rest rooms.

A pontoon boat with a naturalist/guide will take you to parts of the marsh inaccessible by road. Boats leave from downtown Horicon at the junction of WI 33 and Vine Street on the Rock River. Call Blue Heron Tours, (414) 485-2942, for departure times.

0.0   *Right onto Larabee Street at park exit.*

0.1   *Right onto West Lake Street. Continue through downtown Horicon.*

> You will pass the headquarters of John Deere, (414) 485-4411, manufacturers of farm, golf, and turf equipment. Advance reservations are required for factory tours offered daily at 9:30 A.M.

0.5   *To your left is the Ice Cream Station. In the fall, try their special Horicon Hurricane—hot apple cider with cinnamon ice cream and whipped cream.*

0.7   *Left onto Palmatory Street and follow it all the way to the end.*

1.8   *The DNR station offers a scenic overlook of the marsh and provides information on events and activities.*

> For a worthwhile introduction to the marsh ecosystem, attend a lecture or join a hike led by naturalist Bill Volkert or his staff. Programs are offered several times daily during the fall migration. Call (414) 387-7877 for a current schedule. Return on Palmatory Street to Lynn Street.

2.7   *Left onto Lynn Street.*

2.8   *Left onto Clausen Street (WI 28).*

2.9   *Right onto Raasch's Hill Road.*

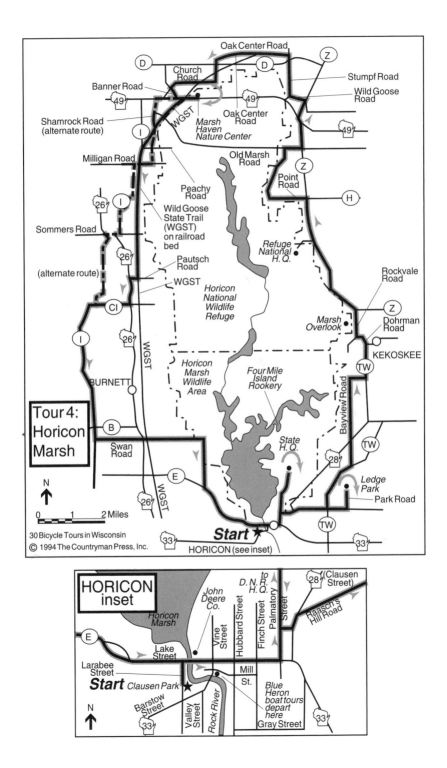

Oak Center Road

D

Church
Road

D

Z

Stumpf Road

Banner Road

Wild Goose
Road

49

WGST

49

Oak Center
Road

Shamrock Road
(alternate route)

Marsh
Haven
Nature Center

I

49

Milligan Road

Old Marsh
Road

Z

26

I

Peachy
Road

Point
Road

H

Sommers Road

Wild Goose
State Trail
(WGST)
on railroad
bed

Refuge
National
H. Q.

26

(alternate route)

WGST

Pautsch
Road

Rockvale
Road

Horicon
National
Wildlife
Refuge

CI

Marsh
Overlook

Z

Dohrman
Road

I

26

KEKOSKEE

BURNETT

Horicon
Marsh
Wildlife
Area

Four Mile
Island
Rookery

Bayview Road

TW

**Tour 4:
Horicon
Marsh**

B

State
H. Q.

TW

Swan
Road

28

Ledge
Park

N

E

Park Road

0   1   2 Miles

26

WGST

TW

30 Bicycle Tours in Wisconsin
© 1994 The Countryman Press, Inc.

33

Start ★

HORICON (see inset)

33

**HORICON
inset**

to
D. N. R.
H. Q.

28

(Clausen
Street)

John
Deere
Co.

Vine Street

Hubbard Street

Finch Street

Palmatory
Street

Haasch's
Hill Road

Horicon
Marsh

E

Lake
Street

Larabee
Street

Mill
St.

Start Clausen Park ★

Blue
Heron
boat tours
depart
here

N

Barstow
Street

Valley
Street

Rock River

Gray Street

33

33

4.2   *Cross County Highway TW. This route takes you to Ledge Park, which provides a nice view from the top of a limestone escarpment. If you don't wish to visit the park, turn left onto TW here and skip to mile 7.1.*

5.0   *Left onto Park Road.*

5.2   *Left into Ledge Park. Stay right toward the campground.*

5.7   *Ponder the view from a park bench on the edge of the ledge.*

6.2   *Right from park on Park Road.*

6.4   *Right onto Raasch's Hill Road.*

7.1   *Right onto County Highway TW.*

8.6   *Left on Bayview Road.*

9.4   *Cross WI 28.*

11.7   *Left onto County Highway TW where Bay View ends (unmarked).*

12.7   *Left onto Dohrman Road.*

13.1   *Right onto Rockvale Road (no sign except < >).*

13.4   *Scenic marsh overlook.*

Sometimes referred to as the "Everglades of the North," Horicon Marsh is an extinct glacial lake that covers approximately 32,000 acres. It is the largest freshwater marsh in the United States. A renewed interest in America's wetlands has helped restore the marsh to its natural state after a legacy of misuse. In 1846, the marsh was dammed to power a sawmill, raising the water level by nine feet and creating a 13-mile-long man-made lake plied by steamboats carrying visitors and supplies. Other industries that sprang up around the marsh were harvesting marsh grasses in the summer and cutting ice in the winter.

A legal dispute forced removal of the dam, which led to the return of wildlife and the next chapter in marsh history—overhunting. From 1870 to the early 1900s, large sections of land were leased to wealthy hunting clubs and for-profit hunters, drastically reducing some species.

As farm prices climbed at the turn of the century, farmers attempted to convert the peaty soil to cropland by draining the marsh through a system of dikes and ditches. It was another experiment that proved useless—the process was expensive and the drained soil deteriorated quickly. An act of the state legislature in 1927 finally paved the way for preservation, dividing jurisdiction of the marsh between the state and federal governments. A "buy a duck" campaign led by a local radio comedian in 1935 helped repopulate the marsh with pairs of waterfowl.

Continue on Rockvale Road.

14.1 **Left onto County Highway Z.**

The marsh is on your left for the next ten miles.

16.4 **Pass the National Refuge Headquarters.**

17.8 **Left onto Point Road (sign hard to read).**

18.8 **Keep right at the T junction.**

21.0 **Left onto County Highway Z.**

21.6 **Left onto County Highway Z/WI 49 for a short distance.**

21.7 **Right onto County Highway Z.**

22.4 **Left onto Wild Goose Road.**

22.9 **Right onto Stumpf Road.**

24.0 **Left onto Oak Center Road.**

26.2 **Left onto Church Road. This turn is easy to miss.**

Pick your own strawberries at Mischler's Berry Farm in June.

28.2 **Left onto Banner Road.**

28.5 **Left onto WI 49. Take care, this is a busier road.**

28.6 **Marsh Barn Antiques.**

29.1 Left into the Marsh Haven Nature Center, (414) 386-2182. This is a nonprofit nature education center, which will eventually have hostel accommodations for groups visiting the marsh. At present, the center offers hiking trails, an observation tower, a small gift shop, a picnic area, and rest rooms.

29.3 Right from Nature Center onto WI 49.

29.6 Left onto the Wild Goose Trail.

If you wish to take the road route, rather than the trail, skip to the "alternate route" section below.

Look for geese feeding in the surrounding farm fields. They consume waste corn, grass, and other vegetation. An adult goose eats about a half pound of food each day, usually feeding in the morning and late afternoon hours. They roost just before sunset; it's not unusual to see several thousand geese in the sky at this time.

30.5 Trail returns to road for short distance.

October is the best time for a ride around Horicon Marsh, a rest stop for migrating Canada geese.

31.0 *Right back onto trail.*

31.6 *Cross Peachy Road.*

34.2 *Pass sign that says: Burnett—6 miles.*

37.5 *Right onto Pautsch Road. (Trail ends here.)*

37.7 *Left onto WI 26 (busier road).*

38.5 *Right onto County Highway CI.*

39.7 *Left onto County Highway I.*

42.4 *Don't go left on County Highway BI (don't follow trail signs any longer).*

43.4 *Cross County Highway B.*

43.9 *Left onto Swan Road.*

45.3 *Cross WI 26.*

48.7 *Left onto County Highway E. Busy, but good shoulder. Becomes Lake Street.*

50.2 *Dangerous railroad tracks.*

50.4 *Enter Horicon.*

50.9 *Right onto Larabee Street.*

51.0 *Left into the park.*

Alternate Road Route

29.6 *Continue on WI 49, past Wild Goose Trail access. Just ahead is Tom Dooley Orchards.*

30.6 *Left onto Shamrock Road.*

31.7 *Right onto Milligan Road.*

32.1 *Left onto County Highway I.*

34.4 *Right onto WI 26.*

34.7 *Left onto County Highway I.*

37.2 Careful, dangerous railroad tracks.

41.1 Left onto Swan Road.

42.5 Cross WI 26.

45.8 Left onto County Highway E (becomes Lake Street in Horicon).

47.3 Take care crossing the tracks again.

47.5 Enter Horicon.

48.0 Right onto Larabee Street by the Rock River Tap.

48.1 Left into the park.

Bicycle Repair Service

Metzgar's Bicycle Shop
1219 Madison, Beaver Dam, WI
(414) 885-9516

5
Northern Kettle Moraine State Forest

Distance: *33.7 miles*
Terrain: *Rolling to hilly*

The landscape in this area, with its matchless variety of glacial features, reads like a geology textbook. Much of this tour takes place in the hilly, ice-carved countryside of the Kettle Moraine State Forest's northern unit. As part of the Ice Age National Scenic Reserve, the Kettle Moraine is under the jurisdiction of the National Park Service.

During the Wisconsin stage of glaciation, about 18,000 to 20,000 years ago, two finger-like lobes of moving ice, the Green Bay lobe and the Lake Michigan lobe, collided along a northeast-southwest line near here. At their junction, billions of tons of sand, gravel, and rock were deposited as the ice slowly melted away, resulting in a long sinuous ridge, known as a moraine. The word "moraine" derives from the Spanish word *morro*, which means "snout."

Other prominent glacial features include drumlins, which are teardrop shaped hills; eskers, which are narrow snakelike ridges; and kames, which are cone-shaped hills. Before or after your bike ride, consider stopping at the Henry S. Reuss Ice Age Vistor Center, (414) 533-8322, located south of Plymouth on WI 67, where a video brings the era of mastodons and massive ice sheets to life.

Plymouth, the pleasant little town where the tour begins, was once the center of the world cheese market. In 1918, the Wisconsin Cheese Exchange, a kind of dairy board of trade, was established here to expand outlets for local cheesemakers. Plymouth remains at the hub of Wisconsin's cheese industry, with five large cheese factories including the international headquarters of Sargento Cheese Company. Sargento was founded in 1848

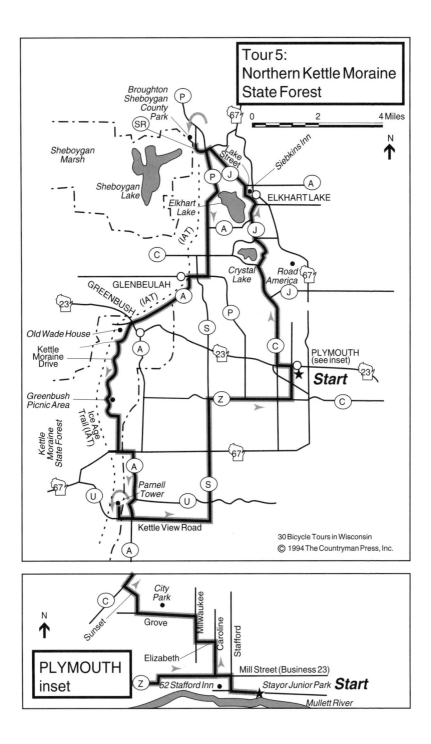

Tour 5:
Northern Kettle Moraine
State Forest

Broughton Sheboygan County Park

Sheboygan Marsh

Sheboygan Lake

Elkhart Lake

ELKHART LAKE

Siebkins Inn

Lake Street

Crystal Lake

Road America

GREENBUSH (IAT)

GLENBEULAH

Old Wade House

Kettle Moraine Drive

Greenbush Picnic Area

Kettle Moraine State Forest

Ice Age Trail (IAT)

Parnell Tower

Kettle View Road

PLYMOUTH (see inset)

Start

0   2   4 Miles

N

30 Bicycle Tours in Wisconsin
© 1994 The Countryman Press, Inc.

PLYMOUTH inset

N

City Park

Sunset

Grove

Elizabeth

Milwaukee

Caroline

Stafford

Mill Street (Business 23)

52 Stafford Inn

Stayor Junior Park *Start*

Mullett River

when Leonard Gentine, Sr., opened the Plymouth Cheese Counter in a small shed behind his funeral parlor, specializing in Italian cheeses.

To get to Plymouth, take WI 23 to Business WI 23, which becomes Mill Street as you enter town. Turn south onto Stafford Street and follow it to Stayor Junior Park, along the river, opposite 52 Stafford, An Irish Guest House. There is a grocery store behind the park.

0.0   *Right onto Stafford Street from the park.*

0.1   *On your left is 52 Stafford.*

> This is an Irish Guest House, (414) 893-0552, a charming bed-and-breakfast inn that offers luxury accommodations (whirlpool baths in every room), terrific food, and a lively Irish pub where bartenders are practiced in the art of pouring a pint of Guiness from the tap. Etched glass windows around the bar depict scenes of Celtic folklore and guest rooms are named after Irish patriots, authors, politicians, and musicians.

0.2   *Left onto Mill Street (Business WI 67).*

0.3   *Right onto Caroline Street.*

0.4   *Left onto Elizabeth Street (still on WI 67).*

0.5   *Right onto Milwaukee Street (your first right).*

0.8   *Left onto Grove Street, passing the city park.*

1.1   *Right onto Sunset Street.*

1.2   *Continue straight at the stop sign, still on Sunset Street.*

2.6   *Right onto County Highway C.*

> The headquarters of the Sargento is just before the turn.

4.0   *Continue on County Highway C at first intersection with County Highway J.*

4.7   *Right onto County Highway J (Crystal Lake Road) where County Highway C goes left (by the Crystal Lake sign).*

> This is a beautiful canopied road with lake views.

5.8   *Right onto County Highway J at the junction of County Highways CJ and J.*

6.4   *County Highway J becomes County Highway A.*

7.1   *Stay left going into Elkhart Lake. Don't take County Highways J and A, which veer to the right.*

> This pretty little resort town, originally called Elk Heart Lake, surrounds a beautiful lake of glacial origin. When the railroad reached here in 1860, Elkhart Lake became a popular summer vacation area for visitors from Milwaukee and Chicago. Auto races on the four-mile track at Road America, (800) 365-RACE or 892-4576, draw competitors and racing aficionados from around the world. Portions of the movie *Winning*, with Paul Newman, were filmed here. Before the track was built, auto races were run through the streets of town!

7.5   *Right onto Lake Street by Siebkin's Hotel, (414) 876-2600.*

> This old-world hotel serves breakfast and lunch on a pleasant wicker-filled porch.

7.7   *Left onto Gottfried Street by the big, gray grain elevator and Kettle Moraine Scenic Drive sign. Gottfried Street becomes County Highway J.*

9.3   *Left onto County Highway SR into Broughton Sheboygan County Park.*

9.7   *The 13,000-acre Sheboygan Marsh is a favorite respite for Canada geese and other migrating waterfowl.*

> The Marsh Lodge restaurant serves breakfast. Rest rooms and picnic tables are available. Backtrack to the park exit.

10.0   *Right onto County Highway J from the park. Then right immediately onto County Highway P.*

11.3   *Rest rooms are available here at the Elkhart Lake boat landing.*

11.7   *All Saint's Chapel, a tiny, stone Episcopal church in a picturesque oak grove, holds services at 9 A.M. in June, July, and August.*

Glaciers formed the challenging hills on this ride.

12.5   *Straight where County Highway A joins County Highway P.*

13.7   *Right on County Highway A through Glenbeulah. This road parallels the glacier's terminal, or end moraine, which takes the form of a wooded ridge.*

14.2   *Left on County Highway A.*

16.0   *Cross WI 23 and continue on County Highway A to Greenbush.*

16.5   *Right onto County Highway T (Plank Road).*

16.6   *Left onto Center Street to the Wade House Stagecoach Inn and Wisconsin Carriage Museum, (414) 526-3271.*

16.7   *Right into the museum parking lot.*

> The Wade House was built by Sylvanus Wade in 1851 to serve stagecoach traffic on the busy Sheboygan to Fond du Lac Plank Road. The site is open daily May through October and offers ongoing demonstrations of spinning, blacksmithing, and candle-making by costumed interpreters. Also on the

property is the Wisconsin Carriage Museum, one of the country's largest collections of restored horse-drawn carriages and wagons. Straight on Washington Street from the museum.

17.1 **Right onto County Highway T.**

17.7 **Left onto Kettle Moraine Drive.**

Gear down for a one-mile climb. Continue past the group campsites and recreation areas to the picnic area at the summit.

19.5 **Stop for a breather at the Greenbush Picnic area, which has hiking trails, a picnic area, and rest rooms.**

20.3 **Don't descend so fast that you whiz by one of the Kettle Moraine's most striking glacial features, the Greenbush Kettle.**

A sign marks the location, to your right, near the bottom of the hill. The kettle was formed when a giant, detached ice block buried under glacial debris melted. This steep-walled cavity is nearly as deep as it is wide.

20.4 **Right, still on Kettle Moraine Drive, at bottom of hill.**

21.2 **Left onto WI 67. Take care, this is a busy road.**

21.7 **Right onto County Highway A.**

23.7 **Right onto County Highway U.**

23.9 **Right into the Parnell Tower Recreation Area, where you will find a picnic area, rest rooms, and a 50-foot wooden observation tower, from which you can survey the surrounding glacial topography.**

24.1 **Left onto County Highway U at exit.**

24.3 **Straight at the stop sign across County Highways A and U onto Kettle View Road.**

Don't turn at first junction with County Highway S.

27.1 **Straight on County Highway S where Kettle View ends.**

27.5 **Silver Springs Trout Farm and Resort, (414) 893-0969, offers fly-**

fishing instruction and a restaurant that serves trout raised on the farm (or they will cook your catch).

Lodging is available in attractive A-frame cottages.

28.8 **Cross WI 67. Take care, this is a busy road.**

30.3 **Right onto County Highway Z.**

33.2 **Right onto Mill Street.**

As you come down the hill into town, glance to the right at the giant fiberglass Holstein that celebrates Plymouth's dairy heritage. Considered the premier dairy cow, the Holstein was imported to Wisconsin from Holland in 1870.

33.5 **Right onto Stafford Street.**

33.7 **Left into Stayor Junior Park.**

Bicycle Repair Services

Johnnie's Bike Shop
1001 Michigan Avenue, Sheboygan, WI
(414) 452-0934

Spoke & Wheel
Northgate Shopping Center, Sheboygan, WI
(414) 458-1515

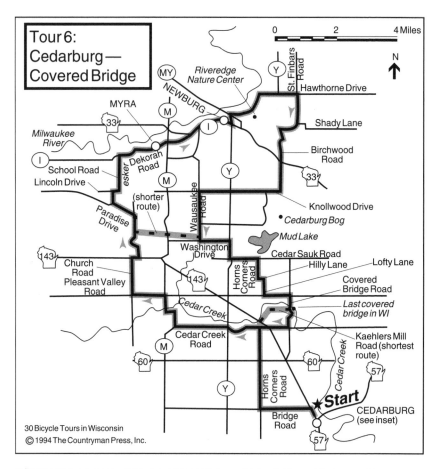

**Tour 6:
Cedarburg—
Covered Bridge**

0 2 4 Miles

N

MY

NEWBURG

*Riveredge
Nature Center*

Y

St. Finbars
Road

Hawthorne Drive

MYRA

M

I

Shady Lane

33

*Milwaukee
River*

I

esker

Dekorah
Road

School Road

Lincoln Drive

M

Birchwood
Road

33

Y

Knollwood Drive

(shorter
route)

Paradise
Drive

Wausaukee
Road

Washington
Drive

• *Cedarburg Bog*

Mud Lake

143

Church
Road

Pleasant Valley
Road

143

Horns
Corners
Road

Cedar Sauk Road

Hilly Lane

Lofty Lane

Covered
Bridge Road

Cedar Creek

*Last covered
bridge in WI*

M

Cedar Creek
Road

60

60

Kaehlers Mill
Road (shortest
route)

Cedar Creek

57

Y

Horns
Corners Road

Bridge
Road

★**Start**

CEDARBURG
(see inset)

57

30 Bicycle Tours in Wisconsin

© 1994 The Countryman Press, Inc.

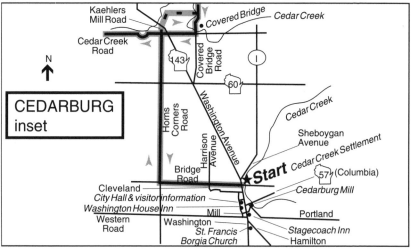

N

**CEDARBURG
inset**

Kaehlers
Mill Road

Cedar Creek
Road

Covered Bridge

Cedar Creek

143

Covered
Bridge Road

I

60

Cedar Creek

Horns
Corners Road

Harrison
Avenue

Washington Avenue

Sheboygan
Avenue

Cedar Creek Settlement

Bridge
Road

★**Start**

Cedar Creek Settlement

57 (Columbia)

Cleveland

City Hall & visitor information

Washington House Inn

Cedarburg Mill

Western
Road

Mill

Washington

*St. Francis
Borgia Church*

Portland

Stagecoach Inn

Hamilton

6
Cedarburg/Covered Bridge

Distance: *13, 24.8, or 39.5 miles*
Terrain: *Flat to rolling*

Just 20 miles north of Milwaukee, this ride is a convenient escape for city dwellers seeking an antidote to urban frenzy. The route passes through fertile bogs fed by the Milwaukee River watershed, where you may be forced to slow your pace as a painted turtle plods across the road. Winding country lanes with an amazing absence of traffic take you past many hundred-year-old farmhouses built of fieldstone, limestone, and Cream City brick, a light-colored brick made from limestone quarried in the Milwaukee area.

Allow an hour or two before or following your ride for a stroll through Cedarburg, a forward-thinking little community whose residents have rallied to save a number of architectural keepsakes from the wrecking ball. Most of the town's historic interest lies in a six-block stretch of Washington Avenue, presided over by the Gothic spires of St. Francis Borgia Catholic Church on the south end. At the opposite end of the historic district is the old Wittenberg Woolen Mill, which now houses a complex of small shops and a winery. The mill dates to 1864, when it was built to capitalize on the demand for wool products brought on by the Civil War. Over a dozen antique shops are further evidence of Cedarburg's bent toward historic preservation.

A half block east of Washington Avenue on Columbia Road, you will find the old Cedarburg Mill. This building, which dates to 1855, is unusual because of its five-story construction. It now houses offices, as well as Landmark Supply, a feed mill which, among other things, offers an incredible selection of bird houses and bird feed. Next to the mill is one of the last remaining pagoda-style filling stations built by Wadham's Oil and Grease

Company of Milwaukee in the 1920s. A walking tour map is available from the Visitor Information Office at city hall on Washington Avenue.

There are also two historic bed-and-breakfast inns, the Washington House Inn, (414) 375-3550, and the Stagecoach Inn, (414) 375-0208. Both are located on Washington Avenue and were formerly stagecoach stops on the dusty, rutted road from Milwaukee to Green Bay. The Washington House Inn sits on the site of Cedarburg's first hotel. Accommodations lean toward the luxurious in this handsome building of Cream City brick. The Stagecoach Inn was originally called the Central House and its literature boasted, "First class accommodations, choice wines, liquors, and cigars. Good stabling and large stockyards." It still offers comfortable lodging and its lively pub is a perfect post-ride watering hole.

The tour begins in the parking lot of Cedar Creek Settlement in downtown Cedarburg. Take I-43 North from Milwaukee and exit on County Highway C (Exit 89). Follow County Highway C to WI 57 North, which takes you into downtown Cedarburg, where it becomes Washington Avenue. Cedar Creek Settlement is on Washington Avenue, just north of the Bridge Road intersection.

If you need a jolt of caffeine to start your ride, walk one block south to the Java House. This pleasant coffeehouse offers espresso, cappuccino, and just plain ol' joe, as well as muffins and other breakfast snacks. This is a bicycle-friendly establishment—as proof, the proprietors have posted a photocopied magazine article on the wall that attributes the success of Italian bike racers to strong, dark coffee. Hint: Gianni Bugno's pre-event brew is a double espresso.

0.0   *Left from the Cedar Creek Settlement parking lot onto Elm Street, then left immediately onto Washington Avenue.*

0.1   *Right at the stoplight onto Bridge Road.*

1.8   *Right onto Horns Corners Road.*

> Notice the many farmhouses, barn foundations, and outbuildings built of fieldstone and local limestone.

4.4   *Left onto Cedar Creek Road. For the 13-mile route that visits just the Covered Bridge, continue straight onto Horns Corners Road to Kaehlers Mill Road. Turn right onto Covered Bridge Road, which*

takes you to Covered Bridge Park. Refer to mileage 34.1 for the return.

This beautiful, winding stretch of road follows Cedar Creek, a quintessential babbling brook. The riverbank is lined with the tamaracks, cedars, and birches that thrive in moist soil. It is the power-producing capacity of this creek that attracted German and Irish immigrants to the Cedarburg area.

7.1   *Right onto Country Aire Drive (County Highway M).*

7.6   *Cross Cedar Creek.*

8.3   *Left onto Pleasant Valley Road.*

9.3   *Right onto Church Road.*

10.4 *Right onto WI 143.*

10.5 *Left onto South Church Road.*

11.6 *Bypass the right turn on Paradise Drive. For the 24.8-mile route, turn right here and follow to Wausaukee Road. Turn right onto Wausaukee and skip to the 28.5-mile mark below for remainder of directions.*

11.8 *Left onto Paradise Drive.*

12.6 *Right onto School Road.*

To your right is a glacial land formation called an esker. This winding ridge of sand and gravel was formed about 10,000 years ago by a glacial stream, which left deposits as it flowed in a tunnel beneath the ice.

13.1 *Right onto Lincoln Drive.*

14.3 *Right onto Decorah Road.*

15.0 *Enter the village of Myra.*

15.9 *Cross County Highway M and continue straight on County Highway I.*

17.3 *Enter village of Newburg.*

17.5 Right onto WI 33.

> This is a busier road but has a good shoulder.

17.7 Left onto Franklin Street by Holy Trinity cemetery.

18.0 Right onto Main Street.

> On your left, just after the turn, notice the building with the colorful storefront done in the San Francisco painted-lady style. The old fire department, one block ahead on the opposite side of the street, has a matching facade.

18.4 Left onto County Highway Y (also West Hawthorne Drive).

> Follow the sign toward the Riveredge Nature Center. In the early spring you will see buckets suspended from many maple trees, collecting sap for maple syrup.

19.6 Right into the Riveredge Nature Center.

> The nature center provides outdoor educational experiences for children and adults from the Milwaukee area. The center includes changing indoor exhibits and extensive hiking trails. This is a good spot to pause for a break or lunch. There are picnic tables and rest rooms.

19.7 Right onto County Highway Y from Nature Center parking lot.

20.1 Straight onto Hawthorne Drive where County Highway Y goes left.

20.8 Right onto St. Finbar's Road.

21.7 Right onto Shady Lane where St. Finbar's ends.

22.3 Shady Lane makes a sharp left turn and becomes Birchwood Drive.

24.4 Birchwood makes a sharp right turn and becomes Knollwood Drive.

26.9 Left onto Wausaukee Road.

28.5 Left onto Washington Drive.

29.4 To your left is Apple Hill Farm, an orchard and fieldstone farmhouse in a picturesque setting. Quench your thirst with sweet cider or crunchy apples in the fall.

29.5 *Right onto County Highway Y.*

30.0 *Left onto Cedar Sauk Road.*

30.7 *Right onto Horns Corners Road.*

31.3 *Left onto Hilly Lane.*

31.6 *Right onto Lofty Lane.*

32.1 *Left onto Pleasant Valley Road.*

33.0 *Right onto Covered Bridge Road.*

34.1 *Covered Bridge Park.*

> Wisconsin's last remaining covered bridge is to your left. While Wisconsin is at the northern end of the covered bridge "belt," there were once over 300 such bridges in the state. This one was built in 1876 to replace previously washed out bridges over Cedar Creek. Look closely at the hardwood pins that are used instead of nails or bolts to secure the bridge's framework. While many people think that the canopy was intended to shelter travelers from storms or provide refuge from Indians, it is more likely that the cover was built to protect the truss structure of the bridge or to prevent oxen from shying at the sight of water.

34.2 *Right onto Cedar Creek Road just beyond bridge.*

35.1 *Left onto Horns Corners Road.*

37.6 *Left onto Bridge Street.*

39.4 *Left onto Washington Avenue.*

39.5 *Right onto Sheboygan Road and into the Cedar Creek Settlement parking lot.*

> Wind down from your ride with wine sampling at the Cedar Creek Winery in the Settlement complex, which features European-style red and white wines.

Bicycle Repair Services

Benz Ski and Cycling
6619 West Mequon Road, Mequon, WI
(414) 242-3310

Grafton Ski & Cyclery
1208 Twelfth Avenue, Grafton, WI
(414) 377-5220

SOUTHWESTERN
WISCONSIN

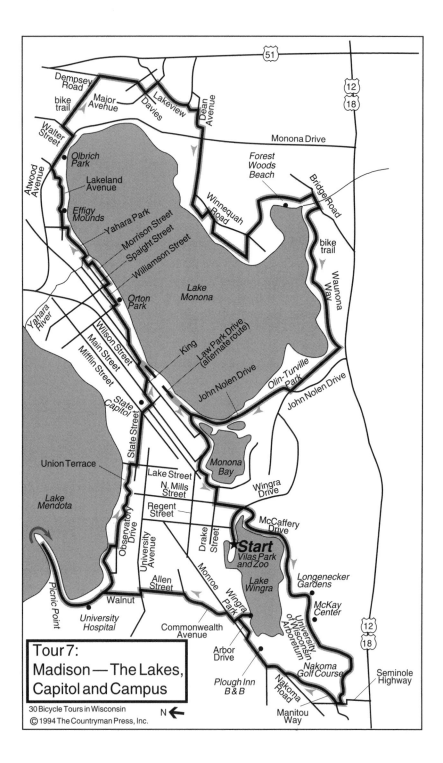

Tour 7:
Madison — The Lakes,
Capitol and Campus

30 Bicycle Tours in Wisconsin
© 1994 The Countryman Press, Inc.

N

7

Madison—The Lakes, Capitol, and Campus

Distance: *14.2 miles or 26.8 miles*
Terrain: *Flat to gently rolling*

Madison straddles four sparkling lakes, with the state capitol, the University of Wisconsin campus, and the downtown shopping district squeezed into a skinny isthmus between the largest two. The city is laced with over 100 miles of well-marked bicycle paths shared with walkers, runners, and sidewalk skaters. And it's one of the few places outside of Beijing where bicyclists are granted their own lane of traffic on major thoroughfares. These features, along with a kind of zany zest for living, have won Madison many "best of" awards, including a spot on *Bicycling Magazine*'s short list for America's top cycling city. The sheer number of cyclists in Madison requires that traffic laws be strictly enforced—fail to heed a stop sign or ride without a light at night and you will soon be acquainted with one of Madison's cycling police officers!

Madison's population is a peppery potpourri of academics, legislators, and litigators—there are more lawyers per capita here than anywhere in the country. The abundance of new and used bookstores demonstrates that Madisonians are a literary lot, buying an average of six books a year each, far above the national average. And it appears that Madison is closing in on Seattle as cappuccino king—there is at least one coffee house on every block in the downtown area.

The University of Wisconsin campus has been the setting of movies (*Back to School* with Rodney Dangerfield), books (*Rads,* which chronicles 1960s antiwar unrest), and Nobel Prize–winning research. One of the largest public universities in the country, with nearly 50,000 students and another 20,000 faculty and staff, the UW dominates Madison's personality and politics.

If you need to rent a bike, check with Budget Bicycle Center, (608) 251-8413, at 1230 Regent Street or Yellow Jersey, which also rents tandems, (608) 257-4737, at 419 State Street. Since the streets weave around the lakes and don't follow a logical grid pattern, we suggest picking up a city map to supplement the one given here. Many of the turns on this tour are very close together, often only a block apart, so stay alert and look for bike route signs. The 14.2-mile route takes in the arboretum, the campus, and the capitol. The 26.8-mile route includes all of the above, plus a loop around Lake Monona.

Madison is easily reached on I-94. Exit on WI 12/18 and follow it around the city to John Nolen Drive. Exit onto John Nolen Drive and follow it past the coliseum and across a narrow causeway to North Shore Drive. Turn left onto North Shore Drive (becomes Proudfit Street) and follow it across West Washington Avenue to Regent Street. At this corner, Trek operates a "company store" selling bicycles and accessories. From Regent Street, turn left onto Mills Street and follow it for about eight blocks. Then turn right onto North Wingra Drive and follow it to the parking area for Henry Vilas Beach.

0.0 *Start at the Henry Vilas Beach bath house, opposite the back entrance to Henry Vilas Zoo. There are rest rooms, changing facilities, a snack bar, and picnic tables here. Right onto Vilas Park Drive from the bath house.*

0.3 *Right onto South Mills Street.*

0.4 *Right into the University of Wisconsin Arboretum.*

> Created on abandoned farmland, the "arb" was designed with the guidance of conservationist Aldo Leopold to include examples of all the ecological communities of Wisconsin. This landmark experiment in land reclamation began in 1932 and much of the initial work was done by Civilian Conservation Corps crews.

1.2 *To the right is Gardner Marsh, part of Lake Wingra, a 345-acre lake adjacent to the arboretum that serves as a living laboratory for students of many disciplines, from art to zoology.*

"Wingra" is the Winnebago word for duck—easy to remember because waterfowl are plentiful on the lake.

2.0 *Here you enter a shady tunnel of trees.*

In Gallistel Woods, to the left, and Wingra Woods, to the right, sugar maples, basswoods, and beeches have been planted beneath an umbrella of oaks. This combination of foliage creates a wonderful color display in the fall.

2.2 *The Longenecker Gardens, to the left, is a 40-acre horticultural collection established by University of Wisconsin professor William Longenecker.*

A favorite time to visit is in May, when hundreds of lilacs and flowering crabapples are in bloom.

2.6 *Tours of the Longenecker Gardens, as well as bird and nature walks, leave from the McKay Center.*

2.8 *Curtis Prairie, to the left, is one of the most successful restoration projects in the arboretum, perhaps because Dane County was originally covered by prairie and savannah.*

Scientists and enthusiasts come from great distances to study the art of prairie-making here.

3.1 *Noe Woods, the last wooded stretch you pass through, is an oak forest typical of southern Wisconsin.*

This kind of forest grew up on the prairie following settlement and the cessation of frequent wildfires. This forest has been left untended to study the cycle of changes that will occur. The magnificent white and black oaks form a canopy 80 feet above the road.

3.4 *Right onto Seminole Highway, for less than a block. Right onto Manitou Way, following bike route sign.*

3.6 *Here you pass the Number 10 Tee at Nakoma Golf Course—your helmet will protect you from errant golf balls!*

4.0 *Right onto the sidewalk, following bike trail sign. The trail parallels Nakoma Road.*

4.2   There is a picturesque duck pond to the right.

4.3   The trail turns right, now running parallel to Monroe Street.

4.4   The Plough Inn, (608) 238-2981, to the left, offers bed-and-breakfast rooms with an arboretum view. Just ahead, turn right onto the bike path as it splits off from the sidewalk.

4.7   Right onto Arbor Drive where the bike path ends, following bike route sign.

4.9   Right onto Knickerbocker Street toward Lake Wingra.

5.0   Lake Wingra Park and Boat House offers canoe and sailboat rental, a snack bar, and rest rooms. Backtrack to Monroe Street from the park.

5.2   Right onto Monroe Street (careful, busy traffic). On this block you will find a cluster of eateries popular with cyclists—Michael's Frozen Custard, Pasqual's Salsaria, and the Laurel Tavern. If you need a bike adjustment, Michael's Cyclery is right across the street.

5.4   Left onto Commonwealth Avenue at the stoplight, opposite Isthmus Sailboards.

5.5   Left on Commonwealth Avenue.

5.7   Railroad tracks with a dangerous angle.

5.9   Left onto South Allen Street at the stop sign.

6.4   Left onto University Avenue (careful, busy traffic). Go one block and turn right onto Walnut Street.

6.9   At the Marsh Lane intersection, continue straight toward the lake on the sidewalk, rather than turning into the parking lot. The behemoth building off to the left is the University of Wisconsin Hospital complex.

7.0   Left onto the bike path. Note: there are separate bike and pedestrian paths that run parallel.

7.4   Right into Picnic Point Wildlife and Recreation Area.

This 129-acre peninsula extending into Lake Mendota has been part of the university since 1939 and bring backs fond memories for many alumni. Picnic Point is accessible only by bike or foot.

7.9 *A bench to right provides an often-photographed view of the capitol and campus. Water is available from an old-fashioned pump ahead to your left. Backtrack when you reach the end of the peninsula.*

8.6 *Stay left at the fork here.*

8.8 *Left onto the bike path. This shaded path follows the shore of Lake Mendota, past a series of dormitories and clubhouses for the UW crew team and sailing organization.*

10.8 *You will need to walk your bike down the steps to the Union Terrace, one of Madison's favorite meeting places for students and nonstudents alike. Bratwurst and other sandwiches are sold at an outdoor snack bar (beer is available only with a University ID card). From the terrace, walk your bike along the lake to Mendota Court.*

11.0 *Right onto Mendota Court (becomes Lake Street) where the terrace ends.*

11.1 *Left onto State Street. Or detour to the right, where exotic aromas emanate from a group of mobile foodcarts. Choices include freshly squeezed juices and, at last check, East African, Hmong, Turkish, South American, and Chinese cuisine. Greek, Nepalese, Italian, Afghan, and American food are available to your left, on State Street.*

State Street is a pedestrian mall that permits bus and bicycle traffic only. About midway up the street, toward the capitol, Canterbury Booksellers and Inn, (608) 258-9911, is located a block to the right at 315 West Gorham Street. This unique "B & B & B" offers bed, breakfast, and bookstore under the same roof in a convenient downtown location.

11.7 *Right onto North Carroll Street.*

The pearly white granite dome of Wisconsin's capitol dominates the surrounding square and the streets that fan out like spokes in a wheel. Its size alone is impressive—just a few feet shorter than our national capitol—an intentional token of respect by designer George Post. The dome is topped with a graceful gilded statue of a woman by Daniel French (sculptor of Lincoln at the Lincoln Memorial).

Enter the capitol from any corner and you are likely to find people lying flat on their backs on the well-worn marble floor, staring at the ceiling. They're not legislators left prostrate by a lengthy filibuster, but tourists taking in a majestic mural, "Resources of Wisconsin" by American artist Edwin Blashfield, 200 feet above, inside the dome.

Every Saturday morning from April through November, the capitol square hosts a farmers' market with over 400 vendors. As the summer progresses, an increasing cornucopia of fresh produce, cheeses, meats, and flowers flows in from surrounding farms. But the market is really much more than vegetables—it's a social happening that involves sipping hot, strong coffee; petting dogs of all sizes and pedigrees; listening to the strains of sidewalk musicians; and watching a passing parade of people. Some 17,000 people visit the market on a busy weekend, but the whole affair is amazingly orderly because everyone strolls the square in a counterclockwise direction.

11.9 Left onto East Main Street. (Use the special lane for bikes and buses.)

12.0 Right onto King Street.

12.2 Left onto East Wilson Street.

12.3 Cross South Blair Street at the light. The bike path resumes on the opposite side of the intersection. Continue straight, parallel to Williamson Street, for the 26.8-mile route.

For the shorter route, bear right on the bike path, through Law Park, along the shore of Lake Monona. Continue on the path for .9 mile, to the second stoplight, at the intersection of John Nolen Drive and North Shore Drive. Use the pedestrian crosswalk to cross John Nolen Drive here. The bike path

The tour of Madison weaves around three lakes and includes the capitol square.

resumes on the opposite side of the intersection. Skip to the 24.9-mile mark for the remaining directions.

12.5 *Right onto Jennifer Street.*

12.6 *Right onto Spaight Street (right turn allowed for buses and bikes only). To your right is Lake Monona, which is in view for most of the remainder of the ride.*

13.0 *Right onto Ingersoll Street.*

13.1 *Left onto Rutledge Street, adjacent to Orton Park.*

13.3 *Right onto Baldwin Street. Baldwin turns left and becomes Morrison Street.*

13.6 *Left onto Thornton Avenue.*

13.7 *Right onto Rutledge Street, over the bridge across the Yahara River.*

13.8 *Right onto Riverside Drive, immediately on the other side of the bridge. Left immediately on Yahara Place.*

14.2 *Left onto Dunning Street.*

Go for one block, then turn right onto Lakeland Avenue. To the right, ahead, is an intricately carved totem pole that marks the location of two Native American effigy (animal-shaped) mounds.

14.2 *Lakeland Avenue turns to the right.*

14.6 *Bike path resumes at intersection of Welch Avenue. Continue around the metal barricades on what looks like a driveway, down a rather steep hill.*

14.7 *Continue on the bike path that parallels Atwood Avenue. You are now at Olbrich Park and Boat Launch.*

Across the street under the glass dome is Olbrich Botanical Gardens, which has permanent and rotating horticultural exhibits.

15.1 *Left on Walter Street at the stoplight, following signs for the Lake Monona bike route. (Busy intersection, take care.)*

15.2 *Right onto the bike trail again, about one block after the intersection.*

15.9 *Right onto the sidewalk that runs parallel to Dempsey Road, where the path ends. You will see a gate to American Family Insurance headquarters. Continue past a busy intersection on Cottage Grove Road.*

16.4 *Right onto Davies Street, following the bike route sign.*

16.5 *Left onto Major Avenue.*

16.7 *Right onto Lakeview Avenue.*

17.1 *Right onto Lance Lane.*

17.3 *Right onto Dean Avenue.*

17.6 *Cross Monona Drive at the stoplight. Take care, busy intersection.*

18.3 *Left onto Tonyawatha Trail.*

18.4 *Left onto Progressive Lane.*

18.5 *Right onto Winnequah Road.*

18.6 *Right onto Tonyawatha Trail.*

19.5 *Left onto Winnequah Trail.*

19.8 *Right onto Winnequah Road.*

20.4 *Forest Woods Beach offers swimming, though weeds are sometimes a problem on Madison lakes by late summer.*

20.8 *Right onto bike trail, parallel to Bridge Street. Right immediately onto the Paunack Park Bike Path.*

22.2 *Straight on Waunona Way where the bike path ends.*

22.7 *The bike path resumes here.*

24.4 *Olin–Turville Park.*

24.9 *Left at stoplight for North Shore Drive, crossing John Nolan Drive. Use pedestrian crosswalk. Bike path resumes on the opposite side of the intersection.*

25.3 *Brittingham Park.*

25.8 *Left onto West Shore Drive where bike path ends. Go one block, then right onto Drake Street.*

25.9 *Cross Park Street. (Busy intersection, take care.)*

26.1 *Left onto Mills Street.*

26.5 *Right onto North Wingra Drive.*

26.8 *Your starting point at Henry Vilas Beach.*

End with a swim or a visit to the zoo, both free of charge.

Bicycle Repair Services

Budget Bicycle
1230 Regent Street
Madison, WI
(608) 251-8413

Michael's Cyclery
2606 Monroe Street
Madison, WI
(608) 231-1101

Middleton Cycle Shop
6649 University Avenue
Middleton, WI
(608) 836-3931

The Trek Company Store
652 West Washington Street
Madison, WI
(608) 259-8735

Village Pedaler
5511 Monona Drive
Monona, WI
(608) 221-0311

Willliamson Bicycle Works
601 William Street
Madison, WI
(608) 255-5292

Yellow Jersey
419 State Street
Madison, WI
(608) 257-4737

Haack's Cycle & Fitness
3729 E. Washington Boulevard
Madison, WI
(608) 241-2138

Haack's Cycle & Fitness
509 S. Gammon Road
Madison, WI
(608) 833-0040

Criterium Cyclery
449 State Street
Madison, WI
(608) 251-7007

8

Mineral Point/Driftless Area

Distance: *38.3 miles*
Terrain: *Rolling to hilly*

If not for a historical misinterpretation, University of Wisconsin athletes would be cheered to victory by a burly lead miner rather than by Bucky Badger, the team's amiable animal mascot. Many proud students and alumni are surprised to learn that Wisconsin earned its nickname, the Badger State, not from the animal at all, but from early lead miners who built caves in the hillsides of southwestern Wisconsin to protect their claims. These burrows resembled badger dens and the miners were commonly referred to as "badgers."

In the 1820s, lead miners swarmed over southwestern Wisconsin in search of lead ore, the elusive mineral that gave Mineral Point its name. The boom continued until 1848 when gold was discovered in California, luring the prospectors to a new promised land.

By the mid-1830s, news of Wisconsin's "lead rush" reached England and enticed skilled hard-rock miners from the Cornwall region to the United States. Besides their mining skills, the Cornish brought an exceptional talent in stone masonry. When they arrived in Mineral Point, they applied their trade to local limestone and made their mark on the community in the form of many charming stone cottages, reminiscent of those in the English countryside. In recent years, Mineral Point has gained a reputation as an artists' community and many of the cottages now house studios and galleries. Oil and watercolor painting, stained glass, sculpture, fiber arts, and pottery are just a few of the mediums represented here.

Take WI 151 to Mineral Point from either the north or south and take Shake Rag Street into town, following the signs to the Pendarvis Historical

79

Site. This tour begins at the historical marker in Soldiers Memorial Park, opposite Pendarvis. You will find plenty of parking, rest rooms, a picnic shelter, and an Olympic-size public swimming pool—a welcome sight after a day of pedaling the roller coaster hills of this driftless, and lakeless, area of Wisconsin. There is also a pool at Centennial Park in Dodgeville, midway through the ride, so bring your swimsuit along on a hot day. If you prefer to explore the area on more level terrain, turn to the description of the Military Ridge Trail; the trail can be picked up at nearby Governor Dodge State Park.

A visit to the Pendarvis site, (608) 987-2122, and the adjacent Merry Christmas Mine, open daily May through October, is a good introduction to area history. Once a stylish restaurant that served Cornish fare to Frank Lloyd Wright, August Derleth, Sinclair Lewis, and other local luminaries, Pendarvis is now museum complex operated by the State Historical Society. Costumed interpreters give guided tours through several Cornish cottages and relate interesting tidbits about the rough and tumble mining era. A walking trail from the Pendarvis parking lot leads to the hillside where lead was first discovered.

0.0 Right onto Shake Rag Street.

> This street's name comes from the lead mining days, when Cornish women who lived in the cluster of cottages here shook dishrags from their doorways as a signal to hungry miners that dinner was ready.

0.2 Right onto Antoine Street at the tennis courts. This road becomes County SS when it leaves town.

> It's time to gear down already. This corner of the state never felt the molding and flattening effect of the glaciers. The result is an undulating topography that consists of multiple sets of ups and downs. Don't despair—with a little practice, you will be able to use your momentum from a downhill run to propel yourself up the next "wave."

3.9 Left onto County D where County SS ends. There is no road sign here.

4.6 Right onto Governor Dodge Road.

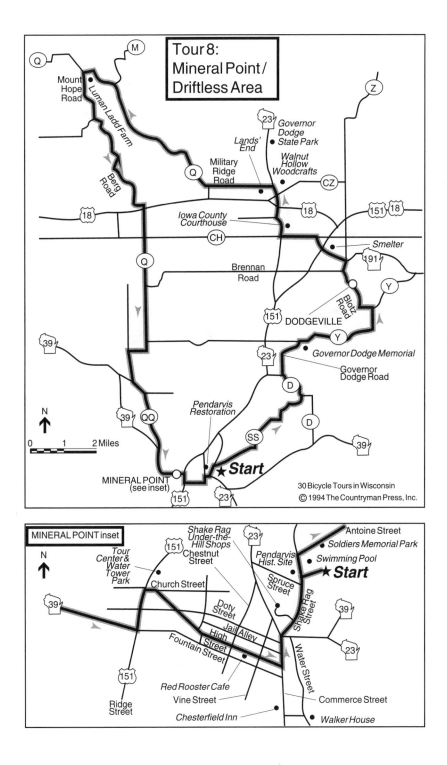

Tour 8:
Mineral Point / Driftless Area

Main map labels:

Q

M

Mount Hope Road

Luman Ladd Farm

Berg Road

Q

Military Ridge Road

23 Governor Dodge State Park

Lands' End

Walnut Hollow Woodcrafts

CZ

Z

18

18

151 18

Iowa County Courthouse

CH

Smelter

191

Q

Brennan Road

Blotz Road

Y

151 DODGEVILLE

Y

39

23 Governor Dodge Memorial

Governor Dodge Road

D

D

39

N

0 1 2 Miles

39

QQ

Pendarvis Restoration

SS

★ Start

MINERAL POINT (see inset)

151

23

30 Bicycle Tours in Wisconsin
© 1994 The Countryman Press, Inc.

MINERAL POINT inset

N

Shake Rag Under-the-Hill Shops

23

Antoine Street

Soldiers Memorial Park

Tour Center & Water Tower Park

151

Chestnut Street

Pendarvis Hist. Site

Swimming Pool

★ Start

39

Church Street

Spruce Street

Doty Street

Jail Alley

39

High Street

Fountain Street

Shake Rag Street

23

Red Rooster Cafe

Water Street

Vine Street

Commerce Street

151

Chesterfield Inn

Walker House

Ridge Street

Watch for pheasant and wild turkey during this ride.

5.8 *Left onto County Y where Governor Dodge Road ends.*

Just past the intersection is the Governor Dodge Memorial, located at the site of his original homestead. Colonel Henry Dodge was inaugurated governor of the Territory of Wisconsin in 1835.

8.7 *Left onto Blotz Road at the top of the hill.*

10.3 *Right at the stop sign. There is no road sign here but you are now on Brennan Road.*

10.6 *Left onto WI 191.*

On your right, shortly after the turn, are the stone remains of a smelter used to melt lead ore.

11.9 *Keep left at the three forks. You are still on WI 191.*

12.2 *Enter the village of Dodgeville. At this point WI 191 turns into Division Street.*

12.2 *Left onto Dacotah Street and follow it to Centennial Park.*

This is a good place for a picnic lunch, a swim, or a nap under one of the many oak trees. Backtrack to the park entrance.

13.0 Left onto East Valley Street.

13.1 Right onto South Iowa Street (Highway 23).

13.4 As you pass through downtown Dodgeville, the Iowa County Courthouse is on your left.

Built by a Cornish stonemason in 1859, this impressive limestone building incorporates the white cupola of a New England church and the fluted columns of a southern mansion.

13.8 Continue straight as Iowa Street turns into Bequette Street.

14.2 Cross WI 18 and continue straight.

14.8 Left onto Military Ridge Road. This turn is easy to miss. It is just past the entrance to the Walnut Hollow Farm Woodcraft Store, (608) 935-2341.

Craft supplies available through the Walnut Hollow catalog are sold at a discount at this factory store.

The large warehouse and office complex off to the left is the corporate headquarters of Lands' End Direct Merchants, a mail-order clothing and luggage company. Sorry, no factory store here.

16.8 Right onto County Highway Q.

For the next few miles, enjoy a beautiful rolling landscape untempered by glacial ice. After a series of expansive vistas from the ridge, the route leads you on an exhilarating downhill cruise through the narrow winding valley along Harker Creek.

22.6 Left onto Mount Hope Road. This is a very easy turn to miss. Begin looking for the road once you pass the County Highway M junction. It turns off directly after the big red barn of the Luman and Ladd Farm.

Both this road and Berg Road (your next turn) have a paved but rather rough surface. Watch for wild turkeys, pheasants, and red-tailed hawks.

24.0 *Left onto Berg Road. There is no sign here but it is the first intersection you come to after turning onto Mount Hope Road.*

28.1 *Cross WI 18 and continue straight on County Highway Q.*

33.3 *Left onto County Highway QQ.*

There is a great downhill stretch as you pass Ludden Lake and the adjoining public golf course. At the bottom of the hill is a lovely farmhouse built from local limestone.

36.0 *Left onto WI 39.*

36.7 *Enter the town of Mineral Point.*

37.3 *Left onto WI 151 for two blocks.*

37.4 *Right onto Church Street at the water tower.*

37.5 *Right onto High Street at the fork and follow it through downtown.*

Notice the zinc cast statue of a dog that guards the Wisconsin Power and Light building. One of Mineral Point's most-loved landmarks, the statue marks the site of the former Gundry and Gray department store, established by two immigrants from Cornwall, England. It was a British custom to identify stores with an animal trademark.

If you have worked up an appetite, stop in for a traditional Cornish pasty (pronounced pass-tee) at the Red Rooster Cafe at 158 High Street or the Chesterfield Inn at 20 Commerce Street (mentioned below). This satisfying fare from lead-mining days consists of meat, potatoes, onions, and seasonings sealed in a pastry crust. It's said that the test of a good pasty was a crust sturdy enough that it would not break apart when dropped down a mine shaft! Fortunately, the pasty of today has a lighter and flakier shell. Finish your meal with another Cornish treat, the figgyhobbin, a pastry log filled with brown sugar, nuts, and raisins and topped with caramel sauce.

38.0 Left on Commerce Street at the bottom of the hill.

To your right is the Chesterfield Inn, (608) 987-3682, a former stagecoach stop, which provides bed-and-breakfast lodging and has a pleasant garden restaurant operated by the Ovens of Brittany, a popular Madison eatery. One block over on Water Street is the Walker House, site of Wisconsin's only legal hanging, in 1842. A crowd of 4,000 turned out to watch murderer William Caffee meet his fate.

38.1 Keep right at the fork by the stop sign, cross WI 39 and continue straight on Shake Rag Street.

On your left is Shake Rag Under-the-Hill, a complex of shops.

38.3 Soldiers Memorial Park is on your right.

Bicycle Repair Service

Dan Atkins Bicycle Shoppe
517 Half Mile Road, Verona, WI
(608) 845-6644

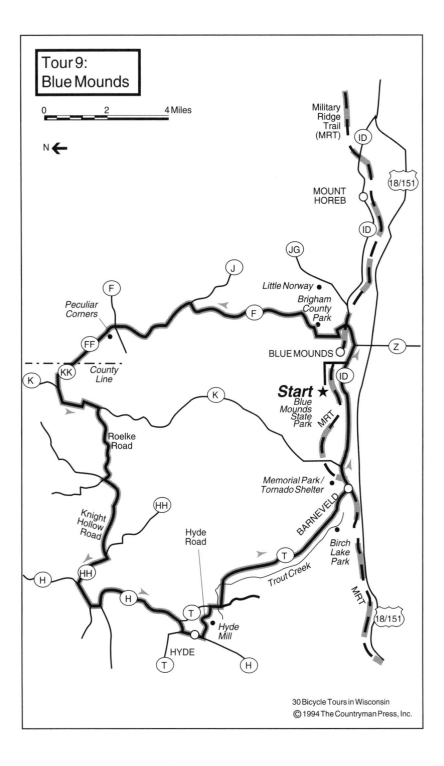

Tour 9:
Blue Mounds

0   2   4 Miles

N ←

Military
Ridge
Trail
(MRT)

ID

18/151

MOUNT
HOREB

ID

JG

Little Norway •

Brigham
County
Park

J

F

Peculiar
Corners

F

FF

BLUE MOUNDS

Z

County
Line

KK

ID

K

Start
Blue
Mounds
State
Park

K

MRT

Roelke
Road

Memorial Park /
Tornado Shelter

HH

Knight
Hollow
Road

Hyde
Road

BARNEVELD

Birch
Lake
Park

H

HH

T

Trout Creek

MRT

H

T

18/151

H

T

Hyde
Mill

HYDE

T

H

30 Bicycle Tours in Wisconsin
© 1994 The Countryman Press, Inc.

9
Blue Mounds

Distance: *35 miles (1 mile dirt surface)*
Terrain: *Rolling to hilly*

"I took view of some mountains…I ascended these and had an extensive view of the country," reported Jonathan Carver, an Englishman exploring the Wisconsin River Valley in 1776.

Mountains, not quite. But the Blue Mounds, two bluish-gray hills that were important landmarks for pioneer travelers, still dominate the skyline of southwestern Wisconsin. Blue Mounds State Park, located atop the westernmost of the two mounds, is the highest point in southern Wisconsin at 1,716 feet. The mounds are made of limestone, which has hardened over millions of years, forming a protective cap and slowing the weathering process.

The Blue Mounds area is known for its deep, sheltered valleys. Your face may be dampened by droplets of foggy mist as you descend into a hollow and quickly dried as you pedal out of the valley onto a plateau with open fields and warm sunshine. Perhaps it is this magical quality that attracted so many Norwegian settlers, with their penchant for elves and trolls, to the area.

Norse descendants in search of their roots may want to visit several attractions that are nearby, but not on this route. Little Norway, (608) 437-8211, located on County Highway JG, encompasses a genuine Norwegian farmstead dating to 1856 and a traditional stavekirke (wooden church) that was part of Norway's exhibit at the 1893 Columbia Exposition in Chicago. Stop in at Schubert's Bakery in Mount Horeb for a loaf of limpa bread or a nourishing lunch of Norwegian meatballs. Mount Horeb also has a Folk Museum and about a dozen antique emporiums. Song of Norway, (608)

437-4600, a musical performance celebrating the life of Norwegian composer Edvard Grieg, is performed on weekends in July.

Be prepared for a number of steep grades on this ride. The weak-kneed may need to walk a few uphill stretches but will still have the pleasure of whizzing down the other side. If you prefer more level terrain, the Military Ridge Trail traverses this area on the flat surface of an abandoned railroad bed.

Keep an eye on the sky if you take this trip on a hot, humid summer day—the area has a reputation for being a "tornado alley." You will pedal past the still-visible devastation of a 1984 twister later in the ride.

The tour begins at Blue Mounds State Park, about one mile northwest of the village of Blue Mounds. Take WI 151 to Blue Mounds, exit north on County Highway Z, and follow it to County Highway ID, where you turn left. This will take you to Mounds Park Road, where you should turn right and follow the signs into the park. Proceed to the picnic area at the top of the hill. Park facilities include an outdoor swimming pool with showers and changing rooms. Call the park office, (608) 437-5711, for camping reservations on holiday weekends.

0.0   *The ride starts at the top of the hill by the East Tower/Vista sign.*

Begin with a great downhill glide, past the ranger station and into the town of Blue Mounds.

0.6   *Continue straight at the stop sign at the park exit. You are now on Mounds Park Road.*

1.4   *Left onto Division Street.*

The village of Blue Mounds was settled by Ebenezer Brigham in 1828. Brigham was the first white settler in the area and sought his fortune as a prospector. When other miners began to arrive, he turned to innkeeping, offering food and lodging along the old Military Ridge Trail. Brigham was also a colonel during the Blackhawk War and prominent in the development of Wisconsin statehood.

Today Blue Mounds is a sleepy little burg with a church, pub, and convenience store. Stop in at the Hooterville Tavern after your ride for some good Wisconsin hospitality. No frosted mugs here—belly up to the bar, drink from the bottle, and find out who's pitching for the Brewers today.

1.7 *Left onto County Highway F and continue under the railway trestle. There is no road sign, but there is one that points toward Mazomanie and Brigham Park. Proceed in that direction.*

2.2 *Left at the fork staying on County Highway F.*

2.8 *Stop to enjoy a panoramic view here at Brigham Park.*

Land for the park was donated by Charles Brigham, a descendant of the village founder. On a clear day you can see 35 miles north toward the Wisconsin River Valley. Brigham Park also contains several mature sugar maples, rarely seen in southern Wisconsin.

2.8 *Continue on County Highway F.*

You're in for a treat now—there's a four-mile downhill run ahead. Halfway down the hill, you'll pass the Saint James Catholic cemetery, with graves dating to the late 1800s.

7.0 *Continue straight on County Highway F at the County Highway J junction.*

9.4 *Straight on County Highway FF where County Highway F turns right.*

Anything seem strange? You have arrived at Peculiar Corners. In 1898, a post office named Peculiar was established in the farmhouse of Tom Davies. Not surprisingly, cyclists relish having their picture taken in front of the Peculiar Corners sign.

11.0 *Continue straight when you enter Iowa County. County Highway FF now becomes County Highway KK.*

11.8 *Left onto County Highway K.*

13.2 *Right onto Roelke Road. The small sign here is easy to miss. If you come to the round barn, you have passed the turn.*

15.3 *Left onto Knight Hollow Road. There are no signs here, but Knight Hollow is the first of the four forks you see. Talk about a peculiar corner!*

17.3 Right onto County Highway HH where Knight Hollow Road ends.

18.7 Left onto County Highway H where County Highway HH ends.

As you round the corner, you'll pass the historic Mill Creek Cheese factory. Continue about 4.5 miles to the tiny village of Hyde.

23.3 Left onto Hyde Road.

The road has a dirt surface that lasts about one mile, but it is worth it to get a glimpse of picturesque Hyde's Mill. If you come to the Hyde Store, you've missed the turn to the mill. Stop for a snack or cool drink and backtrack to Hyde Road. (To avoid the dirt surface turn left onto County Highway T before reaching Hyde.)

Hyde's Mill was built in 1850 by Theodore Sawle. The old millstones used to grind grain are lined up next to the road. If you are lucky, Ted Sawle, a descendant of the original miller, will come out and give you a tour of the mill and his fully equipped blacksmith shop. He also has a water-powered generator that provides electricity to the local utility.

23.6 Continue straight on Hyde Road.

24.3 Right onto County Highway T. This takes you through a beautiful valley along the Trout Creek public fishing area.

29.4 To your right is Birch Lake Park, which has rest rooms and a picnic area. From the park, you have a steep climb up to the village of Barneveld.

30.1 Right onto Grove Street at the hilltop.

30.2 Left onto Main Street.

30.5 Memorial Park.

The first thing that you'll notice about Barneveld is its bald appearance. There are very few large trees and the town's modern ranch and split-level homes look oddly out of place in the midst of older farm communities. Though the buildings are new, the village was founded many years ago. What you

Hyde's Mill is owned by a descendant of the original miller.

see is evidence of the powerful tornado that swept down on Barneveld on June 8, 1984, killing nine people and destroying three churches, the entire commercial district, and 60 percent of the homes.

Residents rallied to the motto "we're not giving up—we're going on." With the help of federal disaster funds they worked together to rebuild the entire town. This park and tornado shelter was built in memorial to those who died. The shelter contains pictures of the downtown area following the tornado, a covered picnic area, and rest rooms.

This route continues back via the roadway. However, you may opt to return to Blue Mounds on the Military Ridge Trail. This adds one mile to the trip.

30.6 Left onto Orbison Street. This turns into County Highway ID.

30.9 Continue straight where WI Highway 18/151 goes right.

33.6 Left onto Mounds Road toward Blue Mounds State Park.

34.4 Continue straight and up, up, up into the park.

35.0 Once you've caught your breath, survey the area you've just covered from the park's two 40-foot observation towers.

Vistas extend as far as the Wisconsin–Iowa border on a clear day. These towers were originally built for another purpose. Vacationers traveled to the area by train from Chicago to watch horses race on a half-mile oval here—the road through the picnic area roughly traces the circuit. The towers offered box-seat viewing for race patrons.

Bicycle Repair Service

Dan Atkins Bicycle Shoppe
517 Half Mile Road, Verona, WI
(608) 845-6644

10
Spring Green/Wisconsin River/ Frank Lloyd Wright Country

Distance: *22.3 or 31.2 miles (.8 mile dirt surface)*
Terrain: *Rolling to hilly*

The Spring Green valley was home to architectural genius Frank Lloyd Wright and the area's pleasing landscape served as his inspiration. Blending in with the rugged bluffs and tucked into niches of wooded hillside are the flat-roof profiles, cantilever projections, and steeple-like spires that identify the designs of Wright and his apprentices.

Unlike his buildings, Wright's lifestyle did not mesh harmoniously with the Spring Green hills. His cohabitation with his mistress, Mamah Borthwick Cheney, was considered scandalous by conservative local standards. After the death of Mamah Cheney in a tragic fire at Taliesin, Wright was married twice and was eventually accepted by the community. Older residents still remember the eccentric shadow Wright cast as he strolled about town in a swirling black cape, carrying a walking stick.

The steep hills and narrow winding valleys of this unglaciated part of Wisconsin often prompt comparisons to Vermont. Those who undertake this ride should have a good understanding of their gears, a dependable pair of knees, and a fair degree of confidence on downhill stretches. Somewhat of a summertime ritual for us, and for many other cyclists from nearby Madison, this ride offers a near-perfect combination of the corporal and cerebral—an afternoon of challenging cycling with stops to admire Wright's masterpieces, followed by a cleansing dip in the Wisconsin River, a sunset picnic on the river's shores, and an evening of Shakespeare under the stars at American Players Theatre.

The tour begins at Tower Hill State Park, (608) 588-2116. If you are

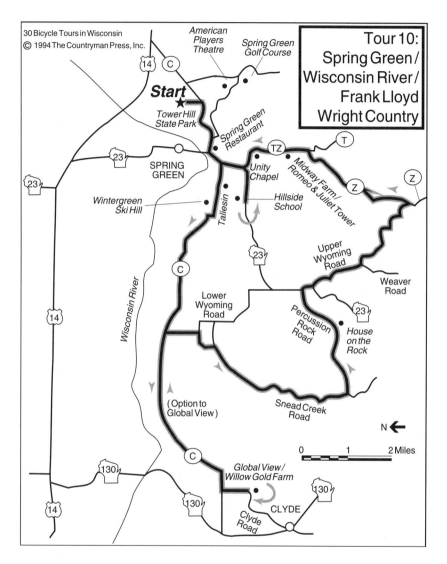

30 Bicycle Tours in Wisconsin
© 1994 The Countryman Press, Inc.

Tour 10:
Spring Green /
Wisconsin River /
Frank Lloyd
Wright Country

American Players Theatre

Spring Green Golf Course

Start

Tower Hill State Park

Spring Green Restaurant

SPRING GREEN

Unity Chapel

Wintergreen Ski Hill

Taliesin

Hillside School

Midway Farm / Romeo & Juliet Tower

Upper Wyoming Road

Weaver Road

Lower Wyoming Road

Percussion Rock Road

House on the Rock

Wisconsin River

(Option to Global View)

Snead Creek Road

N

0   1   2 Miles

Global View / Willow Gold Farm

CLYDE

Clyde Road

heading west on WI 14, turn onto County Highway C and follow it south for about one mile to the park. The park is open from May through October and has campsites, hiking trails, a canoe landing, and pit toilets.

Tower Hill park marks the site of the abandoned village of Helena. When lead was discovered in nearby hills in the 1830s, residents of Helena hung their hopes on a thriving new industry, the manufacture of lead shot. Molten lead was poured through strainers and dropped down a 120-foot shaft into a pool of cold water, where it formed into round pellets. The shot was sorted by size and shipped out for use in the Civil War. A short hike from the parking area takes you to the shot tower and a scenic overlook of the Wisconsin River.

0.0   *Right onto County Highway C at the park exit.*

0.1   *To your left is the entrance to American Players Theatre and the Spring Green Golf Course.*

American Players Theatre, (608) 588-2361, performs the work of Shakespeare and other great playwrights in a spectacular natural setting. The bowl-shaped, multitiered theater is nestled in a wooded hillside where whippoorwills, bullfrogs, falling stars, and fireflies provide the special effects. There is a pleasant picnic area outside the theater where theatergoers can enjoy a preperformance repast.

0.7   *To your right is wonderful view of the lower Wisconsin River. To your left is the Spring Green Restaurant, the only restaurant designed by Frank Lloyd Wright.*

As you look downstream, imagine pinery boys navigating heavily laden lumber rafts around the ever-shifting sandbars. These days the sandbars are populated with sunning canoeists, campers, and snapping turtles. Directly across the river is a beach where you can swim after the ride.

The Spring Green Restaurant was designed by Wright and constructed posthumously from his plans. Restaurant decor includes Wright-inspired furnishings, which are slightly uncomfortable for those over six feet tall—Wright considered anyone of that stature "a weed." Most tables offer a river view and the food is good.

0.8   *Left onto WI 23. Use caution, this is a busy road.*

1.0   *Right onto County Highway C.*

1.2   *Taliesin is to your left.*

Taliesin (tally-ehssen) means "shining brow" in Welsh, the language of Wright's relatives. He chose a high spot on his mother's property for his home, a stunning example of prairie-style architecture, often referred to as his "autobiography in wood and stone." Taliesin was twice destroyed by fire and rebuilt.

Unfortunately, Wright's home has fallen into disrepair in recent years and tours of the home's interior are not offered on a regularly scheduled basis. The State of Wisconsin has committed eight million dollars to renovate the building and Wisconsin's United States senators have introduced legislation that would provide additional funding by making Taliesin an affiliate of the National Park Service.

1.9 *To the right is the entrance to Wintergreen ski area. A series of switchbacks on a paved road will lead you to the top for a panoramic view of the Wisconsin River Valley.*

2.3 *Enjoy this downhill stretch, still on County Highway C.*

4.8 *Junction with Lower Wyoming Road. If you do not wish to visit Global View (described below), turn left here and skip to the 13.7-mile mark. You will eliminate 8.9 miles of the ride. Otherwise, continue straight on County Highway C.*

8.7 *Left onto Clyde Road.*

9.2 *Left into Global View.*

Global View, (608) 583-5311, is a bazaar in a barn, an incongruous yet interesting enterprise in the midst of the Wisconsin countryside. Proprietor Marion Nelson travels to South Asia each year to visit with village artisans who produce the crafts, clothing, jewelry, and textiles that are sold here. The items come from India, Nepal, Thailand, and Indonesia; many are of museum quality. The shop is located on Willow Gold Farm, a pleasant place for lunch. Picnic tables and rest rooms are provided. Exit from the parking lot to the right on Clyde Road and backtrack to County Highway C.

9.8   Right onto County Highway C.

13.7   Right onto Lower Wyoming Road.

15.0   Right onto Snead Creek Road.

16.2   Splendid valley views and picturesque farms to your right for the next two miles. Be sure to stop occasionally and look back at where you've been.

18.8   Continue straight on Percussion Rock Road where it meets Snead Creek Road. Don't turn off to the right here; tilted signs may cause confusion.

21.5   Right onto WI 23 for very short distance.

Before turning, glance back at Percussion Rock, the massive, granite outcropping that gives the road its name. You may also be able to spot the horizontal glass pinnacle of the House on the Rock's "infinity room," which projects out over the surrounding countryside. It's on the left side of the road as

Author Jane Hall in the Spring Green valley

you look back and is easiest to see when leaves on the trees are sparse.

The House on the Rock, (608) 935-3639, was built in the 1940s by sculptor and collector Alex Jordan. It took over 5,000 tons of stone to construct the original building, which consists of 13 rooms, each on a different level. Opened to the public in 1961, today's House on the Rock is a museum complex housing Jordan's personal collections of mechanical musical devices, dolls, guns, and Oriental art, as well as the world's largest carousel. It's not advisable to bike to the entrance, about two miles south of here on WI 23—the traffic is too heavy. If it sounds interesting, return later by car.

21.6 Left onto Upper Wyoming Road.

22.9 Left on Upper Wyoming Road where Weaver Road goes straight.

This road winds through a beautiful valley, passing Wildwood Lodge, formerly a school of pantomime, which offers rustic accommodations.

23.9 Here the road surface turns to dirt for about .8 mile and becomes quite steep. If you're riding a bike with narrow tires, you may want to walk this stretch.

24.7 Left onto County Highway Z and enjoy a great downhill.

27.1 Left onto County Highway T.

28.3 To the left you will see Midway Farm in the foreground, with the Romeo and Juliet Tower behind it.

The 56-foot tower is actually a windmill that stood up to gusty southwest winds for 92 years before it was dismantled and restored in 1991. The windmill was Wright's first attempt at building a structure with no internal bracing, a concept with which he continued to experiment throughout his career. The interlocking diamond and octagon shapes provide the windmill with strength and account for its name, explained in Wright's autobiography. "Romeo will do all the work and Juliet will cuddle along to support and exalt him," he said of the windmill's construction.

28.6 To the left is Unity Chapel and a small cemetery.

This picturesque stone chapel was built in 1866 by the Lloyd-Jones family, including Anna Lloyd-Jones, Frank Lloyd Wright's mother. A contemporary metal sculpture identifies the burial spot of Frank Lloyd Wright. Wright was originally laid to rest here, but his body was later disinterred and moved to Phoenix, Arizona, for burial beside his last wife at Taliesin West. Gravestones for many of his Welsh relatives, most of them named Jones, as well as for Mamah Cheney, are found here.

28.8 Left onto WI 23.

29.2 Right to Hillside Home School.

Hillside School, (608) 588-2511, was built by Wright for his aunts, Jane and Nell Lloyd-Jones, who operated a progressive coed boarding school here. Built of native oak and sandstone, it is a classic example of Wright's fondness for natural building materials. The building is now the summer home of the Frank Lloyd Wright Foundation, which operates a professional architectural firm as well as a school of architecture. There are daily tours of the school, as well as walking tours of the Taliesin grounds.

Left onto WI 23 as you exit the school.

30.4 Right onto County Highway C by the Spring Green Restaurant.

31.2 Left into Tower Hill State Park.

Bicycle Repair Service

Middleton Cycle Shop
6649 University Avenue, Middleton, WI
(608) 836-3931

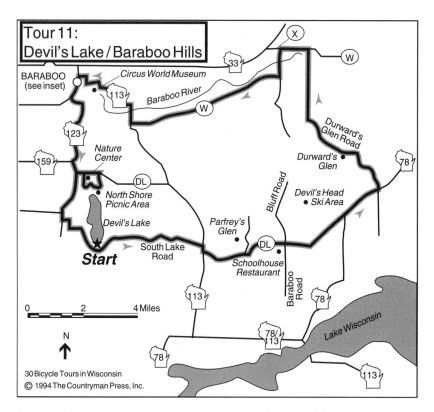

Tour 11:
Devil's Lake / Baraboo Hills

BARABOO
(see inset)

Circus World Museum

113

Baraboo River

33

X

W

W

123

159

Nature Center

DL

North Shore Picnic Area

Devil's Lake

Start

South Lake Road

Parfrey's Glen

Schoolhouse Restaurant

DL

Bluff Road

Durward's Glen Road

Durward's Glen

Devil's Head Ski Area

78

Baraboo Road

78

113

78/113

78

Lake Wisconsin

113

0   2   4 Miles

N

30 Bicycle Tours in Wisconsin
© 1994 The Countryman Press, Inc.

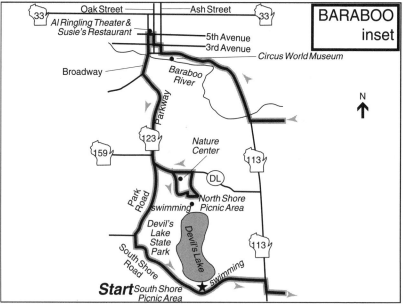

Oak Street

Ash Street

33

33

Al Ringling Theater & Susie's Restaurant

5th Avenue

3rd Avenue

Broadway

Circus World Museum

Baraboo River

BARABOO
inset

N

Parkway

123

159

Nature Center

113

DL

Park Road

swimming

North Shore Picnic Area

Devil's Lake State Park

Devil's Lake

113

South Shore Road

swimming

Start *South Shore Picnic Area*

11
Devil's Lake/Baraboo Hills

Distance: 30.1 miles
Terrain: Rolling to hilly

"Here, in a tremendous gorge…hemmed in on all sides by frowning rocks, of prodigious size, piled up in every conceivable form, nestles one of the loveliest sheets of water in the whole world." This is how Rand McNally's *Tourist Guide to the Northwest*, published in the 1880s, described Devil's Lake. Other tourist literature of that era compares Devil's Lake to California's Lake Tahoe in appearance and origin.

Devil's Lake State Park and the adjacent Baraboo Hills offer some of the most dramatic scenery and challenging cycling in Wisconsin. The lake is situated in a mile-long gap, surrounded on three sides by 500-foot quartzite bluffs. Geologists tell us that the opening was carved by an ancient channel of the Wisconsin River. When the Wisconsin Glacier descended, it rerouted the river outside of the bluffs and deposited a dam of rocks and dirt at each of the two open ends, creating an enclosed basin. The result was a 50-foot deep, crystal-clear spring-fed lake, known today as Devil's Lake.

Winnebago Indian legends provide more action-packed versions of the lake's creation. One tale describes a meteor striking with such force that it sinks deep into the earth, displacing an enormous amount of rock and debris. The meteor's impact is followed by a great rain, which fills the cavernous pit with water. Another legend tells of thunderbirds flying high above the lake, launching lightning bolts into the water and onto the bluffs. Angry water spirits retaliate by hurling rocks and waterspouts into the air. This battle accounts for the bluffs' cracked and tumbled rock faces.

Winnebago Indians called the lake Ta-wa-cun-chuk-dah, which translates as Sacred Lake or Spirit Lake. The present name, Devil's Lake, is thought to be a name invented by turn-of-the-century ad men, who hoped to lure tourists to this nascent resort area with a promise of adventure. Unfortunately, it implies that early Native Americans feared or shunned the lake. In fact, effigy mounds in animal shapes along the South Shore are evidence that it was revered.

Devil's Lake and its surroundings were designated as a state park in 1911. Now attracting over a million visitors a year, it is the busiest park in the Midwest. If you plan to camp, be sure to call the park office, (608) 356-6618, for campsite reservations. Visiting mid-week or slightly off-season will also help avoid the crowds. In addition to cycling on park roads, the park offers several mountain-biking loops on cross-country ski trails. Most cyclists follow a bike ride with a refreshing swim. The bluffs beckon casual day hikers as well as skilled rock climbers. Step carefully, though, to avoid a sunning timber rattlesnake!

This tour begins at the park's South Shore picnic area. Take WI 113 to South Lake Road, turn left if coming from the south, or right if coming from the north, and continue to the South Shore entrance.

0.0 *Mileage begins at the small log office building at the exit for the South Shore picnic area. There are rest rooms, changing facilities, a concession stand, and picnic shelter here.*

> There were once three large hotels on the South Shore, with a total of several hundred hotel rooms. A daily train dropped tourists at their doorstep, until the automobile became popular. Old travel posters advertised Devil's Lake as "just the place where tired brain workers may rest and get strong," a slogan that's still amazingly apt today.

0.1 *Left from exit onto South Lake Road (no sign here).*

> To your left the bluff is covered with loose rock, called talus. This has broken away because of pressure created by tree roots and ice. Enjoy a pleasant coast downhill and out of the park.

2.8 *Right onto WI 113.*

3.2 *Left onto County Highway DL.*

5.3 *If you wish to visit Parfrey's Glen Scientific Area, turn left here.*

A short hike (one-half mile, round-trip) through this sheltered glen is very worthwhile, especially on a hot summer day. "Glen" is a Scottish word for a narrow, rocky ravine. "Parfrey" comes from Robert Parfrey, an Englishman who acquired the property in 1865. The glen's walls are sandstone, embedded with pebbles and boulders of quartzite. This quartzite conglomerate is often called "plum pudding" stone because quartzite "plums" are cemented in sandstone "pudding." This composition is proof that the glen was once submerged in an ancient sea.

Because cool air is trapped in the glen, the plants found here are more typical of the northern part of Wisconsin. Examples are yellow birch, mountain maple, and red elder. The bamboo-like plant that forms low thickets along the creek is scouring rush, a relative of ferns. The presence of silica in the stem enabled pioneers to scour pots and pans with it. Lichens, rarely found in cities because of their sensitivity to air pollutants, grow abundantly here.

5.6 *At the intersection with Bluff Road, the Schoolhouse Restaurant is immediately to your right, and Devil's Head Resort about one mile to your left. Turn only if you're hungry, or interested in exploring.*

The Schoolhouse Restaurant is a conglomerate of another sort—an historic schoolhouse, a jail house, a Lutheran church, and a railroad caboose—that have been patched together to make this popular eatery. The outdoor deck is a pleasant place to enjoy a pizza on a warm day. Devil's Head Lodge is a full-service resort that offers skiing in the winter and golf in the summer.

7.4 *Left onto WI 78 where County Highway DL ends.*

8.7 *Left onto Durward's Glen Road.*

9.6 *Left, following the sign to Durward's Glen.*

9.8 *Right into the visitor parking area at Durward's Glen.*

The lovely chapel built of hand-hewn logs and the surrounding gardens and trickling brook were willed to the Roman

Catholic order of St. Camillus about 70 years ago. The order's primary mission is the healing of the sick, and facilities here are now used for nondenominational workshops and retreats focusing on personal and spiritual growth. The order asks that visitors to Durward's Glen cooperate in maintaining an atmosphere of silence and meditation.

Exit Durward's Glen to the left, and return .2 mile to Durward's Glen Road.

10.0 **Left onto Durward's Glen Road. At the crest of the hill, you are crossing the spine of the Baraboo Range. A two-mile downhill run follows.**

13.8 **Left onto County Highway W at Tucker Hill Cemetery.**

14.6 **Left on County Highway W, following the Baraboo River. County Highway X goes straight here.**

19.6 **Right onto WI 113, which becomes Water Street when you enter Baraboo.**

21.3 **To your left is the Circus World Museum. Opposite the museum is Ochsner Park, which has picnic tables.**

Here along the banks of the Baraboo River are the old brick and wooden buildings where circus workers trained animals, practiced stunts, and carried out off-season repairs from 1884 to 1918, when this sleepy little town served as the winter home of Ringling Brothers and Barnum and Bailey's "Greatest Show on Earth." Baraboo was the birthplace of the five Ringling brothers, whose modest carnival act grew into an enormous enterprise, eventually allowing them to buy out their competition, the Barnum and Bailey troupe.

Today the Circus World Museum, (608) 356-0800, owned by the Wisconsin State Historical Society, occupies this spot and offers a fascinating look back at the days when everyone's summer centered around the circus coming to town. Highlights include the museum's fifty meticulously restored circus parade wagons and the daily big-top show, complete with charismatic ringmaster, death-defying trapeze artists,

A welcome downhill to the end of the ride

exotic wild animals, and ebullient clowns. Other exhibits and demonstrations depict interesting aspects of circus life. The museum is open daily, May through October.

21.6 **Right onto Ash Street to start the loop around Baraboo's historic city square.**

21.8 **Left onto Third Street.**

21.9 **Right onto Oak Street.**

22.0 **Left onto Fourth Street.**

You pass the Al Ringling Theater on your right, built by one of the famous circus siblings for $100,000 in 1915. Modeled after a European opera house, it now functions as a movie theater.

22.1 **Susie's Restaurant, to your left on the corner of Broadway and Fourth Street, is a great place to stop for lunch or just pie and coffee.**

The restaurant serves well-prepared and artfully presented food, including pasta and vegetarian specials, delicious desserts, and specialty coffees. The building that houses Susie's is an historic site in the history of journalism. Ansel N. Kellogg, editor of the *Baraboo News Republic* (which has the present-day distinction of being the state's smallest daily) was dismayed when his partner quit to join Union forces in the Civil War. He kept the newspaper afloat by ordering two pages of preprinted war news each week, and printing local news on the reverse side. The operation later developed into the nation's first news syndicate. To continue from Susie's, turn left onto Broadway (also called Gollmar Boulevard).

22.7 **Left onto WI 123 South (Parkway).**

23.1 **Cross WI 123 carefully and resume cycling on the paved bike path.**

24.9 **Right at fork where the bike path ends. This takes you to Devil's Lake State Park.**

25.5 **The park Nature Center is to your left. The center includes**

dioramas, relief maps, paintings, and other exhibits that depict the area's history and geologic formation.

25.6 *The North Shore picnic area has a swimming beach and rest rooms.*

25.9 *Left toward North Shore area exit.*

26.3 *Left onto Park Road (no road sign) at Devi-Bara Resort.*

26.9 *Left onto South Shore Road.*

Long uphill, followed by downhill with steep switchbacks. Ride in control!

30.0 *Left into South Shore picnic area.*

30.1 *Pass the office building, where your mileage began.*

Bicycle Repair Service

Middleton Cycle Shop
6649 University Avenue, Middleton, WI
(608) 836-3931

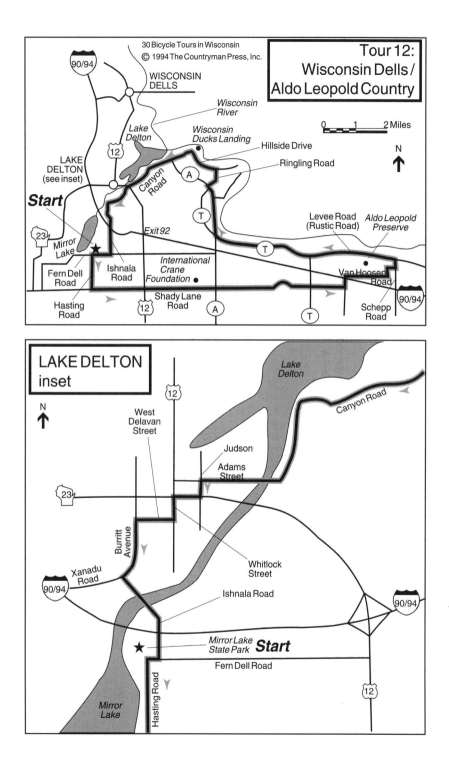

30 Bicycle Tours in Wisconsin
© 1994 The Countryman Press, Inc.

WISCONSIN
DELLS

*Wisconsin
River*

*Lake
Delton*

*Wisconsin
Ducks Landing*

Hillside Drive

Ringling Road

**Tour 12:
Wisconsin Dells /
Aldo Leopold Country**

0   1   2 Miles

N

90/94

12

LAKE
DELTON
(see inset)

Canyon
Road

A

Start

T

Levee Road
(Rustic Road)

*Aldo Leopold
Preserve*

23

Mirror
Lake

Exit 92

T

Fern Dell
Road

Ishnala
Road

*International
Crane
Foundation*

Van Hoosen
Road

90/94

Hasting
Road

Shady Lane
Road

12   A

T

Schepp
Road

**LAKE DELTON
inset**

N

*Lake
Delton*

12

Canyon Road

West
Delavan
Street

Judson

Adams
Street

23

Burritt
Avenue

Whitlock
Street

Xanadu
Road

90/94

Ishnala Road

90/94

★

*Mirror Lake
State Park* **Start**

Fern Dell Road

Hasting Road

12

*Mirror
Lake*

12

Wisconsin Dells/Aldo Leopold Country

Distance: *24.4 miles*
Terrain: *Rolling*

Wisconsin Dells is known for some of Wisconsin's most exquisite natural beauty and some of humankind's most obtrusive, albeit entertaining, additions to it. This tour steers clear of the waterslides and wax museums in favor of the "real" Dells, a spectacular seven-mile stretch of the Wisconsin River lined with cliffs, chasms, pillars, and towers of 500-million-year-old Cambrian sandstone.

The words Dell, Dells and Delton, which appear in local place names, all derive from the French word *dalle*, meaning throat. Winnebego Indian legend provides a colorful explanation of the Dells' creation, claiming that a giant snake slithered along the path of Wisconsin River, parting the rocks with its enormous weight and creating a deep, serpentine depression. Rock structures with imaginative names like Chapel Gorge, Devil's Elbow, Witches' Gulch, and Fat Man's Misery are best seen on boat excursions through the Upper and Lower Dells. Call the Dells Boat Company, (608) 253-1561, Olson Boat Company, (608) 254-8500, or Riverview Boat Line, (608) 254-8336, for schedules and itineraries.

The trip includes a stop at the International Crane Foundation, a world center for the study and preservation of these mystical birds. Try to time your visit with one of the guided tours, which are given daily at 10 A.M., 1 P.M., and 3 P.M. from Memorial Day to Labor Day; and on weekends in May, September, and October. A self-guided tour is also possible.

Much of this route follows a rolling course along the Wisconsin River, passing the humble shack where Aldo Leopold was inspired to write his

A rest stop on the Wisconsin River

conservation classic, *A Sand County Almanac.* There are several picnic spots along the way and restaurants in the town of Lake Delton.

To reach Mirror Lake State Park, take I-90/94 to Exit 92 (WI 12). Follow WI 12 East for about one-half mile, then turn right on Fern Dell Road and continue for about two and a half miles to Mirror Lake State Park. The lake for which the park is named was once a mill pond, formed by the damming of Dell Creek. Swimming is possible, though the water has a tannic cast. Reservations are suggested if you plan to camp at the park on a weekend, (608) 254-2333.

0.0   *Exit the park at the Ranger Station and proceed straight onto Hasting Road.*

1.0   *Left onto Shady Lane Road.*

2.5   *Continue straight at the stop sign. Use caution crossing WI 12.*

3.7   *Left into the International Crane Foundation (ICF).*

What looks like a housing development off in the distance is known as Crane City. These crane "condos" are home to some of the world's last remaining birds of several dwindling crane species, including the whooping crane and Siberian crane. ICF's leading-edge scientific research includes habitat preservation, captive breeding, and educational exchange programs on five continents. Allow about 1½ hours for a tour led by a well-informed aviculturist. The tour includes viewing of about 10 crane species in a display pod (they trumpet dramatic warning signals as you approach) and observing young cranes being walked by their "chick mamas"—humans partly or fully costumed as cranes who coach fledglings in the fundamentals of feeding and flying. Also on the premises are a restored prairie, picnic area, rest rooms, and gift shop. Left out of the parking lot, continuing on Shady Lane.

5.5   *On your left is an abandoned church, now being used as a barn.*

8.3   *Left onto Van Hoosen Road.*

8.4   *Cross I94.*

8.5   *You are now entering the Aldo Leopold Memorial Reserve.*

10.1   *Left onto Schepp Road.*

10.3   *Left onto Levee Road, designated a Rustic Road in 1987 in recognition of the 100th anniversary of ecologist Aldo Leopold's birth. You are now following the course of the Wisconsin River.*

11.3   *Look carefully off to your right and you will see Aldo Leopold's shack, hidden in the trees along the banks of the river.*

The property belongs to Leopold's descendants and is not open to the public. Leopold lived in Wisconsin from 1924 to 1948, when he worked for the University of Wisconsin, first as associate director of the Forest Products Lab and later as chairman of the Game Management Department. He died of a heart attack at the age of 61, while fighting a prairie fire on a neighbor's land.

Leopold is best known as the author of *A Sand County Almanac* and *Round River,* treatises on environmental ethics that have proven to be well ahead of their time. Having just toured the Crane Foundation, you will appreciate this passage from *A Sand County Almanac*, called "Marshland Elegy."

A dawn wind stirs on the great marsh. With almost imperceptible slowness it rolls a bank of fog across the wide morass. Like the white ghost of a glacier the mists advance, riding over phalaxes of tamaracks, sliding across bog-meadows heavy with dew. A single silence hangs from horizon to horizon. Out of some far recess of the sky a tinkling of little bells falls soft upon the listening land. Then again silence. Now comes a baying of some sweet-throated sound, soon the clamor of a responding pack. Then a far clear blast of hunting horns, out of the sky into the fog.

High horns, low horns, silence, and finally a pandemonium of trumpets, rattles, croaks, and cries that almost shakes the bog with its nearness, but without yet disclosing whence it comes. At last a glint of sun reveals the approach of a great echelon of birds. On motionless wing they emerge from the lifting mists, sweep a final arc of sky, and settle in clangorous descending spirals to their feeding grounds. A new day has begun on the crane marsh.

12.9 Right onto County Highway T.

15.7 Right onto County Highway A. This is a busier road.

17.3 Right onto Ringling Road.

17.9 Left onto Hillside Drive.

18.9 This driveway down to the river is an entry point for the Wisconsin Ducks, WWII amphibious landing craft vehicles that offer sightseeing tours. During the summer, you need only wait five or 10 minutes for one to appear.

19.6 Straight onto Canyon Road.

21.2 Right onto East Adams Street into the village of Lake Delton.

Be careful—traffic is heavy here in the summer months. There are several restaurants where you can get a sandwich or a cool drink.

21.5 Left on Judson Street.

21.6 Right onto WI 12 (Wisconsin Dells Parkway).

21.8 Left at the stoplight on Whitlock Street.

21.9 Right onto West Delavan Street.

22.0 To your left is the Lake Delton Fire Department Park, where water, rest rooms, and picnic tables are available.

22.1 Left onto South Burritt Avenue (this becomes Ishnala Road).

23.9 Right onto Fern Dell Road.

24.2 Right into Mirror Lake State Park.

24.4 Ranger Station.

Bicycle Repair Service

Middleton Cycle Shop
6649 University Avenue, Middleton, WI
(608) 836-3931

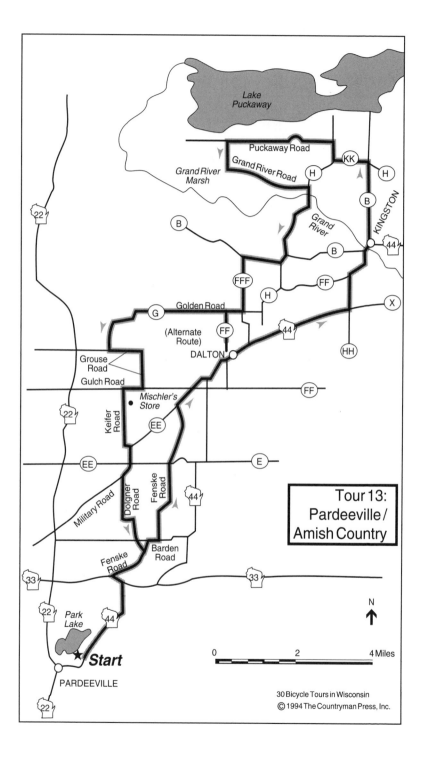

Lake
Puckaway

Puckaway Road

Grand River Road

Grand River
Marsh

KK

H

H

22

B

B

Grand
River

B

FFF

FF

KINGSTON

44

Golden Road

H

G

(Alternate
Route)

FF

44

X

DALTON

HH

Grouse
Road

Gulch Road

FF

Mischler's
Store

22

Keifer
Road

EE

EE

E

Military Road

Dolgner
Road

Fenske
Road

44

Fenske
Road

Barden
Road

33

33

22

Park
Lake

44

★ **Start**

N

PARDEEVILLE

0   2   4 Miles

22

**Tour 13:
Pardeeville /
Amish Country**

30 Bicycle Tours in Wisconsin
© 1994 The Countryman Press, Inc.

13
Pardeeville/Amish Country

Distance: *28.1 or 48.5 miles (.5 mile gravel surface)*
Terrain: *Rolling*

Bicycling brings you face-to-face with Wisconsin's Amish community on this tour through rolling farmland where you'll encounter little traffic other than horse-drawn buggies. There are over 500 Amish people in the area surrounding Kingston and Dalton. Most arrived in Wisconsin from the Shipshewana, Indiana, area in the mid-1970s; others came from Amish colonies in Pennsylvania. In contrast to other Amish settlements, the people who live here do not ride bicycles because of the rubber tires, which they consider an unnecessary luxury.

Most of the Amish are employed in farming or carpentry. Zucchini and other vegetables are raised for their own needs and sold to canning factories. Beautiful bentwood rockers and cedar chests are available from small shops in their homes. Groups of men also hire out to build non-Amish homes. Meticulously tended flower gardens stand in brilliant contrast to the stark colors of Amish dress and plain white paint of their buildings. The Amish are very private people and prefer not to be photographed; please don't do so without asking permission. All Amish-run shops are closed on Sunday.

There are very few commercial attractions along this route and therefore, few notes for the ride. Just relax and take in the peaceful simplicity of the Amish countryside!

The tour begins at Chandler Park in Pardeeville. The park offers a swimming beach, picnic facilities, rest rooms, and water. To reach Pardeeville, take WI 51 north from Madison to WI 22. Follow WI 22 to the junction with WI 44. Turn right onto WI 44, which will take you into Pardeeville, where it becomes East Lake Street. The entrance to Chandler Park is on the left.

0.0   *Exit Chandler Park on Chandler Park Drive. Mileage begins at the stone gate.*

0.1   *Left onto East Lake Street (WI 44) and follow it out of town. You'll be riding around Park Lake.*

1.1   *Pass the Park Lake County Park boat landing.*

3.1   *Left onto County Highway 33 for a short distance.*

3.3   *Right onto Fenske Road.*

7.1   *Right onto County Highway E for .2 mile at the North Scott Baptist Church.*

7.3   *Left onto Fenske Road.*

Many of the large white houses here are Amish homes, added onto many times to accommodate growing families. You may see draft horses in the fields—horses are used to pull buggies, harvest the hay, and skid the lumber.

A Sunday morning in Wisconsin's Amish country

9.0   *Right onto County Highway EE.*

10.1   *Left onto WI 44. This is a busier road but has a good shoulder.*

10.7   *For the 48.5-mile ride, continue straight at the County Highway FF junction.*

> The village of Dalton is off to your left. Snacks are available at Pat's Corner Grocery.
>
> For the 28.1-mile ride, turn left onto County Highway FF. Continue on County Highway FF through Dalton and for one mile north of town. Then turn left onto Golden Road and skip to the 32.1-mile mark for the remaining directions.

16.0   *Enter the village of Kingston.*

> The Kingston House and Camelot Supper Club serve meals. There is no membership required for this supper "club," despite what the name implies!

16.5   *Left onto County Highway B just past the dam.*

18.8   *Left onto County Highway KK.*

19.9   *Right onto County Highway H where County Highway KK ends.*

20.4   *Left onto Puckaway Road.*

> Lake Puckaway is to your right and Grand River Marsh is to your left. During the Ice Age, melting ice formed a depression that eventually filled with silt and decaying vegetation and ultimately became a marsh. When Wisconsin was first settled, the marsh was used for pasture and raising hay. When the land was acquired by the State of Wisconsin, a dam was shut down, releasing enough water to flood 3,500 acres. The marsh is on a major flyway for ducks, geese, and sandhill cranes.

23.5   *Left onto Grand River Road.*

26.8   *Right onto County Highway H where Grand River Road ends.*

28.9   *Right onto County Highway B.*

30.1   *Left onto County Highway FFF.*

31.6 *Right onto County Highway FF.*

32.1 *Continue straight on Golden Road where County Highway FF turns left.*

This is where the shorter ride rejoins the main ride. This road has a gravel stretch for a half mile, just past the railroad tracks.

36.3 *Left onto Grouse Road.*

38.4 *Right onto Gulch Road.*

Mischler's Country Store, which sells bulk foods for the Amish community, is just past the turn. Flours, sugars, spices, and fruit pie fillings are among the foodstuffs sold here. The store is closed on Sunday and Thursday. Fresh baked goods are often sold here on Saturday.

38.9 *Left onto Keifer Road.*

40.6 *Right onto County Highway EE. Careful of the rumble strips and stop sign at the bottom of the hill.*

41.1 *Straight onto Military Road across County Highways EE and E.*

41.4 *Left onto Dolgner Road.*

43.6 *Continue straight on Dolgner Road, the middle fork at the unmarked intersection.*

44.0 *Right onto Fenske Road.*

45.1 *Left onto WI 33.*

45.4 *Right onto WI 44.*

48.4 *Right onto Chandler Park Drive.*

48.5 *You're back.*

Bicycle Repair Services

None in this area.

CENTRAL
WISCONSIN

14
Waupaca Chain of Lakes

Distance: 24.1 miles
Terrain: Gently rolling

This tour takes you through a slice of central Wisconsin forest and farmland that lends itself well to old-fashioned, family-style fun. A lively summer resort area, most activity centers around a chain of 22 clear, spring-fed lakes, as well as numerous rivers and trout streams. Waupaca, the largest town near the Chain O' Lakes, probably took its name from the Native American words "Waubuck Seba," meaning "pale or clear water." Keep an eye out for whitetails on this ride—the area has the state's highest deer population, and it's not unusual to startle a doe and fawn as you round a bend.

The trip begins at Hartman Creek State Park, (715) 258-2372, 1,200 acres of wooded countryside that skirt the terminal moraine of the Wisconsin glacier. Wisconsin's cross-state Ice Age Trail passes through the park. Four spring-fed lakes were formed by damming Hartman Creek when the land was a private fish hatchery, prior to becoming a state park. There is a swimming beach on Hartman Lake and the park offers excellent facilities for family and group camping.

To reach Hartman Creek State Park, take WI 10 to Waupaca. From Waupaca, go west on WI 54 for about four miles, then left on Hartman Creek Road to the park. The tour begins at the ranger station, which you pass when exiting the park.

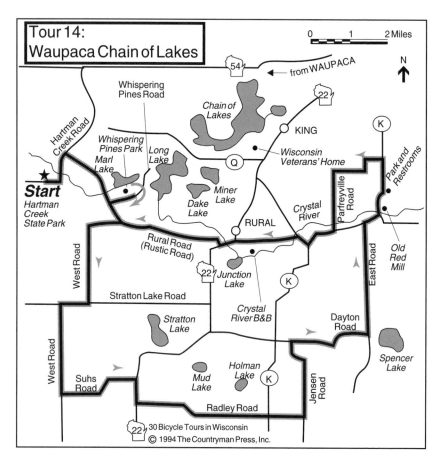

0.4   *Right onto Rural Road.*

1.9   *Right onto West Road.*

3.7   *Right onto Stratton Lake Road.*

4.2   *Left onto West Road.*

5.7   *Left onto Suhs Road.*

7.0   *Right onto WI 22. There is moderate traffic, but the road has a wide shoulder.*

7.6 *Left onto Radley Road.*

10.2 *Left onto Jensen Road.*

11.5 *Right onto Dayton Road.*

12.8 *Left onto East Road.*

14.6 *Right onto County Highway K where East Road ends.*

14.8 *The Old Red Mill, on the banks of the Crystal River, has an interesting history.*

> Built by James Lathrop in 1854, the mill ground feed and graham and buckwheat flour until 1960, when it was converted to the Red Mill Colonial Shop. The buyers of the mill, which now houses a shop selling early American furniture and gifts, were committed to restoring and maintaining the mill's massive 24-foot water wheel. After a long search, a 130-year-old white oak tree on an island near Fremont, Wisconsin, was selected to form a new hub for the wheel. The solid oak hub weighs a ton and a half; the spokes vary in weight from 90 to 120 pounds, depending on the density of the wood. Sixty buckets, set into the rim of the wheel, transport the water, creating a beautiful effect. Also on the Red Mill property is a replica of a covered bridge and a small chapel in the woods. Just beyond the mill, also on the river, is a pleasant park with rest rooms.

15.6 *Left onto Parfreyville Road.*

17.6 *Right onto County Highway K.*

17.9 *Right onto Rural Road where County Highway K goes left.*

> Every Sunday afternoon you will find a row of lawn chairs set up along the riverbank belonging to spectators who gather to watch paddlers navigate the small rapids here in tippy fiberglass canoes. If you have a yen to share the adventure, canoes can be rented from Ding's Dock, (715) 258-2612, on County Highway Q. The dock provides transportation to the river and pick-up at the end of the voyage.

19.0 **Left onto Rural Road (Potts Road) and follow it into the village of Rural.**

> The town was named by James Hinchman Jones, the first settler. He lived in a wooded area near the river and referred to his property as the "rural holdings." Rural was the halfway point on the stagecoach line between Berlin and Stevens Point. It grew up around a gristmill operated by Jones and a stagecoach inn, the Half-Way House. The community flourished briefly when it was rumored that a rail line was going to pass through, but when the gossip didn't pan out, Rural was destined to become the sleepy little hamlet that it is today.
>
> Rural is unique in Wisconsin because of its concentration of homes and buildings dating to the 1800s. The entire village has been deemed the Rural-on-the-Crystal Historic District. Historic structures are marked with plaques, and include the original Half-Way House, built in 1852, which now serves as an antique store. Rural Artists, which features the work of local craftspeople, is housed in the circa-1850 general store. Lodging is available at the Crystal River B & B, (715) 258-5333, an 1853 farmhouse in a pleasant setting.

19.5 **Cross WI 22 and continue straight on Rural Road, one of Wisconsin's Rustic Roads.**

21.5 **Right onto Whispering Pines Road.**

22.1 **Left into Whispering Pines Park.**

> Whispering Pines, now affiliated with Hartman Creek State Park, began as a private park developed by three local citizens who created a lovely labyrinth of gardens and paths beneath a grove of towering cedars and white pines. The developers were a Danish couple, Christ and Emma Hyldegaard, who made their fortune in the milk business. Christ, who retired at age 42, disdained the drugs he was taking for a heart problem and decided to heal himself with fresh air and hard work. With the assistance of a friend, Casey Nowicke, he spent endless hours landscaping and building fences and stairways.

The property has 2,876 feet of frontage on three different lakes. It was willed to the State of Wisconsin when Emma Hyldegaard died in 1975.

A solid rock stairway leads to a swimming dock on Marl Lake, named for the soft white substance on the lake's bottom that gives it a translucent, blue-green color. Marl is a mixture of limestone (calcium carbonate), clay, sand, and organic deposits. The limestone is extracted from alkaline spring water by aquatic plants and by snails, which use the substance to form shells. An effective antidote to soil acidity, marl was once dredged from the lakes for use as a fertilizer.

22.3 *Right onto Whispering Pines Road from the park.*

22.9 *Right onto Rural Road.*

23.7 *Left onto Hartman Creek Road.*

24.1 *Return to the ranger station.*

If you've worked up an appetite, the Wheelhouse on County Highway Q serves great pizza. Also popular is Clearwater

A stop to see the 24-foot water wheel at Red Mill

Harbor on County Highway QQ in the nearby village of King, which has tables on an outdoor deck overlooking Taylor Lake. Stern-wheeler excursion boats also depart from here; call (715) 258-2866 for schedule and price information. A large selection of homemade pies is available at The King's Table, also on County Highway QQ.

Bicycle Repair Service

Harbor Bike and Ski
112 South Main Street, Waupaca, WI
(715) 258-5404

15
Wild Rose/Christmas Tree Country

Distance: *32.2 miles*
Terrain: *Gently rolling*

Just one deep breath of the pine-scented, oxygen-rich air tells you that you're in Waushara County, the Christmas-tree capitol of Wisconsin. The sandy, glacial outwash soil in this area, inhospitable to most crops, is perfectly suited to the ten million pines, firs, and spruces growing here. Wisconsin ranks third nationally in Christmas-tree production and in recent years provided holiday trees for the Johnson, Carter, and Bush White Houses. Most trees require eight to fifteen years to reach harvest size; frequent pruning provides steady summer employment for area young people.

Interspersed with tree plantations and natural forests are hundreds of lakes and hidden trout streams. This is a relaxed, friendly part of Wisconsin with Mayberry-like small towns untainted by tourism and populated by people who always seem to have time to chat—especially about the weather or where the fish are biting.

The Birdsong B & B, (414) 622-3770, on County Highway A, just east of town, offers pleasant lodging in a farmhouse set on 75 acres. Innkeepers Walt and Sallyann Bouwens have put a generous dose of TLC into the inn, named for the indigo buntings, orioles, bluebirds, scarlet tanagers, and other birds that visit the property.

This tour begins at the Wild Rose State Fish Hatchery, (414) 622-3527, a mile and and a half north of the village of Wild Rose on WI 22. You will find ample parking, a picnic area, and rest rooms in a park-like setting. Mileage for the ride begins at the end of the driveway, where it meets WI 22. The hatchery has been stocking area trout streams since 1908. In

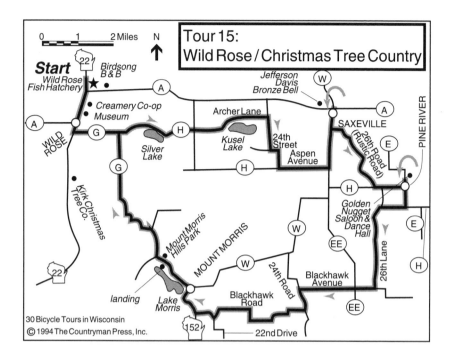

Tour 15:
Wild Rose / Christmas Tree Country

addition to brown trout, the facility now raises Chinook salmon, walleye, northern pike, lake sturgeon, and muskellunge—better known as the muskie. The trout area is open to the public throughout the year; northern pike and muskie cannot be viewed because of the skittishness of the species.

0.0 *Right on WI 22 from the Fish Hatchery driveway. WI 22 becomes Main Street as you enter downtown Wild Rose.*

0.6 *Wild Rose Creamery Co-op is to your left.*

Stop in for a favorite Wisconsin treat—a bag of cheese curds, fresh and squeaky every Friday afternoon. They also offer a nice selection of block cheeses to take home.

0.8 *There are several other places of interest in the village of Wild Rose, given its name by settlers of Welsh and English descent who arrived from Rose, New York.*

To your left is the Pioneer Historical Museum, which consists of several adjacent buildings, including a home furnished in the style of the 1880s, a one-room schoolhouse, a carriage house, a smokehouse, and a blacksmith shop. Next door is the Pioneer Hall, which once housed a bank and a drug store. In a Butch Cassidy–like caper, robbers made an unsuccessful attempt to blow open the bank's vault in 1905. The head outlaw, known as Patsy, was captured, shot, and buried in the local cemetery. The museum is open Wednesday and Saturday, mid-June to Labor Day, for a small admission fee.

Early Wild Rose seemed to attract an individualist crowd. The town was home to an unusual religious sect known as the Standalones, who eschewed religious ritual and declared that every person should "stand alone and believe what he had a mind to." Today's residents are more community-minded. In an exemplary demonstration of civic pride, Wild Rose citizens recently raised enough money to drain, dredge, and clean up the picturesque mill pond that you see from Main Street. The renewed pond is the site of an annual watercross competition where daring drivers jump snowmobiles across open water for prize money.

If you want to begin the ride with breakfast, stop in at the Chatterbox Restaurant, on your left. You can count on a bottomless cup of coffee and a free side dish of local gossip.

0.9   *To your left is the old Wild Rose Mercantile Company, once a general store, now an antique emporium with an adjoining ice cream parlor.*

1.0   *To your right is the Wild Rose Garden.*

Though most agree the town was named after Rose, New York, the beauty of the blooming roses gives credence to an alternate explanation. The unofficial version says the town was christened when men digging the basement for the first store found a wild rose bush blooming out of season.

1.5   *Left onto County Highway G/H.*

Just after the turn is a grocery store; there's an ideal spot for a picnic lunch later in the ride. On your right is the first of many Christmas tree farms you will pass.

The gentle terrain is interspersed with lakes and tree farms.

2.7 *Straight on County Highway H where County Highway G turns right.*

3.4 *Silver Lake is to your right.*

4.8 *Straight on Archer Lane across 22nd Street.*

5.6 *Kusel Lake is to your right.*

6.9 *Right onto 24th Street.*

7.2 *Left onto Aspen Avenue.*

9.0 *Left onto County Highway W.*

9.6 *Downtown Saxeville consists of a general store that doubles as an insurance office.*

Across the road from the store is a bronze bell used to call the slaves from the fields at the Jefferson Davis Plantation in Corinth, Mississippi, before it was captured (or looted, depending on your viewpoint) by Saxeville soldiers in 1862. Backtrack out of town on County Highway W.

10.1 *Left at Hilltop Cemetery on 26th Road.*

This Rustic Road curves between rolling hills that typify the ground moraines found in Wisconsin's central plains region. There are several historic farms on the stretch, including the Spencer Allen Farm and the Ashcroft Farm, which also sells antiques and furniture.

The small wooden boxes mounted on posts are bluebird houses. The bluebird population in Wisconsin declined significantly in the last half-century due to the loss of nest sites such as hollow wooden fence posts, competition from sparrows and starlings, and the use of pesticides. Recently, bird lovers have begun to coax bluebirds back by installing nesting boxes that meet their habitat needs.

12.2 *Left onto County Highway H (a sign indicates the end of the Rustic Road; no other sign). County Highway H becomes Cross Street.*

13.0 *Left onto County Highway E (becomes Main Street as you enter Pine River).*

13.1 *To your left, with the unusual tin siding, is the Golden Nugget Saloon and Dance Hall where local widows kick up their heels on Sunday afternoon. There's a picnic table in a pleasant spot by the dam overlooking the Pine River. Backtrack to the intersection of County Highways E and H.*

13.2 *Continue straight on County Highway H at this intersection and follow it for .5 mile.*

13.7 *Right at your first opportunity on an unmarked road, just before County Highway H makes a sharp left.*

14.4 *Left onto 26th Lane at the stop sign (no road sign).*

16.5 *Right onto Blackhawk Avenue at the stop sign.*

17.0 *Cross County Highway EE, still on Blackhawk Avenue.*

18.5 *Left onto 24th Road; follow for .5 mile.*

19.0 *Right onto Blackhawk Road.*

22.0 *Right on Blackhawk Road where 22nd Drive goes straight.*

22.6 *Right onto WI 152 where Blackhawk Road ends.*

23.2 *You are entering the village of Mount Morris, which has a mill, general store, and several antique shops.*

23.4 *Left onto County Highway G at the Mount Morris Motel.*

Folk music concerts featuring an impressive stable of local talent are frequently held at the Mount Morris town hall on Saturday night. Call the Blackhawk Folk Society for a current schedule, (414) 787-7475.

23.7 *To the left, the Lake Morris public landing is a good spot to rest and enjoy your picnic lunch if your legs aren't up to tackling the steep climb to Mount Morris Hills Park.*

23.8 *If you relish a challenge, turn right into Mount Morris Hills Park.*

A foot race to the top of this steep hill determined the town's name. The honor was clinched by Solomon Morris, and Gunnar Gunderson faded into oblivion.

24.4 *The summit provides an awesome view of the surrounding countryside, as well as a picnic shelter and rest rooms.*

25.0 *Right onto County Highway G.*

29.5 *Left onto County Highway H.*

30.7 *Right onto WI 22.*

32.2 *Left into Wild Rose Fish Hatchery.*

Bicycle Repair Service

Wild Rose Bike Shop
840 Oakwood Avenue, Wild Rose, WI
(414) 622-3638

16

Green Lake/White River Marsh/Princeton

Distance: *6 or 35.7 miles*
Terrain: *Gently rolling*

Sunlight reflecting off Green Lake's sandstone bedrock gives Wisconsin's deepest lake an emerald cast, and hence, its name. The lake fills a seven-and-a-third-mile long, two-mile wide, 237-foot-deep crater carved out by the Wisconsin glacier. Dozens of effigy mounds in the yards of lakefront residents tell us that Winnebago Indians were the first to discover the lake's shimmering water and bountiful stock of fish.

Green Lake has a long history as a resort area, but thankfully the village has succeeded in harnessing the benefits of tourism without succumbing to flashiness. Fishing and boating dominate the local special events calendar. The Green Lake area also boasts three outstanding golf courses within a 10-mile radius—convenient if your companion prefers to be putting while you're pedaling.

Green Lake sits on Wisconsin's central plain, a region that received the full flattening effect of glacial ice. While there are enough ups and downs to keep this ride interesting, there are no real extremes. Three-fourths of Green Lake County's gently rolling prairie land is devoted to agriculture, with red barns and sky-scraping blue silos so abundant that they cease to be useful landmarks. The ride also includes cycling through White River Marsh. Biking through the marsh is not advisable during hunting season, which usually falls in early October. The Department of Natural Resources, (608) 266-1877, can give you the exact dates.

Families with children or those who want a shorter ride should start at the Green Lake Conference Center (mile 28.6) and do the six-mile loop through the grounds. This is a very pleasant ride by itself, with some lovely

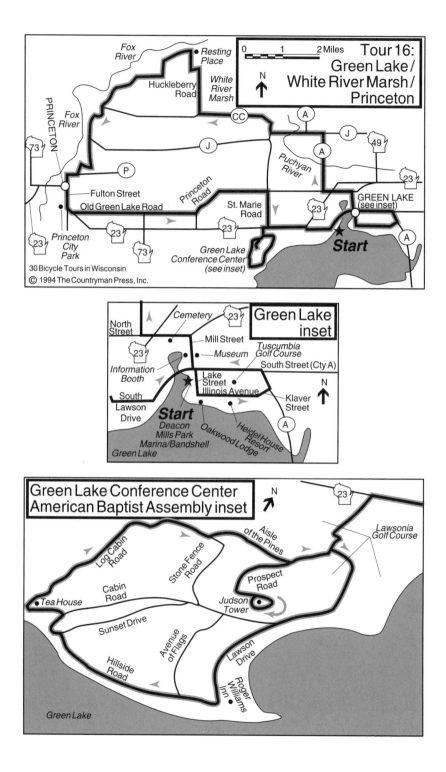

Tour 16:
Green Lake /
White River Marsh /
Princeton

0   1   2 Miles

N

Fox River

Resting Place

Huckleberry Road

White River Marsh

PRINCETON

Fox River

73

CC

A

J

49

J

P

Puchyan River

23

Fulton Street
Old Green Lake Road

Princeton Road

St. Marie Road

GREEN LAKE
(see inset)

23

23

A

23

73

Princeton City Park

Green Lake Conference Center
(see inset)

Start

30 Bicycle Tours in Wisconsin
© 1994 The Countryman Press, Inc.

Green Lake inset

Cemetery

23

North Street

Mill Street

23

Museum

Tuscumbia Golf Course

South Street (Cty A)

Information Booth

Lake Street
Illinois Avenue

N

South Lawson Drive

Start

Deacon Mills Park
Marina/Bandshell

Oakwood Lodge

Heidel House Resort

Klaver Street

A

Green Lake

Green Lake Conference Center
American Baptist Assembly inset

N

23

Aisle of the Pines

Lawsonia Golf Course

Log Cabin Road

Stone Fence Road

Prospect Road

Cabin Road

Tea House

Judson Tower

Sunset Drive

Avenue of Flags

Lawson Drive

Hillside Road

Roger Williams Inn

Green Lake

lake views and a minimum of vehicle traffic (50 cent charge per bicycle).

This tour begins at Deacon Mills Park next to the marina, in downtown Green Lake. To get to the park, take the Business WI 23 exit from WI 23. Business WI 23 turns into South Lawson Drive as you enter town. Look for the park's old-time band shell on your right as you enter the downtown district.

0.0 *Right from the parking lot of Deacon Mills Park, onto South Street.*

Stretch out on the cool grass, stare up at the stars, and listen to the refrains of Sondheim and Sousa when concerts are held here on Wednesday evenings in July and August. The park is also the site of a chili cook-off held annually the first weekend in September, when teams of amateur chefs compete for prizes and put on a fiery feed for the public.

0.1 *Right onto Lake Street.*

As you travel down Lake Street, you're heading out to Oakwood Point, where New Yorker David Greenway opened a rambling wooden frame hotel in 1867, which he touted as "the first resort west of Niagara Falls." Greenway's property included all of the land west of Lake Street and south of the Bay View Motel, totaling 3,500 acres and 2,000 feet of lakefront. The Oakwood Resort Hotel attracted well-heeled tourists from the sweltering cities of Memphis and New Orleans, where a yellow-fever epidemic was raging. In later years, Chicago and St. Louis became the main markets for Greenway's establishment, which at its peak could accommodate nearly 500 guests.

0.6 *Left onto Illinois Avenue at Oakwood Lodge.*

Oakwood Lodge, (414) 294-6580, now a bed-and-breakfast inn, was formerly the St. Louis House, the largest cottage on the Oakwood Resort Hotel property. The home immediately to the west was also one of the original cottages. The main hotel fell into disrepair and was torn down in 1929. In addition to providing overnight lodging, innkeeper Marcy Klepinger serves bountiful country breakfasts to the public on weekends. Ask for a table on the veranda overlooking the lake.

1.2 **To your right is the Heidel House Resort, and to your left, Tuscumbia Golf Course.**

> The Heidel House is a luxurious resort, recently rebuilt after several fires. To see Green Lake from off shore, you can take a narrated cruise on the resort's 52-foot tour boat, the Yachts of Fun. The cruise offers great views of the impressive homes that line the lake shore. Call for the current schedule, (414) 294-3344. Tuscumbia, across the road, is Wisconsin's oldest golf course.

1.8 **Left onto Klaver Street.**

2.0 **Left onto County Highway A.**

2.3 **Left onto County Highway A again (South Street).**

3.4 **Right onto Mill Street (still County Highway A) through downtown Green Lake.**

3.7 **Just past the shopping district, you will see a mill pond and dam to your left, and the Dartford Historical Museum to your right.**

> The dam was built in 1834 by Anson Dart, founder of Dartford (later renamed Green Lake), to power his sawmill, and it is still used to control the level of Green Lake. There is a Chamber of Commerce information booth in the park, which is staffed during the summer season.
>
> Opposite is the historical museum, housed in Dartford's first train station. Chances are good that you will find the museum staffed by part-time mayor Larry Behlen, who can answer your questions about both past and present Green Lake.

3.8 **Continue straight onto Mill Street where WI 23 goes right. Look to the right before crossing. Traffic on WI 23 moves quickly and does not stop at this intersection.**

4.0 **Left onto North Street.**

> To your left is Dartford Cemetery, which includes the grave of one of the area's most beloved Native Americans, Chief

Highknocker. The chief's official Native name was Hanageh, but his habit of wearing an old top hat earned him the affectionate nickname of Highknocker. He died in 1911 and his grave is marked by a large boulder taken from an area along the lake where he liked to camp.

4.5 *Cross WI 23 using caution. This is a very busy stretch and quite wide. When you reach the other side, continue straight ahead.*

4.8 *Right onto County Highway A . There are three forks at this intersection. County Highway A is the first one.*

6.3 *Left onto County Highway J at Bluffton Cemetery.*

7.3 *The road crosses the the Puchyan River.*

7.9 *Right onto County Highway CC.*

Just ahead on the right is a small sawmill and lumberyard. Soon after, the scenery opens up to the expansive White River Marsh, where you'll see numerous duck and goose blinds.

10.3 *Right onto Huckleberry Road.*

The marsh is a nesting area for sandhill cranes, which can be identified by their melancholy call and prehistoric appearance. They are large birds, averaging three feet in height, with an 80-inch wingspan. The best months for viewing cranes are April and October.

12.4 *The road meets the Fox River.*

This is a pleasant spot to pause for a few minutes. Across the road, opposite the river, look behind the tree with the No Trespassing sign for a bubbling spring and a drinking cup, left here for travelers in the hobo tradition. A short distance ahead on the right is a gravel road to the White River Locks Public Fishing Area. There are no services here.

17.1 *Continue straight ahead where Huckleberry Road meets County Highway J. You are now traveling on County Highway J.*

18.5 *Bear left on North Fulton Street where the road forks, as you enter the town of Princeton.*

18.9 Continue straight onto Fulton Street (also WI 23/73) at the stop sign.

19.0 If you wish to take a spin through the downtown business district, turn right onto Water Street. Otherwise, continue straight on Fulton Street.

19.2 Right into Princeton City Park.

Every Saturday from early May through mid-October, this is the site of Wisconsin's largest outdoor flea market. The weekly event draws antiques collectors from miles around to display their wares or to scour the city block full of tables for a rare find. There are also several antique shops and an ice cream parlor adjacent to the park. Right from the park, continuing on South Fulton Street (WI 23).

19.5 Left onto Old Green Lake Road.

23.2 Left onto Princeton Road.

25.5 Right onto St. Marie Road.

26.5 Right onto WI 23, for .3 mile. This is a busy road, but it has an ample paved shoulder.

26.8 Left into the Green Lake Conference Center, also known as the American Baptist Assembly (ABA) or Lawsonia. You are now on Lawson Drive.

There is a charge of 50 cents per bicycle, or $1 per car, for touring the grounds. The gatekeeper will give you a map (very useful if you get turned around) and a pass which you must return on your way out.

As you enter, you will be cycling through the Lawsonia Links Golf Course, opened in 1930 and considered one of the top public courses in the country. The course is laid out in the Scottish links tradition and includes unusually elevated greens with steep-faced bunkers. It is said that an old boxcar is buried beneath the seventh green. Enjoy the pleasant downhill cruise, past the boat house and the chapel car named Grace.

Farm markets abound in central Wisconsin.

The story of the Green Lake Conference Center, (414) 294-3323, began in 1888, when Jessie Lawson of Chicago was enjoying a pleasure-boat cruise on the lake. A sudden storm forced the captain to seek shelter at a spot called Lone Tree Point. Overwhelmed by its beauty, Mrs. Lawson convinced her husband, millionaire *Chicago Daily News* publisher Victor Lawson, to purchase the plot, which they developed into an impressive estate.

When Mr. Lawson died in 1925, the estate was sold to The H.O. Stone Company, which intended to build an exclusive real estate development that they touted as the "Sun Valley of the Midwest." Their plans were stalled by the Great Depression and the property floundered with financial problems until it finally closed during World War II.

Baptist leader Dr. Luther Wesley Smith discovered the estate on a drive through Wisconsin and recognized it as a place where his dream for a national conference center could come true. In 1943, with the assistance of James L. Kraft of Kraft Foods, Dr. Smith arranged purchase of Lawsonia, valued at $11 million, for a mere $300,000. The property is still owned by the American Baptist Church and is used year-round for church-related and non-denominational conferences.

28.4 *To your left is the Roger Williams Inn.*

Inside this 75-room hotel you will find a snack shop and rest rooms. If you wish to climb the 113-foot Judson Tower later on this tour, pick up a key at the registration desk. In addition to the hotel, there are about 20 homes on the grounds, including a replica of Ann Hathaway's cottage, that may be rented by families or other small groups.

28.5 *Right onto Hillside Road, just beyond the inn. Continue straight on Hillside Road where Avenue of Flags goes right.*

There is a narrow stone bridge here, and a slight uphill. On the left is a water tower which you can climb for a great view of Green Lake.

29.0 *Keep left at junctions with Sunset Drive and Cabin Road.*

29.4 *To your right is the Tea House.*

29.5 *Right onto Log Cabin Road.*

Watch for deer in the large, open meadow ahead to your right, especially in the early morning or around sunset.

30.5 *Stay left at the junction with Stone Fence Road. Shortly, you will pass through the Aisle of the Pines.*

31.0 *Right onto Prospect Road.*

31.3 *The road circles around Judson Tower.*

It's 121 steps to the top of this water tower, which once held 75,000 gallons to supply the Lawson estate and to water the lawn with horse-drawn sprinklers. The tower is named after Adoniram Judson, the famous New England missionary who spent more than 30 years in Burma, where he converted many of the hilltribes to Christianity, translated the Bible into Burmese, and in 1849 completed what remains today the standard Burmese–English dictionary.

31.8 *Straight on Prospect at the junction with Aisle of Pines.*

32.2 *Left onto Lawson Drive.*

32.9 *Right onto WI 23 as you exit the grounds. Take care, this is a busy road.*

34.2 *Right onto Business WI 23 (becomes Lawson Drive).*

35.4 *To your right is Hattie Sherwood Park.*

> Here you'll find a swimming beach, picnic area, rest rooms, and a city-run campground with 34 sites, some with electricity.

35.6 *Bear right onto South Street by the McConnell Inn.*

> This charming Victorian home built in 1901 is now operated as a bed-and-breakfast inn, (414) 294-6430.

35.7 *Right into Deacon Mills Park.*

Bicycle Repair Service

Mike's Bike Shop
124 North Capron, Berlin WI
(414) 361-3040

DOOR
COUNTY

17
Southern Door County/ Potawatomi State Park

Distance: *43.4 miles (.75 mile dirt road)*
Terrain: *Flat to gently rolling*

A friend once confessed to a passion for "anything that floats." If you share that persuasion, put this tour on your "to do" list. Boats of every description—intrepid little tugs, cavernous cargo ships, even Ted Turner's sexy yacht, *Tenacious,* have been born in Sturgeon Bay, the starting point of this tour. This unpretentious port of call is the largest shipbuilding center on the Great Lakes and home to three major shipbuilding firms. Commercial fishing, fruit growing, and limestone quarrying round out the local economy.

The rise of the shipbuilding industry began in 1866, when Congress granted 200,000 acres for the construction of the Sturgeon Bay Ship Canal. Prior to that, Native Americans, explorers, missionaries, and fur traders were forced to decide between a demanding portage across the peninsula and a treacherous voyage around its tip, through the passage known as "Death's Door." The corridor was initially large enough for only a rowboat or canoe to pass—today it's a major shipping waterway.

This tour includes one unpaved stretch of road that extends for about three-fourths of a mile along the Lake Michigan shore. Even if you walk this portion, it's well worth it for the lake views. You may notice that the route crosses the Ahnapee Trail. This rails-to-trails project is suitable for snowmobiling and hiking only; the surface hasn't been improved for cycling.

The tour begins at the Door County Maritime Museum, next to the Bay Shipbuilding Company and Sunset Park. Follow Business WI 42/57 into Sturgeon Bay. From the north, turn right on Georgia Street. Continue for four blocks, then turn right on North Third Avenue. The museum is on

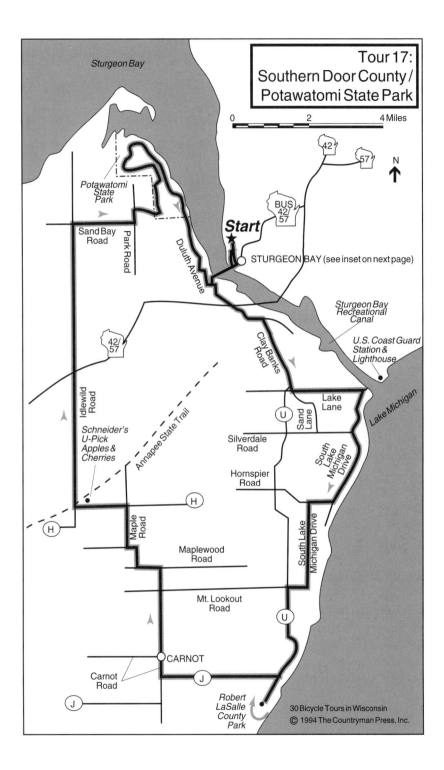

Tour 17:
Southern Door County /
Potawatomi State Park

0   2   4 Miles

N

Sturgeon Bay

Potawatomi State Park

Sand Bay Road

Park Road

Duluth Avenue

42

57

BUS 42/57

Start

STURGEON BAY (see inset on next page)

Sturgeon Bay Recreational Canal

U.S. Coast Guard Station & Lighthouse

42/57

Clay Banks Road

Lake Michigan

Idlewild Road

Annapee State Trail

Schneider's U-Pick Apples & Cherries

U

Lake Lane

Sand Lane

Silverdale Road

South Lake Michigan Drive

Hornspier Road

H

H

Maple Road

Maplewood Road

South Lake Michigan Drive

Mt. Lookout Road

U

CARNOT

Carnot Road

J

J

Robert LaSalle County Park

30 Bicycle Tours in Wisconsin
© 1994 The Countryman Press, Inc.

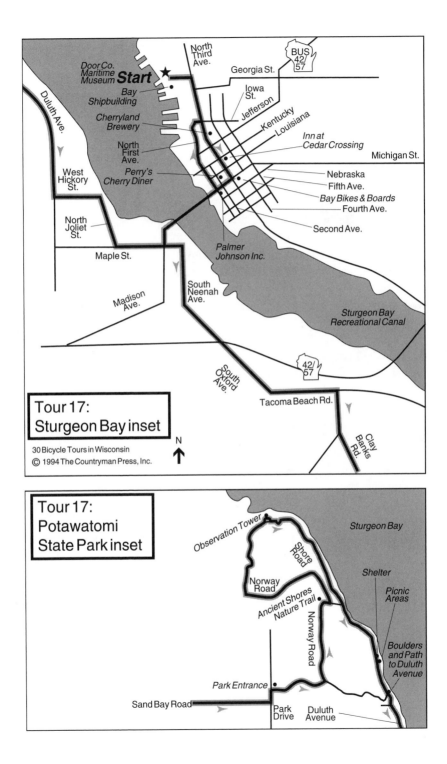

Door Co. Maritime Museum **Start**

Bay Shipbuilding

North Third Ave.

Georgia St.

BUS 42/57

Iowa St.

Jefferson

Kentucky

Louisiana

Cherryland Brewery

Duluth Ave.

North First Ave.

Inn at Cedar Crossing

Michigan St.

West Hickory St.

Perry's Cherry Diner

Nebraska

Fifth Ave.

Bay Bikes & Boards

Fourth Ave.

North Joliet St.

Second Ave.

Maple St.

Palmer Johnson Inc.

Madison Ave.

South Neenah Ave.

Sturgeon Bay Recreational Canal

South Oxford Ave.

42/57

**Tour 17:
Sturgeon Bay inset**

Tacoma Beach Rd.

Clay Banks Rd.

30 Bicycle Tours in Wisconsin
© 1994 The Countryman Press, Inc.

N

**Tour 17:
Potawatomi
State Park inset**

Observation Tower

Shore Road

Sturgeon Bay

Norway Road

Shelter

Picnic Areas

Ancient Shores Nature Trail

Norway Road

Boulders and Path to Duluth Avenue

Park Entrance

Sand Bay Road

Park Drive

Duluth Avenue

your left, just beyond the shipyard. From the south, cross over the Sturgeon Bay canal and turn left on First Avenue, just beyond the bridge. Follow First Avenue until it runs into North Third Avenue. Turn left on Third Avenue and continue several blocks to the museum. Parking, rest rooms, and picnic tables are available.

The museum's lawn is decorated with anchors, propellors, and other artifacts recovered from shipwrecks off the peninsula. Museum highlights include the pilot house from the steamship *Elba*, a 1902 Chris Craft speedboat, and a replica of the office of Captain John Roen, who was known for his ingenuity in solving challenging salvage problems.

One notable feat was his 1943 Houdini-like resurrection of the *George M. Humphrey*, a 586-foot steamer that sank off Michigan's Mackinac Island, carrying 14,000 gross tons of iron ore. Because the wreck posed a danger to passing ferries, the United States War Department sought bids to destroy it with dynamite. Enter Captain John Roen, who offered to remove the boat within one year, if he could claim ownership upon completion of the task. Roen made history by filling the ship's ballast tanks with air and using the buoyancy of the water to lift the *Humphrey* to the surface.

Door County is rich in maritime history.

0.0 *Right onto North Third Avenue at the end of Maritime Museum drive.*

> To your right is the Bay Shipbuilding Company. Facilities include a 7,000-ton floating dry dock and the largest gantry crane in the world. Great Lakes and ocean-going freighters are built and maintained here. Visitors are not allowed in the dock area, but the enormous scale of the shipyard's projects makes it easy to observe from the road.

0.6 *The Inn at Cedar Crossing, (414) 743-4200, is to your left at the junction with Louisiana Street.*

> Innkeeper Teri Wulf has transformed this turn-of-the-century vernacular brick building into a popular restaurant, pub, bakery, and bed-and-breakfast inn.
>
> If you've forgotten an essential cycling accessory or are in need of repairs, Bay Bikes and Boards, (414) 743-4434, a full-service shop, is located at 20 North Third Street, a few blocks south of the inn.

0.7 *Right onto Michigan Street.*

> Look for Perry's Cherry Diner with the red-striped awning on your right, shortly after the turn. The Andropolis family has operated a café at this location for over 20 years. Recently Perry Andropolis, son of the founders, has given this darling little diner a face-lift in the form of a 50s theme. Stop in for a "waffle made in heaven, right here on earth." Another plus for cyclists—Perry's is a non-smoking diner.
>
> On your left just before the bridge is Palmer Johnson, Incorporated, which has been building boats on this location since 1918. Through the years, the company has produced fishing vessels, air-sea rescue boats, freighters, custom sailboats, and world-class racing yachts. The "who's who" of Palmer Johnson boat owners includes King Juan Carlos of Spain, who owns a 100-foot motor yacht named *Fortuna*. Several blocks away is Peterson Builders, Incorporated, whose ship-building vita includes *Seaprobe*, Alcoa's ocean research

vessel, the world's largest tuna-fishing boat, Navy minesweepers, and Alaskan ferries.

Cross the bridge over the Sturgeon Bay Canal, using the walking bridge to the left of car lanes. Do not proceed if the drawbridge is up!

1.3 *Left onto East Maple Street at the stoplight.*

1.4 *Right onto South Neenah Avenue.*

1.7 *Left onto South Oxford Avenue where Neenah Avenue dead-ends.*

2.0 *Cross WI 42/57. Be careful, traffic is heavy here.*

2.1 *Bear left onto South Oxford Avenue on the opposite side of the highway.*

2.5 *South Oxford Avenue becomes Tacoma Beach Road.*

2.8 *Right onto Clay Banks Road.*

4.7 *Left onto Lake Lane.*

Watch for deer on this lovely stretch of birch-lined road.

6.7 *Right onto South Lake Michigan Drive.*

Walk to the shore to see the Lake Michigan entrance to the Sturgeon Bay Recreational Canal, guarded by a picturesque lighthouse and Coast Guard Station.

7.8 *Left onto South Lake Michigan Drive at the junction with Silverdale Road.*

8.9 *An unpaved stretch begins here, lasting about .75 mile.*

9.6 *Right onto Hornspier Road.*

10.3 *Left onto South Lake Michigan Drive.*

12.3 *Left onto Mount Lookout Road.*

13.9 *Left onto County Highway U.*

15.2 *Left into Robert LaSalle County Park.*

Look for a parking area and small sign. Be sure to walk down the hill to the quiet, secluded beach where you will find rest rooms and picnic tables. Right onto County Highway U. Backtrack to County Highway J.

15.7 *Left onto County Highway J.*

18.5 *Right onto Carnot Road (no sign) where County Highway J goes left.*

19.0 *Continue straight on North Carnot Road at Carnot Corners. Don't take the branch of Carnot Road that goes left.*

21.0 *Left onto Maplewood Road where Carnot Road ends.*

21.6 *Right on Maplewood Road.*

22.3 *Right onto Maple Road.*

23.3 *Left onto County Highway H (road sign is behind stop sign).*

24.2 *To the right is Schneider's Cherryland U-Pick Apples and Cherries.*

Most of Door County's famous Red Tart (Mortmorency) cherries are grown in this area. These are baking cherries and are quite sour if eaten uncooked. For snacking, try dried cherries—Wisconsin's counterpart to California raisins. Apple varieties grown in Door County include Delicious, McIntosh, Cortlands, Greenings, and Snows. White apple blossoms open in mid-May, followed by pink cherry blossoms a week or so later. If Mother Nature cooperates, both are in full bloom for Memorial Day weekend.

24.6 *Right onto Idlewild Road where County Highway H goes left.*

27.4 *Cross WI 42/57. Use caution, this is a busy road.*

31.2 *Right on Sand Bay Road.*

32.6 *Left on Park Drive.*

32.8 *Right at entrance to Potawatomi State Park*

The park sits on the edge of the Niagara Escarpment, a 900-mile long slab of dolomite limestone that extends from New York, where it supports the plunging waters of Niagara Falls. Pileated woodpeckers are numerous in the park. Look for a large bird that resembles the cartoon character named Woody, often spotted in places where field meets forest. You may notice large oblong holes in the red pines; these are made by woodpeckers looking for ants and beetles.

33.6 Left on Norway Road toward the tower.

34.4 Left on Norway Road again, by sign for Ancient Shores Nature Trail. Careful, this turn is easy to miss.

36.4 Climb the 75-foot observation tower for a view of Marinette, Wisconsin, and Menominee, Michigan, 16 miles across the bay. Continue on the park loop, following signs to picnic areas.

38.4 On your left is a series of picnic areas with tables, a shelter, water pump, and rest rooms. Continue on the park road beyond fourth picnic area.

38.9 Where road veers right, look for several large boulders marking a small path. Follow the path for about .1 mile to where it meets Duluth Avenue.

40.0 Follow Duluth Avenue back to Sturgeon Bay.

41.3 Left on West Hickory Street.

41.5 Right onto North Joliet Street.

41.8 Left onto Maple Street.

42.1 Left onto North Madison Avenue (WI 42/57) at stoplight. Cross the Sturgeon Bay Canal, using the walking bridge on the right side.

42.6 Left onto First Avenue.

43.0 Right onto Iowa Street.

43.1 Left onto Third Avenue.

If you're thirsty, turn right instead and take a half-block detour to the Cherryland Brewery, (414) 743-1945. This brewpub located in the former Ahnapee and Western Railroad offers tours, tasting, and a half-dozen varieties of beer, brewed right here. The most unusual are fruity brews like Cherry Rail and Apple Bock, which use Door County products. Purists can opt for Silver Rail, a traditional pilsner.

43.4 Left into the Maritime Museum.

Bicycle Repair Service

Bay Bike and Boards
20 North Third, Sturgeon Bay, WI
(414) 743-4434

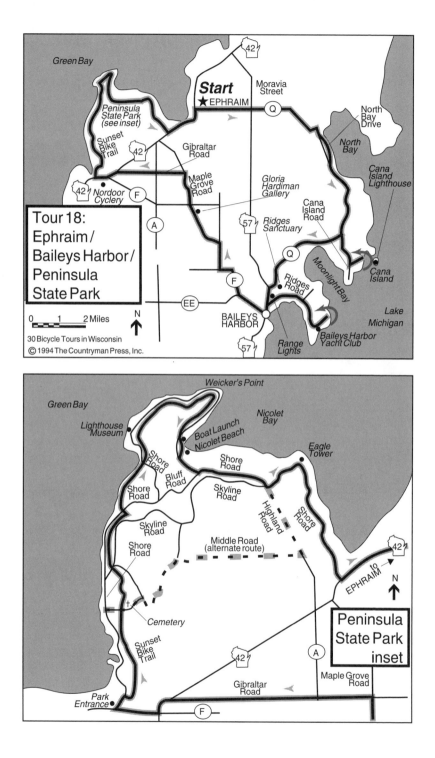

Tour 18:
Ephraim /
Baileys Harbor /
Peninsula
State Park

0   1   2 Miles   N

30 Bicycle Tours in Wisconsin
© 1994 The Countryman Press, Inc.

Green Bay

Peninsula
State Park
(see inset)

Sunset
Bike
Trail

42

Nordoor
Cyclery

F

A

Gibraltar
Road

Maple
Grove
Road

Start
★ EPHRAIM

Moravia
Street

Q

North
Bay
Drive

North
Bay

Gloria
Hardiman
Gallery

57

Ridges
Sanctuary

Cana
Island
Lighthouse

Cana
Island
Road

Cana
Island

Moonlight Bay

Q

F

EE

Ridges
Road

BAILEYS
HARBOR

57

Range
Lights

Baileys Harbor
Yacht Club

Lake
Michigan

Weicker's Point

Green Bay

Lighthouse
Museum

Nicolet
Bay

Boat Launch
Nicolet Beach

Shore
Road

Shore
Road

Bluff
Road

Shore
Road

Skyline
Road

Eagle
Tower

Shore
Road

Skyline
Road

Highland
Road

Shore
Road

42

to
EPHRAIM

N

Shore
Road

Middle Road
(alternate route)

Cemetery

Sunset
Bike
Trail

42

A

Peninsula
State Park
inset

Gibraltar
Road

Maple Grove
Road

Park
Entrance

F

18
Ephraim/Baileys Harbor/
Peninsula State Park

Distance: *11.9 or 38.6 miles (5.2 miles unpaved surface)*
Terrain: *Gently rolling*

Welcome to postcard Door County—neatly white-washed waterfront villages, lighthouses surrounded by swooping gulls, and sailboats bobbing in the harbor, their rigging clanging like soprano wind chimes. On this ride you will meet the contrasting personalities of both the Green Bay and Lake Michigan shores—the bay side a hub of friendly activity, the lake side given to solitude and introspection.

Across the bay from the tour starting point in Ephraim is the 3,763-acre densely wooded peninsula that makes up Peninsula State Park. This view varies with constantly changing weather and light conditions—gray and storm-beaten during a full-force gale, barely visible behind a lace curtain of morning mist, or backlit by a rosy-peach sunset—an appropriate study for a modern-day Monet.

If you plan to cycle this route on a weekend in July or August, don't be discouraged when you arrive in Ephraim to find backed-up traffic and a shortage of parking spots. Take solace in the fact that this ride follows lightly traveled back roads and seldom crosses the main thoroughfares.

The terrain is flat to rolling with the exception of two formidable hills—one near the start of the ride and another in Peninsula State Park. Those looking for a shorter, more leisurely option should consider cycling just the 11.9-mile portion in Peninsula State Park, which follows the level, off-road Sunset Bicycle Trail. The trail surface is a firm, crushed limestone, suitable for all except the thinnest racing tires. Parking and a map are available at the park office. To complete the in-park loop backtrack from Eagle Tower (mile 36.6) and take Highland Road to Middle Road. Middle Road is almost entirely downhill. Beware, the last section is very steep, and there is a sharp left at the bottom of the hill. Turn left onto Mengelberg Lane and take another left onto the Sunset Bike Trail back to the parking lot.

Cyclists wishing to camp in Peninsula State Park should call ahead for reservations, (414) 868-3258; holiday weekends fill early. Hotel and bed-and-breakfast accommodations are plentiful in the area; contact the Door County Chamber of Commerce, (414) 743-4456. The Chamber also publishes a bicycle map for Door County and bike route signs along the roads indicate the loop that's been laid out. Be aware that these signs do not always correspond to this route. In fact, you will sometimes need to turn in the opposite direction.

WI 42 will take you to the village of Ephraim. The tour begins at the municipal parking lot opposite Wilson's Restaurant and the Ephraim Public Library.

0.0   *Left on WI 42.*

0.1   *Right onto Church Street, just beyond the gas station.*

0.2   *Right onto Moravia Street (County Highway Q).*

> Pause here for a moment to muster your energy for the big hill ahead. On your left is a pioneer schoolhouse that served Ephraim for 80 years. Ahead, in the next block, you can see the Ephraim Moravian Church, identified by its white steeple and green shutters.
>
> Ephraim was founded in 1853 by members of the Norwegian Moravian Church under the leadership of the Reverend Andreas M. Iverson. The Moravians formed earlier settlements in Milwaukee and Green Bay, but disbanded because of dissatisfaction with the philosophy of collective ownership espoused by their leader, Nils Otto Tank. When they arrived in Door County, they called their new settlement Ephraim, a word that appears frequently in the Bible and means "doubly fruitful." The strict moral standards of the Moravian community remain today—liquor sales are still forbidden in the village.

0.3 Left on County Highway Q and proceed up the hill.

Don't be discouraged by this steep climb. Once you reach the top, you will be riding on a vast plateau of Niagara limestone that stretches the length of the peninsula.

2.1 Cross WI 57. Use caution, this is a busy road.

4.9 Left onto North Bay Drive.

This short diversion off County Highway Q takes you down to the water's edge.

6.2 Left onto County Highway Q again.

8.3 Left by the Rustic Road sign onto Cana Island Road.

8.4 Straight toward the dead end (don't turn right); follow the Rustic Road sign.

This road passes between Moonlight Bay and North Bay, through a boreal forest filled with magnificent specimens of spruce, cedar, and white pine. These trees are more typical of vegetation found in northern Minnesota or Canada but because of the cooling effect of Lake Michigan, they are able to grow here.

9.4 Left toward the Cana Island lighthouse and Spike Horn Campground (still on Rustic Road), where road ahead becomes dirt.

10.6 Park your bike where the road ends and walk across the channel to the lighthouse.

If the water level is low, you can walk across an isthmus of smooth, wave-worn stones. If it's high, you may need to roll up your cuffs to make the passage! There is an educational display on the island and you are free to wander the lighthouse grounds; the building itself is not open to the public. When you return to the mainland, backtrack on Cana Island Road.

11.9 Right on Cana Island Road where a dirt road goes left.

12.8 Left on Cana Island Road.

12.9 Left onto County Highway Q.

16.3 Left into the Ridges Sanctuary, (414) 839-2802.

> The sanctuary features hiking trails that follow the crests (or ridges) of ancient Lake Michigan shorelines, created as waters rose and fell through the centuries. The sandy soil here, as well as the swales that form in the troughs between the ridges, create a unique habitat for wildflowers and other forest plants. Over 20 species of native orchids bloom in the sanctuary. A self-guided hike takes about an hour; naturalists lead interpretive walks during the summer months. Bring insect repellent!

16.4 Left continuing on County Highway Q as you leave the sanctuary.

16.5 Left onto WI 57.

16.7 Enter the village of Baileys Harbor.

> In the late 1840s, Captain Justice Bailey took refuge from a storm in this picturesque harbor which now bears his name. He was headed from Milwaukee to Buffalo with a boatload of immigrants in search of a new home. Bailey was impressed with the ample supplies of timber and limestone and convinced the owner of his schooner to purchase land and form a settlement here. Baileys Harbor later became a regular refueling stop on the steamship line between Chicago and Buffalo.

17.0 Left on Ridges Road by the Sandpiper Restaurant.

17.3 To the left are two range lights, used to guide ships into harbor.

> The lights were built in 1869, as part of an effort by the federal government to put an end to Door County's history of tragic shipwrecks. The upper range light, also the keeper's home, is located 950 feet inland from the lower light and stands 17 feet higher. Ship captains lined up the towers during the day, or the beacons that shone in them at night, to guide their vessels into port. The lamps were fueled by lard, whale oil, and kerosene, before being converted to electricity in the 1930s. The range lights were used until 1969, when

the single automated light was installed across the road.

18.5 *Right onto Harbor Lane toward the Baileys Harbor Yacht Club.*

18.8 *When you reach the Yacht Club, walk down to the pier and admire the many sailing and motor yachts moored here.*

19.1 *Backtrack from the Yacht Club and go straight on Ridges Road at the stop sign.*

20.6 *Left onto WI 57.*

20.7 *Right onto County Highway EE/F, just beyond the McArdle Library and Tourist Information Office. Rest rooms are available here at the library.*

21.6 *Right onto County Highway F at the stop sign.*

25.3 *Straight onto Maple Grove Road (not right onto Maple Grove East).*
The Gloria Hardiman Gallery at this intersection specializes in hand-woven woolen goods.

The village of Ephraim on Green Bay

26.3 Left onto Gibraltar Road.

27.3 Cross County Highway A.

29.0 Left onto WI 42 at Gibraltar School. The road is busy, but there is an ample paved shoulder.

29.3 To your left is Nor Door Cyclery, a friendly, full-service bicycle shop.

29.5 Right into Peninsula State Park.

> Our route through the park will include some stretches on the Sunset Bike Trail and others on the road. There are no entrance or trail fees for cyclists. If you prefer not to ride on unpaved surface you can take the Shore Road through the park, but there is a great deal of camper traffic during the summer.

29.6 Right onto the Sunset Bicycle Trail, just past the entrance.

30.8 Cross the road by the cemetery.

33.1 To your left is the Eagle Lighthouse and Museum.

> The lighthouse was built in 1868 in the interest of maritime safety. The museum is is open to visitors, June through Labor Day, for a small admission fee. From the museum, continue on the Sunset Bicycle Trail.

33.7 Welkers Point Picnic Area, on your left, makes a good lunch stop.

34.2 Follow signs down to the boat landing and Nicolet Bay campsites #600-677.

34.3 Right again onto the Sunset Bicycle Trail.

34.6 The trail leads to Nicolet Beach, with a sandy area for swimming, picnic area, and rest rooms.

> It is named for Jean Nicolet, who arrived in Door County in 1634 dressed in a mandarin robe, in preparation for his arrival in China! Backtrack to exit and turn left onto Shore Road.

34.7 Left again onto Shore Road toward Eagle Tower.

Get ready for the second big hill of the ride.

35.9 Bear left at Skyline Road junction.

36.1 Eagle Bluff Lookout and the 75-foot Eagle Tower.
Both offer stunning views of the Green Bay shoreline, including Chambers, Horseshoe, Little Strawberry, Pirate, Jack, and Adventure Islands. From the tower, it's all downhill back to Ephraim. As you coast past the park's golf course, notice the 40-foot totem pole on your left, topped with a carved bear, clan symbol of the Potawatomi tribe. The pole marks the grave of Chief Simon Kahquados.

37.4 Left onto WI 42. This is a busier road, but has a shoulder for cyclists.

38.6 Left into the parking area where you began.
An ice cream cone from Wilson's is a Door County must-do— a jelly bean is cleverly included in the bottom of your cone to prevent dripping.

Bicycle Repair Service

Nor Door Cyclery
4007 WI 42, Fish Creek, WI
(414) 868-2275

19
Ellison Bay/Gills Rock/ Newport State Park Ride

Distance: 19 miles
Terrain: Flat to gently rolling

Door County's tranquil "top of the thumb" area is a world apart from the bustling villages farther south on the peninsula. While you'll come across the occasional pottery shop or ice cream parlor, the attractions here are natural rather than than commercial.

The water is never far away on this short ride that takes in both the Green Bay and Lake Michigan shores and the turbulent channel known as Death's Door. On a foggy morning, with only a gentle stretch of the imagination, you'd think you were on the coast of Oregon or Maine. With the exception of one hill, which is steep enough to be a "walker" for most, the terrain is flat and the traffic light to nonexistent. Most visitors who make it this far north are headed for the ferry to Washington Island, but for those with an afternoon to spare, there's plenty worth exploring before you pull anchor. For those with the inclination to do both, the Washington Island ride can easily be combined with this one.

The tour begins at the Women's Club Park, located just south of Ellison Bay on WI 42. If you're traveling north from Sister Bay, be sure to stop at the Grand View Motel, just south of Ellison Bay, for a panoramic view of Green Bay and offshore islands. As you descend a large hill from the motel, Women's Club Park is on your left.

0.0   Left on WI 42 leaving the park.

> Ellison Bay was founded in 1872 by Danish immigrant John
> Eliason, a local timber baron who made his fortune in the

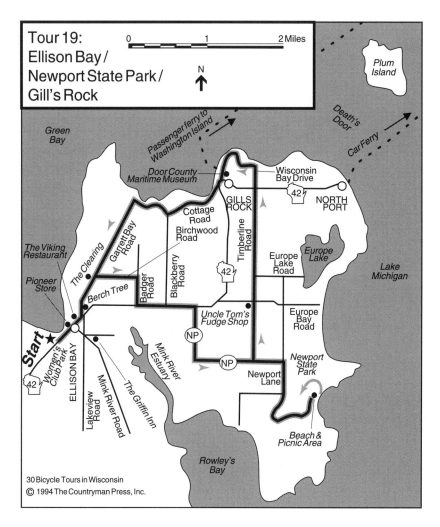

Tour 19:
Ellison Bay /
Newport State Park /
Gill's Rock

0   1   2 Miles

N

Green
Bay

Passenger ferry to
Washington Island

Death's
Door

Car Ferry

Plum
Island

Door County
Maritime Museum

Wisconsin
Bay Drive

42

GILLS
ROCK

NORTH
PORT

Cottage
Road

Birchwood
Road

Timberline
Road

The Viking
Restaurant

Garrett Bay
Road

The Clearing

Europe
Lake
Road

Europe
Lake

Lake
Michigan

Pioneer
Store

Berch Tree

Badger
Road

Blackberry
Road

42

Uncle Tom's
Fudge Shop

Europe
Bay
Road

Start

Women's
Club Park

ELLISON BAY

42

Lakeview
Road

Mink River
Road

The Griffin Inn

Mink River
Estuary

NP

NP

Newport
Lane

Newport
State
Park

Beach &
Picnic Area

Rowley's
Bay

30 Bicycle Tours in Wisconsin
© 1994 The Countryman Press, Inc.

telephone-pole business. The Pioneer Store, on your left, is a good spot to stock up on provisions for your ride. Built in 1900, this old-time general store epitomizes the axiom, "if they don't have it, you don't need it." Besides buying comestibles, you can drop off your dry cleaning here, and if you need his services, the grocer is a notary public.

Across the street is the Viking Restaurant, home of Door

County's longest running fish boil. Inquire about dinner seating times when you pass by—this is a great place to satisfy a cyclist's post-ride appetite. The fish boil became a Door County tradition in turn-of-the-century lumber camps, where local whitefish provided an inexpensive yet filling meal for the lumberjacks. The camp cook tossed potatoes, onions, large chunks of whitefish, and, in those days, enormous quantities of salt, into a huge kettle over a raging bonfire. When all the ingredients were cooked, wood was added to the fire, causing the kettle to boil over. Along with the foamy water that spewed forth went the strong, "fishy" taste associated with this rather rough fish. The "boil over" remains the grand finale and prime photo opportunity of the present-day fish boil.

If you turn right on Mink River Road (opposite the Viking) and follow it for about two blocks, you'll come to the Griffin Inn, (414) 854-4306, where you'll feel welcome the moment you walk in the door. This New England–style inn, named for a fur-trading vessel that went missing in Door County waters in the 1600s, is highly recommended for its cozy atmosphere and delicious country breakfasts.

0.3   *Left on Garrett Bay Road, by the old Gus Klenke garage.*

Just beyond the garage is the Berch Tree, where a dollar buys a double-decker ice cream cone. If it's too early for ice cream, the shop also sells hand-crafted home furnishings.

Ahead and to your left on Garrett Bay Road is The Clearing, (414) 854-4088, originally the summer home of Jens Jensen, the prominent American landscape architect. According to Jensen, the word "Clearing" refers to a clearing of the mind. He built the home as a place where his students could "withdraw from the manmade world." Today The Clearing is a school where students pursue writing and artistic endeavors in an inspirational natural setting. Tours are available on Saturday and Sunday afternoons during the summer months.

A break beside Lake Michigan

1.2   *Right onto Birchwood Road.*

2.0   *Right onto Badger Road.*

Here you'll pass apple and cherry orchards, some regrettably abandoned in recent years.

2.4   *Left and follow WI 42 for about one mile.*

This is a busier road, so stay in single file. Along this stretch look for roadside stands and orchard stores selling apples, cider, and homemade preserves, especially in the fall.

3.5   *Right onto County NP.*

6.1   *Right onto Newport Lane.*

6.3   *Enter Newport State Park and continue on Newport Lane.*

There is no entry fee for bicycles, but you may want to pick up a park map at the entry gate. Because the campsites here can only be reached by backpacking, Newport State Park draws fewer visitors than other Door County parks. The park was a logging village in the 1800s. Old dock cribs, lilac hedges, and a few remains of cabin foundations can still be found here.

7.8 Newport Lane ends at parking area #3.

Here you will find a beautiful sandy beach that extends for several miles. There are changing facilities if you dare to take a polar-bear dip in Lake Michigan. For the not-so-daring, beachcombing here nets all sorts of unusual treasures. Those with mountain bikes can try out a new off-road bicycle trail through the park. Signs point to the trail from the beach area. Backtrack out of the park on Newport Lane.

9.4 Left onto Newport Drive.

9.9 Right onto Timberline Road.

10.7 Uncle Tom's Fudge Shop is on your left, opposite Europe Bay Road.

This little blue Newport Schoolhouse, dating to 1858, is where Uncle Tom, unofficially known as "the Socrates of Door County," peddled his own brand of pancake mix, peanut brittle, fudge, and homespun philosophy until he died in 1991. Among Tom's favorite customers were cyclists, who often spent hours warming up around his pot-bellied stove and listening to his snippets of wisdom like "gratitude is attitude." The walls of the store are papered with photos of Uncle Tom with friends, politicians, and celebrities. The store still operates under the tutelage of Aunt Marge, and is well worth a stop.

12.8 Cross WI 42 and go straight on Wisconsin Bay Drive.

This road winds along a rugged bluff past some of Door County's most beautiful homes, including that of well-known watercolorist Tom Lynch.

14.6 On your left, just as you enter the village of Gills Rock, the Door County Maritime Museum is on your left.

Exhibits at the museum, (414) 854-2860, focus on the area's commercial fishing industry and include a 60-year-old refurbished commercial fishing tug called *Hope*.

14.7 Right onto WI 42.

14.8 Right into Gills Rock where WI 42 goes left.

Gregarious gulls will greet you as you arrive at the Gills Rock Harbor, to the left just below the Shoreline Resort. Both commercial and sport fishing boats depart from here and if you arrive in the mid-afternoon, you are likely to see them coming in with the day's catch. Near the dock are several souvenir shops and Charlie's Smokehouse, where you can buy a piece of delicious smoked whitefish. This gourmet delight travels well in a handlebar bag, or it can be enjoyed pierside with rye crackers and a cold drink.

From Gills Rock you can catch a glimpse of the treacherous passage between the Door Peninsula and Washington Island that the French explorers called Porte des Morts (Death's Door). Strong variable currents make the coastal waters here tricky to navigate, particularly during winter storms. Between 1837 and 1914, 24 vessels were lost in the Porte des Morts and another 40 boats ran aground on nearby reefs, shoals, and islands. The three passenger ferry lines that now service Washington Island from Gills Rock have a much better safety record. Backtrack from Gills Rock on WI 42.

14.9 Straight onto WI 42 where it also turns left towards Northport.

15.0 Right onto Cottage Road.

This road traces a craggy shoreline, then turns inland to a deep boreal forest.

16.1 Right again onto Cottage Road at the Blackberry Road junction, by the "Hill" sign.

Luckily, the sign indicates a downhill, but be aware that the hill is very steep and there is often loose gravel at the edges of the road. Anticipate a sharp, 90-degree turn at the bottom.

16.3 Left at the hill bottom onto Garrett Bay Road.

From here it's a pleasant coast back to Ellison Bay under a canopy of massive maples. This stretch is especially delightful in mid-May, when delicate white trillium blossoms poke their noses out among the the tree trunks. As you approach the highway, it's your last chance for ice cream at the Berch Tree.

18.7 Right onto WI 42.

19.0 Right into Women's Club Park.

Bicycle Repair Service

Nor Door Cyclery
4007 WI 42, Fish Creek, WI
(414) 868-2275

20
Washington Island

Distance: *24 miles*
Terrain: *Flat to rolling*

While Washington Island's isolated locale may have discouraged less in-trepid immigrants, the hearty Icelandic settlers who arrived here in the mid-1800s felt right at home. Today the island has a population of about 650 permanent residents who earn their living from tourism, commercial fishing, and various artistic endeavors. Washington Island remains the oldest, and one of the largest, Icelandic communities outside of Reykjavik. The island was called Potawatomi Island for its resident tribe until 1816 when a Navy fleet stranded here renamed it Washington Island in honor of its flagship.

A complete circumnavigation of the island is only 24 miles, making a bicycle the ideal way to explore. Those hungry for more mileage can easily combine this ride with the northern Door County route.

Three ferry companies provide service to Washington Island and all allow you to bring your bike on board. The most comfortable way to travel is on the upper deck of the passenger-only Island Clipper, (414) 854-2972, which departs from Gills Rock. Captain Charlie Voight gives a brief commentary along the way. If the Clipper's schedule doesn't work, try the C.G. Richter, (414) 847-2546, which also leaves from Gills Rock. A car ferry, operated by the Washington Island Ferry Line, departs from Northport, (414) 847-2546. This boat operates earlier and later in the season and is also more likely to go in inclement weather. The passage, through the infamous Death's Door strait, takes about 30 minutes. Don't worry—all of the recommended vessels have a good safety record.

There are several restaurants and a grocery store on the island. Lodging

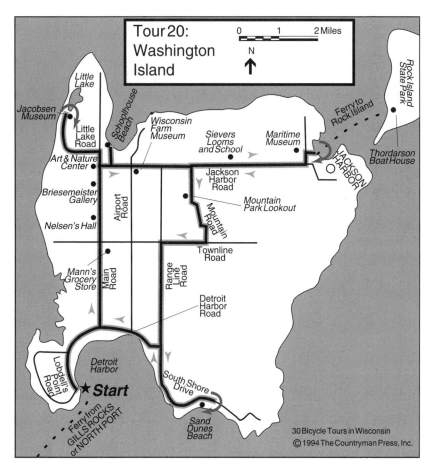

Tour 20:
Washington
Island

0   1   2 Miles

N ↑

Little Lake

Jacobsen Museum

Schoolhouse Beach

Little Lake Road

Wisconsin Farm Museum

Sievers Looms and School

Maritime Museum

Ferry to Rock Island

Rock Island State Park

Art & Nature Center

Jackson Harbor Road

JACKSON HARBOR

Thordarson Boat House

Briesemeister Gallery

Airport Road

Mountain Park Lookout

Nelsen's Hall

Mountain Road

Townline Road

Mann's Grocery Store

Main Road

Range Line Road

Detroit Harbor Road

Lobdell's Point Road

Detroit Harbor

★ **Start**

South Shore Drive

Ferry from GILLS ROCKS or NORTHPORT

Sand Dunes Beach

30 Bicycle Tours in Wisconsin
© 1994 The Countryman Press, Inc.

is available at the Dor-Cros Chalet, (414) 847-2126, and Findlay's Holiday Inn, (414) 847-2526.

To get to Gills Rock, take WI 42 North. To reach Northport, continue on WI 42 for about two miles beyond Gills Rock, where the road ends. This tour begins at Detroit Harbor on Washington Island, near the bike rental concession at the Island Clipper pier.

0.0   Right onto Lobdell Point Road.

1.5   Left onto Main Road through "downtown."

Mann's Grocery Store has a deli counter if you need to pick

up lunch supplies. Mann's Mercantile in the Den Norske Grenda (Norwegian Village) complex offers souvenirs.

2.6   *To your left is Nelsen's Hall, Bitter's Pub and Restaurant.*

Bicyclists have waited out many a rain shower at this legendary bar that began as a bootlegging operation during prohibition. The establishment gained a reputation for "treating" thirsty patrons with angostura bitters, which was considered to have medicinal value and, despite its high alcohol content, was not banned. Take the cure—a shot glass of bitters followed by a chaser of beer—and you will receive a Bitter's Club Membership Card for your wallet. Hot chocolate, soup, and sandwiches are also available.

3.7   *To your left is the Briesemeister Gallery, which sells island-made paintings, pottery, and textiles.*

4.2   *To your left is Art and Nature Center, (414) 847-2025.*

This 90-year-old schoolhouse contains exhibits devoted to island history and rotating displays of artwork by island residents. If you're lucky, you may catch one of the artists performing a new composition on the piano or demonstrating watercolor painting.

Continue straight on Main Road.

4.5   *Left onto Little Lake Road. Stay right at the fork.*

6.0   *Jacobsen Museum, on Little Lake, (414) 847-2213.*

This tiny cedar log cabin museum is chock-a-block full of natural and historic artifacts from the island. Every faded photograph tells a story, which the curators are quick to relate if you show curiosity. Backtrack on Little Lake Road to Main Road.

7.5   *Right onto Main Road.*

7.8   *Left onto Jackson Harbor Road.*

7.9   *Left toward Schoolhouse Beach.*

The shore here is covered with smooth, rounded, white rocks, which are better for stone skipping than beach sitting. Wait for Sand Dunes Beach, later in the ride, if you plan on sunbathing. Backtrack to Jackson Harbor Road and turn left.

At the junction with Airport Road is the Wisconsin Farm Museum, which has old horse-drawn farm machinery and displays on island farming.

10.1 Sievers Looms and School of Fiber Arts is to your left.

Sievers Looms is the distributor of island-built birch and cherry weaving looms. A small shop on the premises sells yarns spun from the wool of island sheep and items made by students and teachers. The School of Fiber Arts offers week-long and weekend classes on weaving, quilting, spinning, knitting, basketry, and papermaking during the summer months.

11.7 Continue on Jackson Harbor Road to Jackson Harbor.

Here the sprightly little Karfi ferry, (414) 847-2252, will take you to Rock Island State Park, a 10-minute trip. This 905-acre island was once the private estate of millionaire investor Chester Thordarson, whose castle-like boathouse is visible from Jackson Harbor. Now the island offers hiking, mountain biking (there are no paved roads), and primitive camping.

Also at Jackson Harbor is a small maritime museum housed in converted fishing sheds. Methods of setting nets and processing fish for market are shown in photographs and exhibits. Backtrack on Jackson Harbor Road to Mountain Road.

14.1 Left on Mountain Road.

14.6 Tower Wayside.

Climb the observation tower for a sea gull's view of the island. Rest rooms and picnic area.

Right from Wayside onto Mountain Road.

15.6 Right onto Townline Road.

16.3 Left onto Rangeline Road.

Cyclists board the ferry for the half-hour ride to the start of this tour.

Continue past the marina. Rangeline Road becomes South Shore Road.

19.6 Sand Dunes Beach.

Take off your shoes and wiggle your toes in the sugar-fine sand at this scenic swimming beach. Remember to allow about 20 minutes to get back to the ferry pier from here! Exit the beach area and backtrack on South Shore and Rangeline Roads.

21.0 Left onto Detroit Harbor Road (becomes Lobdell Point Road).

24.0 Left toward the Detroit Harbor ferry piers.

Bicycle Repair Service

Nor Door Cyclery
4007 WI 42, Fish Creek, WI
(414) 868-2275

NORTHERN
WISCONSIN

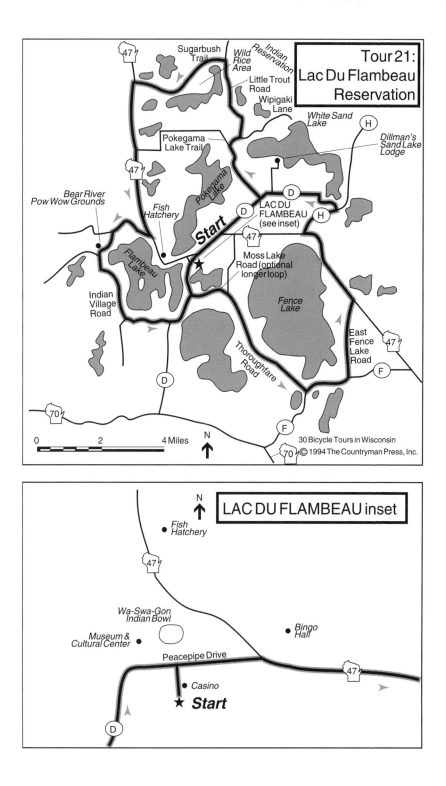

21
Lac du Flambeau Reservation

Distance: *20.8 or 35.1 miles*
Terrain: *Flat to gently rolling*

Deerskin moccasins bounce to the beat of ceremonial drums each week when powwows are held on the reservation of the Lac du Flambeau band of the Lake Superior Chippewa. This entire tour takes place within reservation boundaries and offers rare opportunities to glimpse a bald eagle circling over the site of a fierce Indian battle or to see a canoe slipping silently through a marsh during the wild rice harvest.

The route skirts the shores of the 10-lake Lac du Flambeau chain. The terrain is almost perfectly flat and the road paved, though subject to frequent frost heaves. The route is heavily forested with pines and birches.

The Chippewa are an Algonquin-language eastern tribe, originally called Ojibway, a word that translates as "to roast until puckered up," referring to the characteristically puckered seams of their moccasins. The word Ojibway was mispronounced by white traders and became Chippewa. The Chippewa referred to themselves as "the writing people" because of their habit of drawing on birch bark. The Lac du Flambeau people have grown from a small band to a tribe of just over two thousand members, governed by a tribal council of twelve.

French fur traders named the lake that dominates the area, Lac du Flambeau, French for "lake of the torches," when they observed the Chippewa spearfishing at night by the light of flaming torches. Recent years have seen a renewed interest in spearfishing and other Chippewa customs. Like other Wisconsin tribes, the Chippewa have benefited from rulings permitting reservation gaming and have recently opened a casino and bingo hall.

To reach Lac du Flambeau, take WI 47 to County Highway D, which becomes Peace Pipe Drive as you enter town. You may park at the Lake of the Torches Casino. The casino is open 24 hours every day and offers blackjack, slot machines, and video poker.

Directly across the street from the casino is the Lac du Flambeau Museum and Cultural Center, (715) 588-3333, a well-organized facility that includes an authentic 24-foot dugout canoe, examples of Native American clothing, and an exhibit depicting Chippewa activities during various times of the year. There is also a gift shop that sells traditional Native American crafts. Hours are Monday through Saturday, 10 A.M. to 4 P.M. Adjacent to the museum is the Wa-Swa-Gon Indian Bowl (call the Cultural Center for information), where powwows are held on Tuesday evening at 7 P.M., mid-June through mid-August. The Indian Bowl also contains a replica of a Native American village with wigwams, hide and fish racks, and wild rice finishing areas.

0.0 *Right onto Peace Pipe Drive (County Highway D) from the casino parking lot.*

0.3 *Right onto WI 47.*

0.8 *Bear left onto County Highway D.*

2.4 *Left onto Pokegama Lake Trail.*

4.1 *Right onto Wipigaki Lane where Pokegama Trail becomes dirt.*

4.4 *Left onto Little Trout Road.*

Wild rice is harvested from the marshes along this stretch beginning in mid-August. Tribe members ply the waterways in pairs of canoes. When the rice plants are located, the four-to-eight-foot stalks are bent over one canoe and beaten with a stick to loosen the kernels, which fall to the bottom of the boat. The stalks are then beaten in the opposite direction over the other canoe. Sacks of the purplish-black delicacy (some of which is now planted, not really wild) are available for sale in local shops.

6.3 *Left onto Sugarbush Trail at the bottom of the hill. This turn is easy to miss.*

9.7 Left onto WI 47.

13.8 Right onto Indian Village Road.

15.7 The parallel road to your left leads to the site of an old Indian village; nothing remains today.

> The Chippewa lived a nomadic existence, traveling between the shores of Lake Superior where they fished in the summer and Lac du Flambeau where they fished, tapped trees for maple sugar, hunted, and harvested wild rice during other seasons. They used birch bark to construct their homes, called wigwams, and their canoes. A small group led by Chief Sharpened Stone arrived here in 1745 and found the area so appealing they decided to settle permanently. Their presence was challenged by the Sioux, culminating in a fierce battle on the lake's Strawberry Island (visible at various points of this ride) where the Chippewa emerged as victors.
>
> The French claimed sovereignty of the area during a ceremony held at Sault St. Marie in 1671. The fur trade

Wild rice is harvested in mid-August.

181

peaked in 1815 when John Jacob Astor's American Fur Company dominated area commerce. An 1853 treaty established the Chippewa on reservations, including the one at Lac du Flambeau. The greatest upheaval in Flambeau history was probably the opening of the reservation to logging in the 1880s. The industry thrived to the benefit of timber barons and the detriment of the forest, which was severely overcut. Visitors to the Flambeau Lumber Company were housed at a local hotel and were the first to broadcast the area's fishing and vacation appeal.

To your right, looking across the Bear River to the peninsula, are the Bear River Powwow grounds where large intertribal gatherings are held. The Bear River was an important water route, linking Lac du Flambeau with the Wisconsin River and eventually Lake Superior.

19.0 *Left onto County Highway D.*

19.8 *Moss Lake Road. If you are taking the longer loop, turn right here and skip to directions below.*

20.7 *Right onto Peace Pipe Road.*

20.8 *Right into the casino parking lot.*

Longer Loop

19.8 *Right onto Moss Lake Road.*

20.2 *Mink farm.*

20.9 *Right onto Thoroughfare Road.*

24.2 *Left onto County Highway F.*

25.3 *Left onto East Fence Lake Road.*

On this road is the Lighthouse Resort, purchased in 1950 by the Johnson Wax Company of Racine, Wisconsin, as a vacation retreat for its employees.

27.4 *Left onto WI 47.*

29.4 Right onto County Highway H.

30.5 Left onto County Highway D.

32.5 Though the route continues straight, a right turn here will take you to Dillman's Sand Lake Lodge.

> This is a top-notch resort with a stunning location on a 1,200-acre peninsula jutting out into White Sand Lake. Established in 1934, this was one of the first resorts in the area, and it continues to be run by the founding family. The resort has carved out a unique niche by offering artists' workshops led by well-known painters.

34.4 Right onto WI 47.

34.8 Left onto County Highway D toward the casino.

35.1 Left into the casino parking lot.

> A worthwhile side trip is a visit to the Tribal Council Fish Hatchery, (715) 588-3307, at the lower end of Pokegama Lake on WI 47. Over 40 million trout, walleye, and muskellunge eggs are hatched annually, raised to fingerling sizes, and planted in local lakes. The facility also has a catch-and-keep trout-fishing pond.

Bicycle Repair Service

BJ's Sport Shop
917 WI 51 North, Minocqua, WI
(715) 356-3900

183

22
Nicolet National Forest

Distance: *37.9 miles (2 miles gravel road)*
Terrain: *Gently rolling*

Pristine lakes and tall pines highlight the scenery on this leisurely tour through the heart of Wisconsin's North Woods. The route skirts a network of 28 glacial lakes (the largest freshwater chain in the world) and weaves through the 656,000-acre Nicolet National Forest on quiet, curvy back roads. Only northern Minnesota, the province of Ontario, and a district in southern Finland can boast more lakes per square mile.

The terrain is flat and the roads are well-shaded by balsam pines, paper birches, and century-old hemlocks. Other than a two-mile (and quite manageable) stretch of gravel, roads are paved and in surprisingly good condition, despite the harsh winters here.

The tour begins in Three Lakes, an unassuming little town named for three bodies of water discovered by early railroad surveyors. There are a couple of cafés serving breakfast and lunch basics, and several worthy points of interest. At the Fruit of the Woods Winery, (715) 546-3080, located downtown in the old railroad depot, you can sample cranberry wine produced from local fruit and purchase related products like jams, chutneys, and syrups.

Just down the block and around the corner on Huron Street is the Three Lakes Historical Museum. Housed in a replica of a Civilian Conservation Corps (CCC) barracks building, the museum is a North Woods encyclopedia with captivating exhibits on lumbering, cranberry growing, and local personalities. There is also a still that was confiscated near here during prohibition—our curiosity prompted the older man minding the museum to recall several entertaining tales about bootleggers who made moonlight

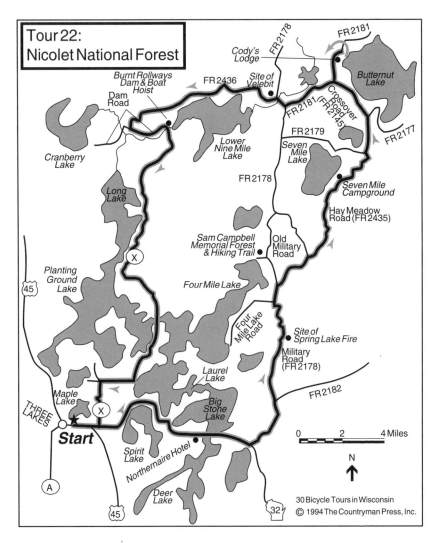

Tour 22:
Nicolet National Forest

Cody's Lodge

FR 2178

FR 2181

Burnt Rollways Dam & Boat Hoist

FR 2436

Site of Velebit

Butternut Lake

Dam Road

Crossover Road (FR 2245)

FR 2181

FR 2177

Cranberry Lake

Lower Nine Mile Lake

FR 2179

Seven Mile Lake

FR 2178

Long Lake

Seven Mile Campground

Hay Meadow Road (FR 2435)

Planting Ground Lake

45

X

Sam Campbell Memorial Forest & Hiking Trail

Old Military Road

Four Mile Lake

Four Mile Lake Road

Site of Spring Lake Fire

Military Road (FR 2178)

Laurel Lake

FR 2182

Maple Lake

THREE LAKES

X

Big Stone Lake

0   2   4 Miles

N

Start

Spirit Lake

Northernaire Hotel

A

Deer Lake

45

32

30 Bicycle Tours in Wisconsin
© 1994 The Countryman Press, Inc.

boat runs across local lakes. Hours are 10 A.M. to 4 P.M. daily, Memorial Day through Labor Day.

The tour begins at the Chamber of Commerce building and the Cy Williams Memorial Park on Superior Street (WI 45) in Three Lakes. It's easy to find—the entire town encompasses several blocks. Check with the Chamber of Commerce, (715) 546-3344, for information on camping in the national forest or lodging in the Three Lakes area. The park faces Maple Lake; there are rest rooms and a nice swimming beach.

The park is named in honor of Cy Williams, a professional baseball player for the Chicago Cubs and later the Philadelphia Phillies who spent most of his life here. After a successful baseball career (he was the first player to hit over 200 home runs), Williams settled in Three Lakes where he made a lasting impression as an architect and builder. Among his designs are the Oneida Village Hotel, the original part of the Black Forest Restaurant, and the elegant Northernaire Resort Hotel. The unusual architectural style of the Northernaire is a striking contrast to the rustic look of most North Woods buildings.

0.0   *Left onto Superior Street.*

0.4   *Left onto WI 32 South.*

> This stretch offers intermittent views of Spirit Lake and Laurel Lake.

3.8   *On the channel between Big Stone and Deer Lakes is the Northernaire Hotel.*

> Once, this was a swank resort that drew star-studded entertainment and moneyed clientele, earning a reputation as the "Waldorf of the Wilderness." Unfortunately, the resort recently closed after a decade of decline.
>
> Sports celebrities and Hollywood types frequented the property in its heyday under founder Carl Marty. Marty's show-biz side contrasted with a tender love of the woods and its creatures. He rescued dozens of orphaned wild animals, which he nurtured back to health with the help of Bernese, his Saint Bernard, and Ginger, his cocker spaniel, who served as foster mothers. Marty's menagerie was chronicled by many authors and featured in wildlife films by Walt Disney and Marlin Perkins. During Marty's reign, it wasn't unusual to see a wobbly-kneed fawn wandering through the hotel lobby.

4.7   *Left onto Military Road (Forest Road 2178), designated as a National Forest Scenic Byway in 1992.*

> This road follows the Lake Superior Trail, an old Native

American trade route that runs from Green Bay to the Keweenaw Peninsula on Lake Superior. The route was traced on high ground to avoid building bridges or fording numerous surrounding lakes, swamps, and bogs. Around 1861 it was established as an overland mail route. Early mail carriers described the journey as "unbroken forest."

During the Civil War, a wagon road was built over the route so that supplies, ammunition, and mail could be transported from Green Bay to Lake Superior in case the water passage was cut off by enemy troops. Since Britain sympathized with the Confederacy, and Canada allied itself with Britain, the Military Road was considered a key element in the national defense. The road later opened up the north country to European settlers and lumber interests.

8.0   This is the site of the Spring Lake Fire on May 6, 1986.

The Nicolet National Forest's worst recorded burn covered 1,176 acres, most of which were replanted the following year.

A flat, shady ride through Wisconsin's North Woods

It is a good example of forest regeneration through a combination of hand planting and nature's healing power.

8.7 *Continue straight on Military Road at Fourmile Lake Road junction.*

8.9 *Stay right on Military Road where Old Military Road intersects.*

A detour on Old Military Road (Forest Road 2207), which veers to the left, takes you to the Sam Campbell Memorial Forest and Hiking Trail Complex. Campbell (1865–1962) was an author, lecturer, conservationist, and nature photographer known locally as the "philosopher of the forest." He maintained a summer home on an island in Fourmile Lake, where he and his wife took the photos and made the films that accompanied his lectures.

10.1 *Nicolet National Forest historic marker.*

The forest was severely overcut by early lumbering interests but was later successfully replanted by the Civilian Conservation Corps team. During the height of the program in the 1930s, there were 22 CCC camps within the boundaries of the Nicolet National Forest. Like all national forests, the Nicolet operates under a multiple-use policy that permits controlled harvest of forest products such as timber or minerals, as well as a broad range of recreational opportunities. Go straight on Hay Meadow (Forest Road 2435).

12.3 *To the left is Sevenmile Campground.*

13.2 *Right onto Forest Road 2179 toward Cody's Lodge.*

14.5 *Left onto Crossover Road (Forest Road 2145).*

16.3 *Right onto Forest Road 2181.*

16.7 *Right into Cody's Butternut Lodge.*

This small lakeside fishing resort run by friendly folks has rustic cabins and a lodge overlooking Butternut Lake. The bar serves light lunches and refreshments.

16.8 *Left at the lodge exit and backtrack on Forest Road 2181.*

189

17.3 Straight on Butternut Lake Road (Forest Road 2181) at the junction with Crossover Road.

20.5 Right onto Forest Road 2178.

> This corner marks the site of an early twentieth-century Croatian settlement named Velebit, named after a mountain range in Yugoslavia. An early settler named Yosef Habrisch assisted the immigrants in building homesteads on cutover timberlands. They worked in logging camps and mined iron and copper in Michigan's Upper Peninsula in the winter. The settlement began in 1916 and vanished by 1925.

20.7 Left onto Forest Road 2436. This road is unpaved for exactly two miles.

21.8 Ninemile Lake Boat Landing. Rest rooms.

22.7 Surface returns to pavement.

23.4 Left on Dam Road.

25.0 Right where Dam Road ends.

25.1 The dam operated by the Wisconsin Valley Improvement Company between Long Lake and Cranberry Lake regulates the water level in the Eagle River/Three Lakes chain.

> The twenty lakes in the Three Lakes portion of the chain are also known as the Burnt Rollways Reservoir. The name comes from the lumberjack era, when a group of loggers took action against a jobber who couldn't pay them after they had stacked his timber on the rollways (inclines used to unload logs headed downstream to the mill). Their revenge—burning his logs on the rollways—led to the name Burnt Rollways.
>
> A boat hoist here transports boats traveling the chain from one side of the dam to the other. The original hoist, built in 1911, was an inclined marine railway powered by steam. From 1911 to 1949, the hoist was powered by a water wheel. Today's hoist is driven by electric motors and transports boats over a 165-foot trestle. There are picnic tables and rest rooms here. Backtrack from boat hoist.

25.2 *Straight toward Honey Rock Camp. Dam Road becomes County Highway X.*

35.6 *Right onto WI 32.*

37.5 *Right onto WI 32/45.*

37.9 *Right into the Chamber of Commerce.*

Bicycle Repair Service

Maxson's Cyclery
5016 WI 70 West, Eagle River, WI
(715) 479-4533

23
Boulder Junction/Manitowish Waters

Distance: *47.4 miles*
Terrain: *Gently rolling to rolling*

Flannel shirts are haute couture in this area to which most Midwesterners simply refer as "up north." For many, just breathing the pine-scented air brings back childhood memories of summers spent at the family cabin, fishing with a cane pole or floating idly in an inner tube.

Wisconsin writer Robert Gard summed up the feeling this area evokes. "Something happens to me when I go up to northern Wisconsin," he wrote. "Perhaps it's because the sky and woods and lakes still have an edge of wildness...you can definitely experience a feeling that you are alone, and for a moment, you have intimate knowledge of the secret of solitude."

Manitowish Waters and Presque Isle are small towns with a few shops selling such unlikely combinations as baked goods, bait, and souvenirs. Boulder Junction is slightly larger and has several lodging options, including the Northern Highlands Motor Lodge, (715) 385-2150, which has a living room with fireplace, a swimming pool, and a Jacuzzi. Owner Jim Galloway can suggest other road bike or mountain bike trips. Satisfy your post-ride appetite with dinner at the Guide's Inn, (715) 385-2233, where chef Jimmy Dean VanRosson prepares walleyed pike and other north country specialties with a flair. Call ahead for reservations.

The tour begins at the Boulder Junction Chamber of Commerce and Information Center, located on County Highway M, just south of the center of town. To get there, take WI 51 to County Highway M. Follow County Highway M north to Boulder Junction. The Information Center is adjacent to a park with rest rooms and a picnic area.

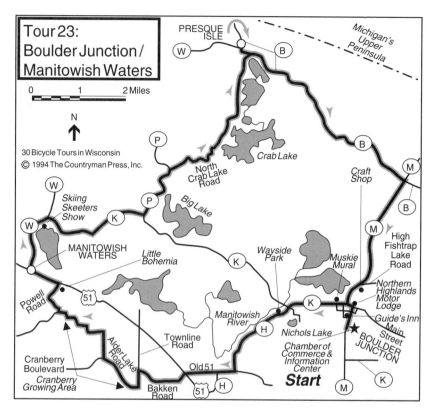

**Tour 23:
Boulder Junction /
Manitowish Waters**

0   1   2 Miles

N

30 Bicycle Tours in Wisconsin
© 1994 The Countryman Press, Inc.

0.0   Right onto County Highway M.

0.4   Left onto Main Street.

0.6   Straight on County Highway K where County Highway M goes right.

1.0   On the water tank to your right is a mural depicting the town mascot, the muskie—short for muskellunge, Wisconsin's top trophy fish.

> Boulder Junction has dubbed itself "the muskie capital of the world," a title it holds with the official endorsement of the United States Trademark Office.
>
> The Native American word for this predaceous member of the pike family is "masquinong." Muskies commonly reach a weight of 70 pounds and a length exceeding four feet. The

194

head has long, thin, powerful jaws that house a set of needle-sharp teeth. Owing to its position at the top of the food chain and its reputation as a moody loner, hundreds of legends have evolved around the annual "muskie hunt." The heaviest concentration of muskie lakes is the headwater region of the Chippewa, Flambeau, and Wisconsin Rivers.

2.8   Left onto County Highway H.

The wayside park on the right borders the Manitowish River. A canoe trip down this wild and scenic river is a wonderful afternoon voyage. Eagle sightings are almost guaranteed. Call Schauss Woodworking, (715) 385-2434, for canoe rental and transport. On the opposite side of the road, a one-mile detour will take you to Nichols Lake picnic area, which has rest rooms.

6.8   Straight onto Old 51 Road where County Highway H goes left.

7.8   Stay on the paved road here.

7.9   Cross WI 51 and continue straight onto Bakken Road.

10.1   Left onto Townline Road.

10.7   Right onto Alder Lake Road (Cranberry Boulevard).

Six cranberry growers are represented on this stretch of road. The cranberry harvest takes place in late September when the bogs are artificially flooded, causing berry-laden vines to float to the surface. Several methods of "wet picking" are used.

One method employs a machine, which is either pushed or ridden by the operator, and which uses teeth to lift berries from the vine. This is a variation on the hand rake, a box-like apparatus commonly used to scoop up berries from the bog before the process was mechanized. Hand rakes are still used for hard-to-reach places. The berries are deposited into plastic boats, which are towed by tractors to a loading area.

Another method, called the water reel, lifts berries off the vine to float on top of the flooded bed. They are then corralled to a corner and loaded into trucks by elevators.

The bait shop in Manitowish Waters

Growers are paid according to the quantity, quality, and color of berries they deliver to the processing plants.

15.6   Right onto Powell Road.

16.9   Left onto WI 51. Busy road with shoulder.

To the right about one mile is Little Bohemia Restaurant and Lodge, (715) 543-8433, a resort on Little Star Lake where notorious underworld character John Dillinger escaped under the noses of FBI agents in 1934. Dillinger, Baby Face Nelson, and several other gangsters had rented rooms at the hotel. Federal agents got a tip that Dillinger was in the area and were hot on his trail. When they fired on a suspicious car, killing one innocent local and wounding two more, Dillinger, who was inside the lodge, heard the shots and fled. In his haste, he left behind a toothbrush and a box of laxatives, which are on display, along with other memorabilia, in the restaurant's Dillinger Room.

18.0 *Right onto County Highway W.*

18.5 *The town of Manitowish Waters consists mainly of lakefront vacation properties.*

> The village center is small, with several restaurants and a grocery store. Manitowish is a Native American word meaning "evil spirit."

18.6 *The Frank B. Koller Memorial Park is "downtown," next to the bait shop with the giant fiberglass bass outside it.*

> Continue on County Highway W on the outskirts of town.

18.8 *Veer right on County Highway W.*

19.1 *The Skiing Skeeters, a local water ski club, performs here during the summer months.*

> Visitors to Wisconsin's North Woods will be impressed with the professional caliber of small-town ski shows. Many of these talented youngsters, who begin skiing as tots, go on to win national competitions or ski at Florida's Cypress Gardens. There is usually no admission charge—a hat is passed to cover club expenses. Check with local Chambers of Commerce for show schedules.

20.1 *Right onto County Highway K.*

24.3 *Left onto County Highway P at the school.*

25.6 *Big Lake Campground is to your right. There are rest rooms and a nice swimming beach. It is about a mile-and-a-half in and out.*

26.6 *Straight on Crab Lake Road where County Highway P goes left.*

> Crab Lake Road ranks among our favorite cycling roads in Wisconsin. Just as you've fallen into a rhythmic, effortless cadence on this flat to barely rolling route, here it is—another of Wisconsin's geographic anomalies. The bold ridge and kettle topography along this road follows the spine of a terminal moraine, more typical of the scenery in southern Wisconsin. In addition to its pleasing contours, the road is

shaded by enormous hardwoods, which successfully eluded the chain saw when the lumberjacks quested for pine. High points along the ridge overlook Crab Lake which has several picturesque islands. This hilly pocket of the North Woods, combined with fertile plains for grain growing nearby, attracted a group of Kentuckians, who ran an extensive moonshine operation here during Prohibition.

32.7 Left onto County Highway B.

33.1 Presque Isle, French for "nearly an island," has a park, grocery store, and restaurant. At this point you are about one mile south of the border with Michigan's Upper Peninsula.

In keeping with the fish theme, Presque Isle calls itself the "walleye capital of the world." Don't be deceived when you pick up the *Walleye Street Journal*—you won't find NYSE listings in Presque Isle's newsy little weekly. Backtrack on County Highway B from downtown Presque Isle.

41.9 Right onto County Highway M.

45.8 To your left on High Fishtrap Lake Road is the Homestead.

This shop features local crafts to decorate your vacation home, ranging from a life-sized wooden Indian to a loon-shaped napkin holder.

46.7 Left onto County Highway K into downtown Boulder Junction.

47.0 Right onto County Highway M.

47.4 Left into the Chamber of Commerce.

Bicycle Repair Service

BJ's Sport Shop
917 WI, 51 North, Minocqua, WI
(715) 356-3900

24
Chequamegon National Forest

Distance: *39.6 or 76.1 miles*
Terrain: *Rolling*

This tour traverses the Chequamegon National Forest, an 844,000-acre parcel of public land larger than the state of Rhode Island. Chequamegon, a tongue twister used by Wisconsin Public Radio as a test for apprentice announcers, comes from the Chippewa language. The accepted pronunciation is "Sho-wa-me-gon," with the accent on the second syllable. Translations vary from "long strip of land" to "soft beaver dam."

The population of Cable, starting point of the tour, swells from its normal 800 residents to as many as 20,000 during two world-class sporting events held annually, the American Birkebeiner cross-country ski marathon in February and the Chequamegon Fat-Tire Festival in September. The Birkebeiner follows a 55-kilometer course through the forest between Telemark Lodge in Cable and the town of Hayward. A 27-kilometer course called the Kortelopet is also offered. The event is patterned after the Birkebeiner held each year in Lillehammer, Norway, which celebrates the rescue of a Norwegian prince from enemy soldiers in 1206. The word *birkebeiner*, which means "birch legs," refers to the primitive hand-crafted skis worn by early Norsemen.

Telemark Lodge also hosts the Chequamegon Fat Tire Festival, which has made a name for the area as the Midwest's mountain biking mecca. Mountain bike enthusiasts can pick up a comprehensive trail map from the Chamber of Commerce or write to CAMBA (Chequamegon Area Mountain Bike Association) at P.O. Box 141, Cable, WI 54821. This organization has produced a map that shows the location of trailheads in the Chequamegon region. If you're looking for an off-road diversion, mountain bikes may be

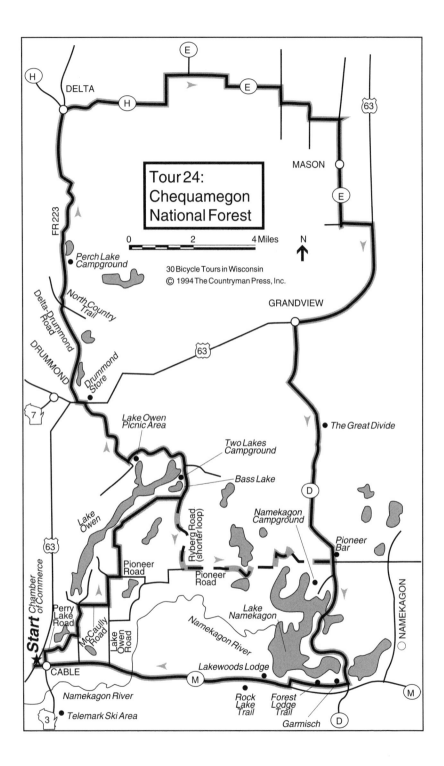

Tour 24:
Chequamegon
National Forest

0   2   4 Miles

N

30 Bicycle Tours in Wisconsin
© 1994 The Countryman Press, Inc.

H

DELTA

E

E

63

H

MASON

E

FR 223

Perch Lake
Campground

North Country
Trail

Delta-Drummond
Road

GRANDVIEW

DRUMMOND

63

7

Drummond
Store

The Great Divide

Lake Owen
Picnic Area

Two Lakes
Campground

Bass Lake

Namekagon
Campground

D

Pioneer
Bar

Lake
Owen

Ryberg Road
(shorter loop)

Pioneer
Road

Pioneer
Road

Lake
Namekagon

NAMEKAGON

63

Perry
Lake
Road

McCaully
Road

Lake
Owen Road

Namekagon River

Start Chamber
of Commerce

CABLE

Lakewoods Lodge

M

M

Namekagon River

3

Telemark Ski Area

Rock
Lake
Trail

Forest
Lodge
Trail

Garmisch

D

rented from Glacier Pines Outfitters, (715) 794-2055, on County Highway M and New Moon Mountain Biking, (715) 798-3811, at Telemark Lodge.

This tour begins at the Cable Area Chamber of Commerce on WI 63 in downtown Cable.

0.0   *Right onto First Avenue, past the Bon Nuit Motel.*

0.5   *Right onto Perry Lake Road (no sign) at the intersection where First Avenue ends.*

1.4   *Perry Lake Road makes a sharp turn to the left. The boat landing and beach are ahead.*

2.2   *Left where Perry Lake Road ends.*

3.2   *Right onto McCauley Road at the stop sign, where Resort Road goes left and Trail Inn Road goes straight.*

4.2   *Left onto Lake Owen Drive where McCauley Road ends.*

5.7   *Left onto Lake Owen Drive toward Eagle Knob, where Pioneer Road goes straight.*

11.1   *Continue straight on Lake Owen Drive at the Two Lakes Campground, (715) 739-6334, for the 76.1-mile ride. For the 39.6-mile ride, skip to the directions for the shorter loop, given below.*

> Located between Lake Owen and Bass Lake, this is one of many beautiful campgrounds in the Chequamegon National Forest. All have primitive facilities, with water pumps and pit toilets. For those who prefer pure wilderness, camping is allowed anywhere in the national forest, as long as you are at least 50 feet from a lake or stream.

13.5   *Left into the Lake Owen Picnic Ground.*

> There are rest rooms and a picnic shelter here, along with a beautiful swimming beach. Lake Owen is a spring-fed, fjord-shaped lake with 1,250 surface acres, 24 miles of shoreline, and a depth of 95 feet.

13.7   *Left onto Lake Owen Drive once you leave the picnic area.*

17.0   *Left onto WI 63.*

A half-mile detour straight ahead will take you to the village of Drummond. The Drummond General Store has an exceptionally good deli counter—pick up lunch fixings there. While in Drummond, stop by the Drummond Museum, located in the library building. Displays depict a hundred years in the history of this logging town, which once had one of the largest sawmills of its time.

17.3 Turn right onto the Delta–Drummond Road.

This superb cycling road weaves through the rolling, glacial terrain of the 6,580-acre Rainbow Wilderness Area. The preserve includes 15 lakes interspersed with mixed northern hardwood forest.

17.4 North Country Trail.

This trail was established by Congress in 1980 to link the Appalachian Trail with the proposed Lewis and Clark Trail in North Dakota. A 60-mile section passes through the Penokee Range of northern Wisconsin. The Ice Age Trail, which crosses Wisconsin from east to west, also passes through the Chequamegon region.

22.0 There are rest rooms at the Perch Lake Campground, (715) 373-2667.

27.0 White River Fishery Area.

28.1 Right onto County Highway H where Delta–Drummond Road ends.

28.8 Delta Town Hall.

33.7 Straight on County Highway E where County Highway H ends.

42.2 Enter the small town of Mason.

43.1 Right onto WI 63. This is a busier road with a good shoulder.

49.6 Left onto County Highway D in the village of Grandview, named for its location on a rise overlooking the broad swampland of the White River Valley.

Previously named Pratt, for the general manager of the Neill and Pratt Lumber Company, the town hosts a very popular

A birch-lined road on the Chequamegon *(Sho-wa-me-gon)* ride.

annual biking tour and race, called the Fire House Fifty. The area is also known for its trout streams, well-stocked with wily German browns.

54.2 *Here a marker notes the Great Divide of northern Wisconsin.*
Formed by the Penokee Range, which separates water flowing north to Lake Superior, the St. Lawrence River, and the Atlantic Ocean from water flowing south to the Mississippi River and, ultimately, the Gulf of Mexico, the divide adjoins the Porcupine Lake Wilderness, which is covered by vast stands of sugar maple, red maples, and yellow birch.

58.5 *Pioneer Bar. This is where the shorter loop rejoins the route.*

59.1 *Lake Namekagon Campground and Picnic area.*

61.4 *The Hilltop Inn serves typical North Woods supper-club fare, with a nice view of Lake Namekagon from the dining room.*

64.8 *Right onto Garmisch Road just before reaching County Highway M.*

65.8 This is the road to Garmisch USA.

This old-world style Bavarian lodge dates to the 1920s, when it was a private vacation retreat for a wealthy Chicago family. It's worth a peek into the Great Room of the main lodge, where the decor centers around an unusual stuffed menagerie!

66.5 Forest Lodge Nature Trail.

This self-guided trail, operated by the Cable Natural History Museum, gives a good introduction to north country fauna with a walk through a restored prairie, bog, and hemlock forest.

67.4 Right onto County Highway M.

68.2 The Rock Lake Trail is a favorite with mountain bikers, hikers, and cross-country skiers.

73.8 Telemark Ski Area.

Telemark has a world-class network of cross-country ski trails where international competitions such as the American Birkebeiner are held each year. There is also downhill skiing The cross-country ski trails are open to mountain bikers during the warmer months.

76.1 You're back in the village of Cable.

Shorter Route

11.5 Follow the road into Two Lakes Campground.

Rest rooms and water are available at the beach. Backtrack out of the campground.

12.1 Right onto Lake Owen Drive at the campground exit.

12.9 Left onto Ryberg Road.

15.4 Left on Pioneer Road where Ryberg Road ends.

21.1 Right onto County Highway D at the Pioneer Bar. From this point, follow the directions for the longer route beginning at the 58.5-mile mark. Your total mileage will be 39.6 miles.

Bicycle Repair Services

Bay City Cycles
412 Main Street West, Ashland, WI
(715) 682-2091

Skinny's Bike Shop
204 West Third Street, Hayward, WI
(715) 682-2091

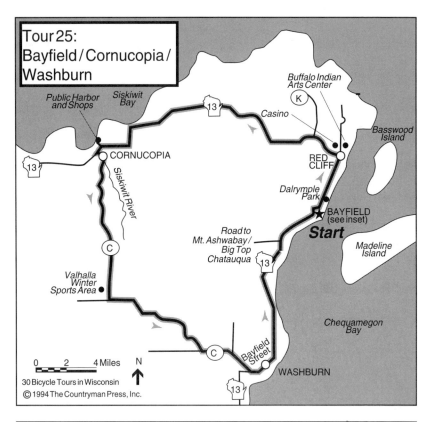

Tour 25:
Bayfield / Cornucopia / Washburn

Public Harbor and Shops

Siskiwit Bay

Buffalo Indian Arts Center

K

Casino

13

Basswood Island

CORNUCOPIA

13

Siskiwit River

RED CLIFF

Dalrymple Park

BAYFIELD (see inset)

Start

C

Road to Mt. Ashwabay / Big Top Chatauqua

13

Madeline Island

Valhalla Winter Sports Area

Chequamegon Bay

C

Bayfield Street

WASHBURN

13

0 2 4 Miles   **N**

30 Bicycle Tours in Wisconsin
© 1994 The Countryman Press, Inc.

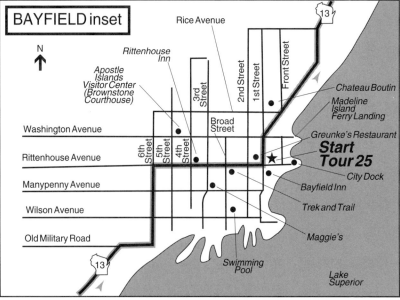

BAYFIELD inset

N

Rice Avenue

13

Rittenhouse Inn

Apostle Islands Visitor Center (Brownstone Courthouse)

3rd Street

2nd Street

1st Street

Front Street

Chateau Boutin

Madeline Island Ferry Landing

Washington Avenue

Broad Street

Greunke's Restaurant

Rittenhouse Avenue

6th Street

5th Street

4th Street

Start Tour 25

City Dock

Manypenny Avenue

Bayfield Inn

Wilson Avenue

Trek and Trail

Old Military Road

Maggie's

13

Swimming Pool

Lake Superior

25
Bayfield/Cornucopia/Washburn

Distance: *54.7 miles*
Terrain: *Rolling*

After a century of boom and bust economies based on fur trading, lumbering, commercial fishing, and brownstone quarrying, Bayfield has finally settled comfortably and profitably into the tourism niche. Today's visitor is content to reap only the spectacular views of Lake Superior and the glittering offshore archipelago known as the Apostle Islands.

Biking in the Bayfield area is best combined with some offshore exploration aboard one of several vessels. The Apostle Islands Cruise Service, (715) 779-3925, offers several sightseeing voyages daily departing from the Bayfield dock. These cruises are extremely popular—advance booking is suggested. Sailing charters and sea kayak trips can be arranged through Trek and Trail, (715) 779-3320, on Rittenhouse Avenue, or Sailboats, Inc., (715) 779-3269), on Front Street.

Relentless lobbying by Wisconsin Senator Gaylord Nelson led to the creation of the Apostle Islands National Lakeshore by the United States Senate in 1969. All of the islands except the most developed, Madeline Island, are included in this designation. How the Apostles got their name is always fodder for a feud, since no matter how you count, there are more than a dozen of them. While several transitory sand spits are sometimes included and sometimes not, the generally accepted total is 22, including Madeline Island.

Some say the label originated with a French explorer and priest who followed tradition by granting the islands a name with religious significance. Others say the name came from a gang of thieves known as the Apostles who used the islands as their base. In 1820, scientist and explorer

Henry Schoolcraft suggested calling the chain the Federation Islands and giving each island the name of a state—his proposal garnered little support.

A walking-tour guide titled "Bargeboard and Brownstone," available from local businesses, guides the visitor past Bayfield's most impressive buildings.

Turn-of-the-century timber barons favored the eye-catching Queen Anne style, characterized by a variety of surface textures, multiple gables, turrets, and sweeping porches that allowed them to savor both the view and the cool lake breezes. People of more modest means built rectangular, one-and-a-half story houses with steep roofs to shed heavy snows in the winter. These homes were traditionally made of wood logged from local forests, and painted white.

The former Bayfield County Courthouse, located on Washington Avenue between Fourth and Fifth Streets, is a stunning example of local brownstone construction. The building has served as a school, World War II German prisoner-of-war camp, and currently as the Apostle Islands Lakeshore Visitor Center.

The town was named after Lieutenant Henry Bayfield of the British Navy, who made the first accurate navigational charts of the Apostle Islands and Chequamegon Bay. Lieutenant Bayfield joined forces with Minnesota legislator Henry Rice to establish the town in hopes of it becoming a major Great Lakes port to compete with Duluth and Chicago.

Follow WI 13 North to Bayfield. The tour begins at the junction of First Street and Rittenhouse Avenue, in front of the Bayfield Inn. Behind the inn is a gazebo known as the Waiting Pavilion. Built in 1913 by the Bayfield Civic League at a cost of $300, it is still used as a speaker's platform, band shell, and shelter for boat passengers.

0.0   Left onto WI 13 (First Street) as you face the harbor.

> As you climb the hill out of town, enjoy a spectacular view of the lake to your right. There's little doubt why lumber baron Frank Boutin, Jr. chose this site for the splendid yellow house that stands on the hillside above you. Called Chateau Boutin, the building is now a bed-and-breakfast inn, operated in conjunction with the Old Rittenhouse Inn. The home's combination of sandstone, brick, and clapboard construction is characteristic of the Queen Anne style.

0.6 *Dalrymple Park Campground, (715) 779-5712, is to your right.*

This 30-site facility with a prime location on the Lake Superior shore is operated by the city of Bayfield. The campground is named for entrepreneur William Dalrymple, who in 1883 began construction on a railroad to connect the port of Bayfield with his huge wheat farms in Minnesota and North Dakota. Only four miles of track were laid before Dalrymple's death and an economic crisis put an end to the grand scheme.

2.7 *You are now entering the reservation of the Red Cliff band of the Lake Superior Chippewa.*

The Chippewa arrived here in the 1500s, escaping the threat of the Iroquois who dominated the east. They found the Superior area populated by the Dakota nation, who they easily suppressed. When the French arrived, the Chippewa established a friendly and beneficial trading relationship that lasted over a century. Pressure to open up northern Wisconsin to logging and settlement led to the Treaty of 1854 when the reservation was formed. About 600 Chippewa tribe members now live on the 7,000-acre reservation.

3.4 *Right from WI 13 and then right again into the Buffalo Art Center.*

The center offers contemporary art displays, artifacts, and a gift shop selling Native American–made items. Across the road is the newly built Isle Vista Casino, which offers blackjack and slot machine gaming. A bingo hall is adjacent to the casino.

3.5 *Right on WI 13 after backtracking from the art center.*

5.8 *The Buffalo Store is your last chance to buy provisions for the next 15 miles.*

20.2 *Known locally as "Cornie," Cornucopia is Wisconsin's northernmost community.*

This old fishing village is located on Siskiwit Bay, where the Siskiwit River flows into Lake Superior. The Chippewa called the bay "Siskawekaning," which means "where the fish can be

Pleasure boats in Bayfield Harbor

caught." Polish and Czechoslovakian immigrants who worked in the lumber industry built the impressive Russian Orthodox church with its octagonal tower that still stands on Erie Avenue.

21.1 *Right onto Siskiwit Bay Parkway, which leads to the Cornucopia Wayside Park. Here you will find water, rest rooms, and a picnic shelter. Follow the driveway to Cornucopia Public Harbor shops.*

21.3 *The Good Earth Shop, Blue Raven Antiques, and Hart Handweaving are all worth a visit.*

The Good Earth sells books, cards, juices, and healthy snacks. Take a breather at an outdoor table overlooking the Cornucopia marina, where stubby white Great Lakes fishing boats brush elbows with snazzy sailboats.

21.7 *Left onto County Highway C. The Village Inn, on this corner, serves up a good hot lunch.*

32.5 *Enter Chequamegon National Forest. This road follows the course of the Siskiwit River.*

33.0 *Right into Mount Valhalla Recreation Area, which has rest rooms and picnic tables.*

33.3 *Right onto County Highway C, which becomes Eighth Avenue in Washburn.*

Residents of this spunky little city at the mouth of Chequamegon Bay rarely miss a chance to rib friends in Bayfield about how they stole the county seat in 1892. The long-standing grudge goes back to Washburn's heyday as a lumber town, when mills hummed around the clock, turning out over 100 million board feet a year. The town is named for Cadwallader Washburn, Wisconsin's governor from 1872 to 1874.

41.7 *Left onto WI 13 (West Bayfield Street).*

42.1 *Karlyn's Pottery Shop features pottery and paintings by local artists.*

42.4 *The 1890 bank to your left is built of local Potsdam sandstone, often called brownstone.*

A high demand for the stone, used in courthouses, schools, and fashionable row houses in cities like Chicago, St. Louis, and New York, spurred the expansion of the stonecutting industry in the 1880s and 1890s. A narrow belt of sandstone extends for about eight miles along Chequamegon Bay and the south shore of Lake Superior to Port Wing. There are also extensive sandstone deposits on several of the Apostle Islands.

The stone varies in color and texture, though the local variety is usually reddish. It is a desirable building material because it maintains its color, disintegrates slowly, and hardens with time. At the turn of the century, quarries near Washburn shipped out trainloads of the rock to major cities all over the country. Sandstone was rarely used in this area except for civic buildings. Examples in Washburn include this bank and the business block across the street.

46.2 *On your right is a historical marker and a view of Madeline Island in the distance.*

51.3 *The road to your left leads to Mount Ashwabay Ski Area.*

This is the site of Lake Superior Big Top Chautauqua, (715) 373-5851. The Big Top features top-notch entertainment, from bards to banjo pickers, nearly every night during the summer months. Performers include both homegrown talent and nationally known acts.

54.0 *Smoked whitefish and trout are available at the Fish Market.*

54.1 *Left onto South Sixth Avenue.*

54.4 *Right onto Rittenhouse Avenue.*

54.5 *Old Rittenhouse Inn at junction with Third Street.*

This elegant Queen Anne–style mansion was built in 1890 by Allen Fuller, adjutant general for Illinois during the Civil War. Fuller vacationed in Bayfield, where he found relief from his bouts with asthma. The steeply pitched roof with prominent gables, enormous wraparound porch, and bay windows are characteristic of this turn-of-the-century style.

In 1974, the home was purchased by Jerry and Mary Phillips, who have developed it into one of the Midwest's premier bed-and-breakfast inns. Guest rooms are lavishly decorated with antiques and working fireplaces. Whether or not you stay at the Old Rittenhouse Inn, dinner there is a Bayfield "must do." Dining room staff recite an everchanging verbal menu with theatrical flair, an inn tradition that began when printed menus failed to arrive in time for opening day. The menus always incorporate fresh, local ingredients.

54.7 The corner of Rittenhouse Avenue and First Street—your starting point.

A local benefactor has provided Bayfield with an Olympic-size indoor swimming pool that is open to the public. Soak out the stiffness in the whirlpool or swim a few laps after your ride! The pool is located downtown, on the corner of Broad Street and Wilson Avenue. Call (715) 779-3201 for current hours.

For good food and a lively atmosphere, try Maggie's, (715) 779-5641, on Mannypenny Avenue. Another personal favorite is Greunke's First Street Inn, (715) 779-5480, which offers quaint lodging and a fish boil featuring Lake Superior whitefish nightly; their other specialty is deep-fried whitefish livers, a local delicacy. Bayfield is the only place on the lake where commercial fishermen take the time to save the livers.

Bicycle Repair Services

Bay City Cycles
412 Main Street West, Ashland, WI
(715) 682-2091

Trek & Trail
Rittenhouse Avenue, Bayfield, WI
(715) 779-3320
Rentals only

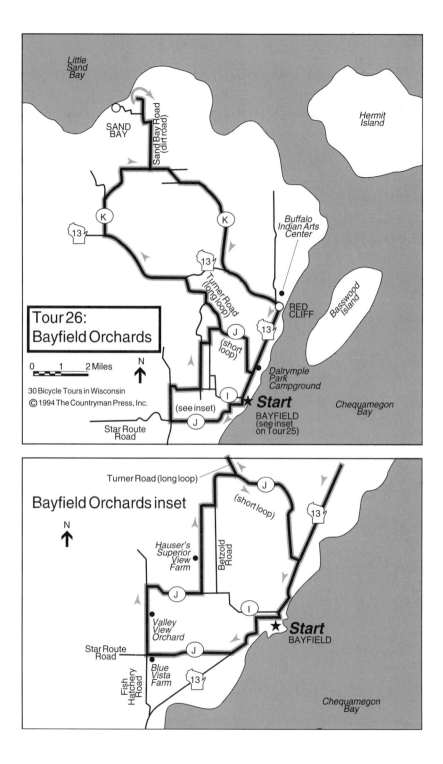

Little Sand Bay

SAND BAY

Sand Bay Road (dirt road)

Hermit Island

K

13

K

Buffalo Indian Arts Center

13

Turner Road (long loop)

RED CLIFF

Basswood Island

Tour 26: Bayfield Orchards

0   1   2 Miles

N

30 Bicycle Tours in Wisconsin

© 1994 The Countryman Press, Inc.

J

(short loop)

13

Dalrymple Park Campground

I

(see inset)

★ **Start**

BAYFIELD (see inset on Tour 25)

Chequamegon Bay

J

Star Route Road

J

Bayfield Orchards inset

Turner Road (long loop)

J

13

N

(short loop)

Hauser's Superior View Farm

Betzold Road

J

I

★ **Start**

BAYFIELD

Valley View Orchard

Star Route Road

J

Fish Hatchery Road

Blue Vista Farm

13

Chequamegon Bay

26
Bayfield Orchards

Distance: *10.6 or 32.2 miles (4 miles on dirt road)*
Terrain: *Rolling to hilly*

This short spin takes you through the heart of Bayfield's fruit-growing area, where every month of the cycling season offers something fresh and juicy to pluck from the tree or vine. Strawberries ripen in late June or early July; followed by raspberries and blueberries in mid-July; cherries in early August; apples throughout September; and pears later in September. Because Bayfield is located on a peninsula, a "lake effect" moderates the temperature and results in a longer growing season than that of farms farther inland.

Cider flows freely at the Bayfield Apple Festival, celebrated during the first weekend of October for over 30 years. This community event extraordinaire includes a parade, street fair, apple-peeling and pie-baking contests, and of course, the coronation of the Apple Queen. It's worth planning a trip around the festival, since the dates usually correspond perfectly with the peak of autumn color. Contact the Bayfield Chamber of Commerce, (715) 779-3335, for lodging suggestions.

This route follows paved (though occasionally rough) roads, with the exception of the road leading to Little Sand Bay, which has a dirt surface. It's well worth a couple miles of jostling around, but you can easily bypass this turn if your tires aren't up to it. Be prepared for a number of long, steep hills with sensational views of Bayfield and the Apostle Islands from the summits.

Follow WI 13 north to Bayfield, and begin at the corner of Rittenhouse Avenue (WI 13) and First Street, next to the Bayfield Inn.

0.0   *Straight on Rittenhouse Avenue (WI 13).*

0.4   *Left onto South Sixth Street.*

0.9 Eckels Pot Shop. This well-known shop sells pottery made by several generations of the Eckels family.

1.4 Right onto County Highway J.

2.8 Right onto County Highway J (Hatchery Road) where Star Route goes straight, just past Blue Vista Farm. The ski runs of Mount Ashwabay Ski Area are visible off to the left.

3.7 A detour down this road leads to Valley View Orchard, Organic Strawberry Farm, and North Wind Orchard.

5.0 Left onto County Highway J at the County Highway I junction.

5.6 Hauser's Superior View Farm. Stop for a moment and admire the far-reaching vista. The farm sells perennial plants by mail order.

7.5 Left onto Turner Road, if you plan to do the 32.2-mile route. If you plan to do the 10.6-mile loop, Continue straight on County Highway J and follow it for two miles. Right on WI 13, which will take you back to your starting point in Bayfield.

9.6 Left onto WI 13.

12.8 Right onto County Highway K. Rough road.

16.0 Left onto Little Sand Bay Road. Dirt road.

18.0 Little Sand Bay.

Along the waterfront, with a commemorative plaque, you will find the hatch cover of the *Sevona*, a 373-foot steamer that was shipwrecked in Julian Bay, off Stockton Island, in 1905. Scuba divers and snorkelers still explore the wreck. The dock here is the jumping-off point for the Inner Island Shuttle, which delivers backpackers to some of the lesser-visited Apostle Islands.

Get a close-up view of the commercial fishing industry in the Apostles region on a tour of Hokenson Brothers Fishery. Here Eskel, Leo, and Roy Hokenson ran a successful fishing operation for over 35 years until they retired in the 1960s. Sons of Swedish immigrants, they came to the area to farm, but turned to fishing when farming didn't pay the bills. The tour, led by a National Park Service guide, takes in the twine shed, where nets were constructed, mended, and stored; the ice house, where ice cut from the lake during the winter months was kept; a dock with a herring shed, where fish were cleaned, salted, and packed for market; and the fishing tug *Twilite* used by the Hokensons for herring fishing.

Scandinavian immigrants brought their fishing skills to the Bayfield area in the late 1800s. During this period, fishermen abandoned sailing vessels in favor of larger boats with steam engines and fishing companies organized individual fishermen into a single enterprise. Company boats made daily pickups from fishing camps located among the Apostle Islands. The Bodin and Booth fisheries were two of the largest operations, together employing over 500 people.

The fishing industry still exists in Bayfield and many restaurants serve a fresh "catch of the day." But as time goes on, fewer and fewer people are willing to put in the long hours required for mending nets and maintaining equipment, with no certainty that their efforts will pay off.

The Bayfield Apple Festival is the first weekend in October.

Whitefish, lake trout, and herring have always been the mainstays of the fishing industry here. The abundance of each has varied through the years and each has at one time been the most lucrative catch. Fish populations were greatly reduced in the 1950s and 1960s because of overfishing and the destructive sea lamprey (an eel-like creature that invaded the Great Lakes through the St. Lawrence Seaway), but lamprey control measures and restocking programs have restored most species. Backtrack to County Highway K.

21.5 *Left onto County Highway K.*

26.4 *Left onto WI 13.*

28.4 *To your left is the Buffalo Art Center.*

The center offers contemporary art displays, artifacts, and a gift shop selling Native American–made items. Across the road is the newly built Isle Vista Casino, which offers blackjack and slot machine gaming. A bingo hall is adjacent to the casino.

29.8 *The Jam Factory sells homemade jams and jellies, a thriving cottage industry here.*

31.1 *Dalrymple Park Campground, (715) 779-5712, is to your left. This 30-site facility with a prime location on the Lake Superior shore is operated by the city of Bayfield.*

32.2 *WI 13 becomes First Street. The tour ends at the intersection with Rittenhouse Avenue, in front of the Bayfield Inn.*

Bicycle Repair Services

Bay City Cycles
412 Main Street West, Ashland, WI
(715) 682-2091

Trek & Trail
Rittenhouse Avenue, Bayfield, WI
(715) 779-3320
Rentals only

27
Madeline Island

Distance: *30.4 miles*
Terrain: *Flat*

Madeline Island might be called Wisconsin with a French accent. Roadsides lined with nodding lupines and tiger lilies seem born of the impressionist's brush and a flotilla of sailboats whose boldly painted hulls bear names like *Esprit* and *Joie d'Vivre* bob in the harbor. A longtime association with France has given the island a Gallic flair that is easier felt than defined.

Just a 20-minute ferry ride from the Bayfield peninsula, Madeline Island packs more history per square mile than any other corner of the state. The Chippewas called it Monignwana Neisha, home of the golden-breasted woodpecker, for the many flickers that nested near Grant's Point. The current name was bestowed in 1793 when Michel Cadotte, a fur trader for the North West Company, married Equaysayway, daughter of Chief White Crane, a Chippewa leader. Cadotte's bride was baptized at the time of their marriage and given the Christian name Madeleine. The island was named in her honor, though the spelling has changed slightly through the years.

There are now about 150 year-round residents on Madeline Island, a mere fraction of its population during the height of the Chippewa reign, when 13,000 Native Americans struggled to survive here. In the winter, residents and high school students travel to the peninsula across the ice on a plowed ice road. When the ice begins to thaw in the spring, an engine-driven windsled, similar to an Everglades airboat, is used to make the crossing.

Madeline Island's past was molded by fur traders and missionaries. The first Europeans to tread on the island were French explorers Radisson and Groseilliers (jokingly referred to as "Radishes and Gooseberries" in some old

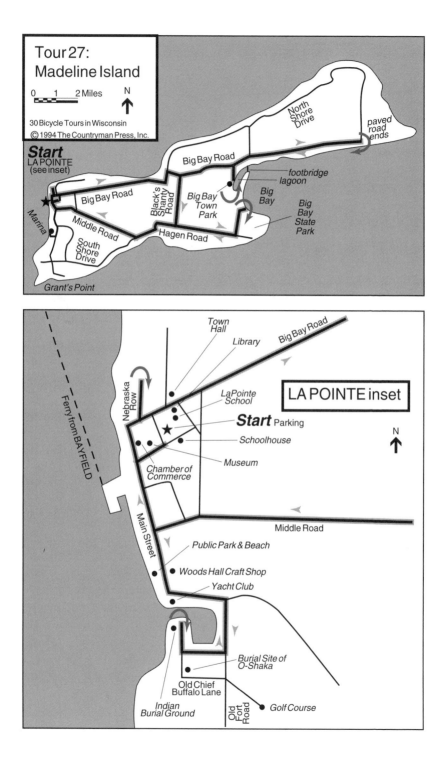

Tour 27:
Madeline Island

0   1   2 Miles

N

30 Bicycle Tours in Wisconsin
© 1994 The Countryman Press, Inc.

Start
LA POINTE
(see inset)

North Shore Drive

paved road ends

Big Bay Road

footbridge
lagoon

Marina

Big Bay Road

Black's Shanty Road

Big Bay Town Park

Big Bay

Big Bay State Park

Middle Road

Hagen Road

South Shore Drive

Grant's Point

Town Hall

Library

Big Bay Road

LA POINTE inset

Ferry from BAYFIELD

Nebraska Row

LaPointe School

Start Parking

N

Schoolhouse

Museum

Chamber of Commerce

Main Street

Middle Road

Public Park & Beach

Woods Hall Craft Shop

Yacht Club

Burial Site of O-Shaka

Old Chief Buffalo Lane

Indian Burial Ground

Old Fort Road

Golf Course

journals) in 1638. They were followed by Fathers Allouez and Marquette, who attempted to convert the Chippewas to Christianity in the 1660s and 1670s. The "black robes" eventually left with little success.

In 1693, Pierre Le Sueur took over as commander with a trading post near Grant's Point, launching the island into the lucrative fur trade. Furs were so abundant that in just three short years, Le Sueur glutted the market and Louis XIV cancelled all fur trade licenses. By 1717 the fur market had recovered and a new Frenchman, Louis Denis, Sieur de la Ronde took over. On his heels came Michel Cadotte, credited with establishing the first permanent settlement on the island, near the present Old Fort Road. The fur boom continued well into the 1800s, when beaver pelts were in great demand because the animal's soft underhairs could be compressed into the stiff fabric used in fashionable top hats.

Boats operated by the Madeline Island Ferry Line, (715) 747-2051, leave from the pier at the west end of Front Street in Bayfield at least once an hour during the summer months. A visit to the island can be a leisurely full-day trip if you stop to savor all the sights or a half-day excursion if you don't linger too long. All of the roads included in this route are paved and the terrain is absolutely flat. There are several casual restaurants in the village of La Pointe near the ferry pier.

If you find yourself waiting a while for the next ferry, check out the Cooperage Museum, located adjacent to the ferry pier parking area. This building once housed the Booth Fishery, which salted and packed fish in handmade barrels for shipment to market. On weekends you can see two coopers at work, assembling barrels over an open hearth. At one time, five coopers turned out 50,000 to 75,000 barrels a year. Refrigerated transportation, new packing methods, and the decline of the fishing industry led to the closing of the facility in the 1950s. The Cooperage includes a museum (no charge) and gift shop.

0.0 *When you arrive on Madeline Island, turn left onto Main Street in the village of La Pointe. Or proceed straight ahead if you wish to begin with a side trip to the Madeline Island Historical Museum.*

> A 20-minute multi-media show called "Spirit of the Island" is shown in the Capser Center, added to the museum in 1991. Fast-paced, with a lively, locally composed score, the show takes you through three centuries of life on the island.

Originally called Monignwana Neisha by the resident Chippewa, Madeline Island was renamed in 1793.

Exhibits in the new wing of the museum include examples of European and Indian trade goods. The older wing, built in 1955 on the site of the American Fur Company building, includes some rare specimens of Native American clothing, beadwork, and tools.There is also a nice gift shop.

If you chose to visit the museum, you will need to backtrack to Main Street. Continue on Main Street, which becomes Big Bay Road (also County Highway H), as it makes a sharp right turn.

Straight ahead, as you turn, is a short dead-end street called Nebraska Row. This stretch of vacation homes is named for Colonel Frederick Woods of Lincoln, Nebraska. After renting a small cottage on the island, Woods broadcast the summer appeal of this spot and convinced many well-to-do families to build homes here. Among them was Hunter Gary, the founder of General Telephone, who, along with Woods, hosted Calvin Coolidge on his 1928 visit.

0.2   *The Town Hall, to your left, was built in 1909 for $2,000. The Public Library, to your right, is housed in an old school, dating to 1872. The present La Pointe grade school is just behind it.*

4.2   *Stay left at the junction with Black Shanty Road. Follow the signs toward Big Bay Town Park.*

6.4   *Right into Big Bay Town Park, operated by the village of La Pointe.*

6.5   *A wooden footbridge crosses a lagoon, leading to the beach.*

When Madeline Island reappeared from under the Wisconsin glacier, about 15,000 years ago, this lagoon was a large, shallow, open bay. Shoreline currents and waves built the barrier beach that now separates the lagoon from the lake. There are rest rooms and a picnic area at the park.

6.6   *Right onto Big Bay Road as you exit the park.*

10.7 *This is where the paved road ends. Backtrack.*

16.2 *Left onto Black's Shanty Road toward Big Bay State Park beach and park office.*

18.0 *Left onto Hagen Road toward Big Bay State Park, Wisconsin's northernmost state park.*

20.0 *Left into the park and follow the road to the barrier beach.*

21.0 *This mile-and-half-long strand is a beachcomber's delight.*

There are rest rooms here. A second picnic area is located at the point, where there are sandstone bluffs and caves at the water's edge.

22.0 *Right onto Hagen Road at the park exit.*

24.1 *Hagen Road becomes Middle Road. Continue straight here.*

28.5 *Left onto Main Street.*

28.5 *Pricey pleasure craft are moored at the Madeline Island Yacht Club.*

28.6 *Right onto Old Fort Road.*

28.8 *Right onto Old Chief Buffalo Lane.*

29.0 Here you will find the Old Indian Cemetery, established in 1836.

Notice the miniature houses, used as grave covers to protect the dead, as well as the food left with the dead for nourishment on their four-day journey to the afterlife. A very weathered gravestone marks the burial spot of Chief Great Buffalo, a principal chief in the Great Lakes area, who signed the treaty creating Wisconsin's reservations in 1854. You will also find the grave of Michel Cadotte and his Chippewa wife, Madeleine. Chief Buffalo's son, O-Shaka, is buried in the clearing to your left as you leave the cemetery, between two pines marked with a colorful banner.

These days, most people come to this end of the island for the Robert Trent Jones golf course and the upscale Clubhouse Restaurant, which has an excellent reputation.

29.2 Left onto Old Fort Road after backtracking from the cemetery.

29.5 Left onto Main Street.

29.8 The La Pointe Public Park, to your left, has picnic tables and rest rooms. The Woods Hall Craft Shop, to your right, features local arts and crafts.

30.4 You're back at the ferry pier.

Bicycle Repair Services

Bay City Cycles
412 Main Street West, Ashland, WI
(715) 682-2091

Trek & Trail
Rittenhouse Avenue, Bayfield, WI
(715) 779-3320
Rentals only

WESTERN
WISCONSIN

28
Lake Pepin/Stockholm/Great River Road

Distance: *25.7 or 41 miles*
Terrain: *Rolling to hilly*

One of Lake Pepin's most ardent admirers was William Cullen Bryant, who said its shores "ought to be visited in the summer by every painter and poet in the land." Bryant's suggestion was pure prophesy. The 1970s marked a wave of artistic immigration, as students of the Minneapolis Institute of Art, attracted by the wild beauty of the lake and its surrounding valleys, began to move into the area. Many have settled into drafty old farmhouses, converting them into studios as time and money allow.

The tiny crossroads village of Stockholm, where the tour begins, hosts an annual art fair on the third Saturday of July. The rest of the year, local artwork is available for sale at the Red Balloon Gallery. Amish-made goods, including quilts and hickory furniture, are sold at Amish Country. For nourishment, try the Jenny Lind Café, which serves whole-grain breads and great soups. Although its hours are a bit erratic, the Stockholm Café is also worth a visit for stir-fried catfish cheeks, its updated version of a Great River Road specialty.

The oldest Swedish settlement in western Wisconsin, Stockholm was founded in 1851 by Eric Peterson and a group of immigrants from Kalskoga, Sweden. In the summer of 1939, Crown Prince Gustav of Sweden and his family visited the village. This fact is mentioned prominently in all of the town's promotional literature—a clue that nothing quite as exciting has happened since. Once a thriving community, Stockholm couldn't keep up with towns on the Minnesota side of the river and now claims only 104 residents. Stop in at the Stockholm Institute, a historical preservation society located in the old post office, for more information about Stockholm's past.

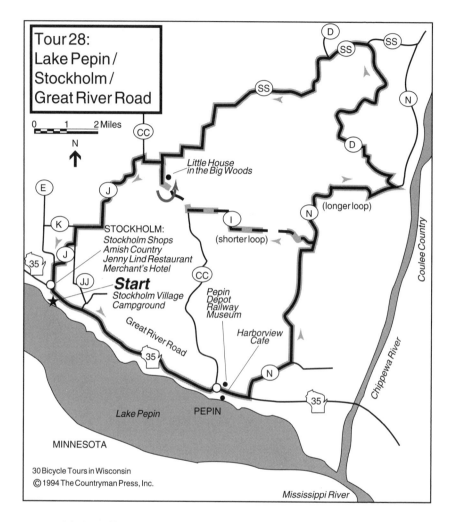

Tour 28:
Lake Pepin /
Stockholm /
Great River Road

0   1   2 Miles

N

CC

D

SS

SS

SS

N

D

N

(longer loop)

Little House
in the Big Woods

E

J

K

J

JJ

35

35

I

(shorter loop)

N

STOCKHOLM:
*Stockholm Shops
Amish Country
Jenny Lind Restaurant
Merchant's Hotel*

Start
*Stockholm Village
Campground*

CC

Pepin
Depot
Railway
Museum

Great River Road

35

Harborview
Cafe

N

35

Lake Pepin   PEPIN

MINNESOTA

30 Bicycle Tours in Wisconsin
© 1994 The Countryman Press, Inc.

Coulee Country

Chippewa River

Mississippi River

Stockholm offers two lodging options—both highly recommended. The Merchant's Hotel, (715) 442-2113 or (715) 448-2508, is a great little bed-and-breakfast inn with slightly eclectic decor run by Lucy Elliott, proprietor of the antique shop next door. There is a communal kitchen where guests can make their own breakfast—even the appliances have personality—and a screened porch with wicker furniture, antique books, games, and trout-shaped twinkle lights. Just south of town on WI 35 is the Great River Farm, (800) 657-4756, where Leland Krebs rents out two elegantly furnished rooms in an old farmhouse. There's no sign, so just look for the Irish flag or drop in at the Harbor View Café in Pepin, where Krebs is the bartender. Light sleepers should note both hotels' proximity to the train tracks!

The tour begins at the Stockholm Village Campground, just off WI 35, on the shore of Lake Pepin. Simple campsites, rest rooms, parking, and water are available here. Mileage for the tour begins as you turn onto WI 35, after leaving the campground. Just before the intersection, on your right, is the Mississippi River Pearl Jewelry Company, which sells rings, earrings, and necklaces created from the small asymmetrical pearls of freshwater clams.

0.0 *Right onto WI 35 South. There is moderate traffic, but the road has a generous shoulder.*

2.3 *A scenic overlook and historic marker here indicate the site of Fort St. Antoine, built here by Nicholas Perrot to establish French sovereignty over the region.*

> A ceremony on May 8, 1869, officially informed both the Indians and the English that Perrot had claimed the entire region west of the Great Lakes, "no matter how remote," in the name of Louis XIV. Continue on WI 35.

5.1 *Lake Pepin Wayside.*

> Lake Pepin is formed by the faster-moving waters of the Chippewa that flow into the Mississippi, causing a backup of the sand and gravel carried down from Wisconsin farmlands. Named for Pepin le Bref, a French king, the lake is a boaters' paradise, dotted with billowing spinnakers on a breezy day. It's not surprising that this alluring body of water inspired 18-year-old Ralph Samuelson to strap a set of boards on his feet and skim across its surface, inventing the popular sport of waterskiing here in 1922.
>
> A variety of products has been harvested from Lake Pepin and adjacent stretches of river through the years. River carp were seined from the lake and sold to kosher markets on the East Coast; freshwater clams were collected and the shells sold to button factories in Lake City, Minnesota; and commercial fishing continues to provide many with their livelihood.

Clamming has made a comeback in the last twenty years, though these days clam shells are ground into pellets and sold to Japan for use in culturing pearls. The pellets are inserted into saltwater clams to begin pearl formation.

5.9 *Enter the village of Pepin.*

6.3 *Pepin Depot Railway Museum and Laura Ingalls Wilder Historic Marker are to the left.*

The depot includes a ticket office that looks much as it did a century ago. There is more information about Wilder at her birthplace, later in the ride. A picnic area, water, and rest rooms are also available.

6.5 *Right onto Pine Street toward the Pepin business district.*

6.6 *Left onto Second Street through downtown.*

6.7 *Right onto Main Street to the marina and the Harbor View Café.*

Twin Cities sailors tie up outside for dinner at this popular waterfront restaurant. There's nearly always a wait of an hour or more for a Californiaesque menu of innovative salads, pastas, and fine wines. Take a stroll through town, watch the sunset over Wisconsin's "west coast," or browse through the stacks in the library-cum-waiting area. There are also several more casual eateries on the harbor.

6.8 *Left onto First Avenue at the waterfront.*

6.9 *Left onto Prairie Avenue and up the hill.*

7.0 *Right onto WI 35.*

7.2 *Left onto County Highway N (Dunn Street). The last .7 mile is quite steep. At the hilltop, veer left by the Evangelical Free Church. County Highway N is called Pepin Hill Road at this intersection.*

13.1 *For the 41-mile route, continue straight on County Highway N. For the 25.7-mile loop, left onto County Highway I. Follow County Highway I for 4.4 miles, then right onto County Highway CC. This will take you to the Little House in the Big Woods Wayside on your*

Winding through the valleys of coulee country

right. Skip to the 33.6-mile mark for the remainder of the route.

17.1 *Left onto County Highway D.*

24.1 *Left onto County Highway SS.*

25.4 *Straight on County Highway SS where County Highway D goes right.*

32.6 *Left onto County Highway CC South.*

33.6 *Little House in the Big Woods Wayside is to your left. The shorter loop rejoins here. Turn right on County Highway CC at Wayside exit.*

> Author Laura Ingalls Wilder, whose books have endeared her to several generations, was born on this spot in 1867. The log cabin is a replica of that on which Wilder based her childhood memories of the Pepin area in *Little House in the Big Woods*. This was the first book in the *Little House* series, which Wilder began writing at age 65. Wilder's family moved to Kansas (her inspiration for *Little House on the Prairie*), but later returned to Pepin.

34.6 Left onto County Highway CC.

35.2 Straight on County Highway J where County Highway CC goes right.

38.7 Left on County Highway J where County Highway K goes straight at Sabylund Cemetery.

39.2 Right on County Highway J where County Highway JJ goes straight.

41. Cross WI 35 in Stockholm to your starting point at the campground.

Bicycle Repair Services

Bike LTD
1001 LaCrosse Street, LaCrosse, WI
(608) 785-2326

Vagabond Touring
539 Main Street, LaCrosse, WI
(608) 782-2453

Valley Ski & Bike
321 Main Street, LaCrosse, WI
(608) 782-5500

29
Alma/Great River Road

Distance: *31.4 or 43.7 miles*
Terrain: *Gently rolling to hilly*

If you're a romantic who can't resist the shrill whistle of a train or the throaty horn of a heavily laden barge, you'll feel right at home in this part of Wisconsin. Short of hopping a freight or signing on as an oarsman, bicycling is the best way to explore the scenery and history of the Upper Mississippi River Valley. Tourism dollars have just begun to reach this area, so you won't find trendy cafés, slick brochures, or fudge shops. Instead, the tiny river towns seem to be covered with a fine layer of silt, giving them the hue and charm of a sepia print. The landscape here is a medley of the mellow, gently rolling Great River Road and the challenging climbs of the "coulee country," steep, winding valleys where water flows only in the spring.

Squeezed between the river below and the bluffs above, Alma, the starting point of this tour, is seven miles long and just two streets wide. There are so many turn-of-the-century frame and brick houses that the entire town is on the National Register of Historic Places. Among the historic structures is the Italianate Laue House, (608) 685-4923, at 1111 South Main Street (WI 35). This is a laid-back bed-and-breakfast inn where you may find a note telling you to settle in to the room of your choice and help yourself to the player piano in the parlor. More upscale is the Gallery House B & B, (608) 685-4975, at 215 North Main Street, tucked away on the airy second floor of a brick mercantile building that houses a watercolor and photography gallery and a spice shop on the street level.

Though named for a river town in Russia, Alma was originally settled by Swiss and German immigrants who followed the Mississippi north from

233

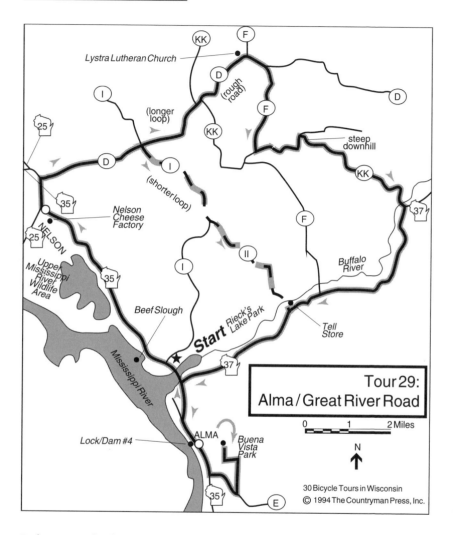

Dubuque with plans to cut and sell cordwood to passing steamboats. One of the town's unique attractions is a fishing float in the river that rents the tackle, sells bait, and serves up a hearty breakfast to early-bird anglers. To get to the float, walk to the end of Alma's municipal pier and wave your arms wildly—someone will come by with a boat to pick you up!

Take WI 35 to the tour starting point at Rieck's Lake Park (Alma Rod and Gun Club), just a few miles north of Alma at the junction with WI 37.

Parking, rest rooms, water, and a picnic shelter are available. People gather here in late autumn to watch the migration of rare tundra swans.

0.0   *Right onto WI 35 and follow the river north, passing through the Upper Mississippi Wildlife Refuge.*

The refuge, which includes 194,000 acres of bottom land from Wabasha, Minnesota, to Rock Island, Illinois, was established by the US Department of Interior, Fish and Wildlife Service in 1924. This area was set aside for the perpetuation of migratory birds, native wildlife, and fishes.

About one mile north of Alma, you will pass Beef Slough, a sluggish branch of the Chippewa River. This was an excellent storage pond for logs being floated downstream from northern logging camps on the Chippewa, Eau Claire, and St. Croix Rivers. Each log was marked to identify its logger and the sawmill to which it was destined. The person charged with marking had to determine which side of the log would float upward and mark that side. Logs were laid side by side until enough were collected to make a 50- by 500-foot raft, called a brail. Four to six brails were chained together to form an even larger raft, which a steamboat pushed to a sawmill downriver. At its height, Beef Slough was the largest log sorting and rafting works in the world.

A conflict between the Eau Claire and Beef Slough Lumber Companies over where logs were to be sold (here or farther south) led to the Beef Slough War of 1868. The dispute was ended by lumber baron Frederic Weyerhauser, who turned Wisconsin's logging industry into an interstate industry.

5.5   *Enter the village of Nelson.*

Old-timers remember when Nelson wasn't on the river at all—that was before the lock-and-dam system flooded the area now known as Nelson Bottoms, a huge section of backwater adjoining the Mississippi River, with thousands of acres of woods and abundant wildlife. Nelson is also popular with hang-gliding enthusiasts who soar off the high cliff behind town.

5.8   *Castleberg Park has rest rooms and picnic tables.*

5.9   *Nelson Cheese Factory.*

> This fifth-generation cheese-making operation, begun by Hubert Greenheck in the mid-1850s, offers huge double-dip ice cream cones at bargain prices, as well as assorted cheeses.

6.1   *Right onto WI Highways 25/35 through town.*

6.7   *Right onto County Highway D.*

10.0   *At the junction with County Highway I, the 43.7-mile route continues straight on County Highway D where you will enjoy a nice downhill and see several picturesque round barns. For the shorter, 31.6-mile route, skip to directions below.*

12.4   *Pass the first junction with County Highway KK and continue straight on County Highway D. The road surface is rough for the next two miles, but this stretch offers some spectacular views.*

14.3   *Right on County Highway DF at the Lystra Lutheran Church. There is a picnic shelter here.*

The high bluffs overlook the Mississippi River valley.

14.9   Right onto County Highway F.

17.7   Left onto County Highway KK at the hilltop.

19.0   A long downhill stretch starts here. Ride in control and watch for loose gravel on the turns.

24.0   Right onto WI 37 just after crossing the Buffalo River.

29.3   The Tell Store has rest rooms and sells snacks. The shorter option rejoins the route here.

33.3   Left on WI 35 and continue into the village of Alma.

34.9   At United States Government Lock and Dam #4 in downtown Alma, you can watch riverboats, barges, and pleasure craft passing through the locks from an observation platform.

> Barges heading upstream are often carrying coal from the coal fields of southern Illinois and western Kentucky. Those heading downstream typically carry corn, oats, wheat, barley, and rye grown in Minnesota and Wisconsin. Diesel towboats guide as many as 12 to 15 barges at a time, totaling 20,000 tons of freight.

35.4   Left onto County Highway E.

35.5   Right onto Second Street.

35.7   Left onto Eagan (County Highway E) and begin the ascent to Buena Vista.

36.7   Left onto Buena Vista Road. The last mile of the climb, after this turn, is very steep. Even if your knees demand you walk this stretch, it's well worth it for the view from the top. We promise!

38.0   Buena Vista Park. Looking over Alma's shoulder from a towering bluff 500 feet above town, the park offers an awesome view of the Mississippi River and the Minnesota shore.

39.3   Right onto County Highway E as you exit the park. Enjoy the downhill!

40.3   Right onto Second Street (County Highway E).

40.5 *Stay left at the fork, still on County Highway E.*

40.1 *Right onto WI 35.*

43.7 *Right into Rieck's Lake Park.*

Shorter Route

10.0 *Right onto County Highway I.*

13.1 *Straight on County Highway II where County Highway I turns right.*

17.0 *Right on WI 37 at the Tell Store. The short route rejoins the longer route here. Refer to the 29.3-mile mark above.*

Bicycle Repair Services

Bike LTD
1001 LaCrosse Street, LaCrosse, WI
(608) 785-2326

Vagabond Touring
539 Main Street, LaCrosse, WI
(608) 782-2453

Valley Ski & Bike
321 Main Street, LaCrosse, WI
(608) 782-5500

30

Wyalusing State Park/Great River Road

Distance: 12.9, 33.1, or 55.2 miles (2.7-mile dirt road on two longer rides)
Terrain: Hilly

Wyalusing State Park enjoys a unique setting at the confluence of the Wisconsin and Mississippi Rivers with panoramic views of Iowa across the river and the city of Prairie du Chien on the plain below. Father Jacques Marquette and fellow explorer Louis Joliet were among the first white men to behold the spectacular view from the bluffs when they arrived here in 1673, after a journey from Green Bay via the Fox and Wisconsin Rivers.

Archaeological digs show that the park was inhabited as early as 9,000 B.C. However, it is the Woodlawn Indians of the late prehistoric period (600 B.C. to 1300 A.D.) that left the most impressive mark, a network of 28 mounds along a prominent ridge overlooking the Mississippi River. Some of the mounds are conical or linear in shape; others, called effigy mounds, are shaped like deer, bears, birds, and turtles.

While the conical mounds contain skeletons, many of the animal-shaped mounds do not and therefore probably served a purpose other than burial. It's possible that effigy mounds were used to delineate territory or as the focal point of a religious territory. Take a few minutes before or following your ride to hike the Sentinel Ridge Trail, where the series of mounds is well-marked. There is also a memorial here to the last passenger pigeon. While that species has unfortunately been lost to extinction, a project to reintroduce the wild turkey has been very successful and turkeys are now abundant in the park. Wyalusing has individual and group campsites, as well as a dormitory building. Reservations are recommended, (608) 996-2261.

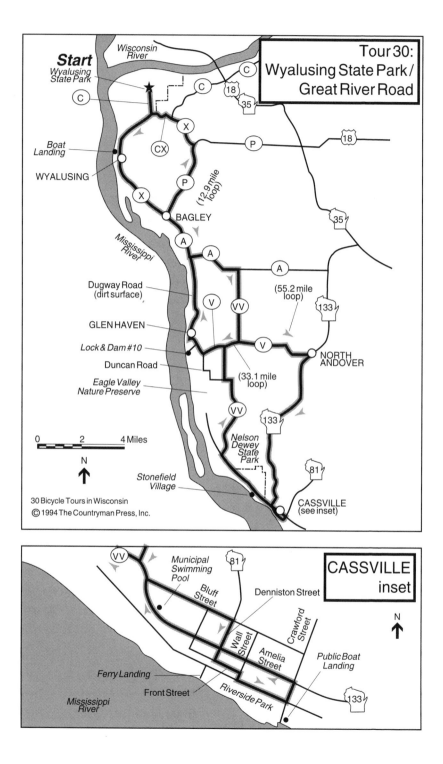

Start
Wisconsin River
Wyalusing State Park

Tour 30:
Wyalusing State Park /
Great River Road

C

C

18

35

C

X

CX

Boat Landing

P

18

WYALUSING

P

(12.9 mile loop)

X

35

BAGLEY

A

Mississippi River

A

A

Dugway Road (dirt surface)

V

VV

(55.2 mile loop)

133

GLEN HAVEN

Lock & Dam #10

V

NORTH ANDOVER

Duncan Road

(33.1 mile loop)

Eagle Valley Nature Preserve

VV

133

0   2   4 Miles

N

Nelson Dewey State Park

Stonefield Village

81

30 Bicycle Tours in Wisconsin
© 1994 The Countryman Press, Inc.

CASSVILLE
(see inset)

VV

81

Municipal Swimming Pool

Bluff Street

Denniston Street

CASSVILLE
inset

N

Wall Street

Crawford Street

Amelia Street

Public Boat Landing

Ferry Landing

Front Street

Riverside Park

133

Mississippi River

To reach Wyalusing State Park, take WI 18 west from Madison to County Highway P. Take County Highway P to County Highway X and continue until you see signs for the park. The park can also be reached by traveling south on WI 35 to Prairie du Chien, where it meets WI 18. Mileage for the tour begins at the ranger station.

0.0 *Follow the road out of the park (County Highway C).*

1.4 *Right onto County Highway X. Enjoy a beautiful, two-mile downhill past the bluffs.*

3.7 *The village of Wyalusing.*

Cradled in a bend of the river, Wyalusing includes several interesting native stone houses and a church that sits partway up the bluff. Though not as well-known as Jean Lafitte and his band on the lower Mississippi, there are numerous accounts of river pirates operating out of the village of Wyalusing. Among them was a notorious Dr. Bell, who kept a den of stolen cargo on Big Island in the river just off town.

3.8 *The recreational area and boat landing here has rest rooms.*

7.3 *The village of Bagley has several bars that serve light lunches, and a small grocery, Grandpa's General Store.*

7.6 *Left onto Chicago Street (County Highway A).*

8.0 *At the intersection with County Highway P, continue straight ahead if you plan to take the 33.1- or 44.2-mile routes. If you plan to take the 12.9-mile route, turn left onto County Highway P and skip ahead to the 47.3-mile mark.*

12.7 *Right onto County Highway VV.*

16.2 *Left onto County Highway V for the 55.2-mile route. For the 33.1-mile route, right onto County Highway V and follow it into Glen Haven. Then skip to the 40.7-mile mark below.*

19.8 *Right on WI 133 by Randy's Bar in North Andover.*

26.6 *A long downhill run into Cassville begins here.*

27.5 *Left onto West Bluff Street, as you enter Cassville.*

Daniels, Denniston, and Co., land speculators from the east, platted Cassville and promoted the sale of lots in the 1830s in hopes that the town would be chosen as capital of the new Wisconsin Territory. Cassville lost out to Madison on that count, but continued to prosper as a robust little river town. Seeing double? It may reassure you to know that Cassville is the site of the national Twin-O-Rama gathering each July!

28.1 *Right onto Denniston Street. The Geiger House, (608) 725-5419, on your right, is a friendly bed-and-breakfast establishment in a home dating to 1855.*

28.2 *Left onto Front Street.*

28.4 *Right onto Wall Street. Riverside Park has picnic tables and rest rooms.*

The Cassville Car Ferry, which crosses the river to Millville, Iowa (just south of Guttenberg), departs from here daily from Memorial Day to Labor Day and on weekends in May, September, and October. The schedule is continuous during daylight hours. The fare is reasonable—take it just for the ride and for an opportunity to view the bluffs from offshore.

28.7 *Left onto Crawford Street.*

28.8 *Left onto Amelia Street. There are several cafés to choose from here.*

29.6 *Cassville Community Swimming Pool is open to the public for a small fee.*

29.9 *Left onto County Highway VV.*

31.2 *Right into the parking area for Nelson Dewey State Park.*

Nelson Dewey was Wisconsin's first governor, in 1848 at age 35. This park is the site of a southern-style plantation developed by Dewey, which totaled 2,000 acres and employed over fifty people. Stonefield included a number of stone outbuildings and an elaborate brick house, all designed in the

Gothic Revival style. Dewey stocked his farm with dairy cows and imported horses, and planted a vineyard producing wine for sale.

Dewey's wife decided she preferred city life to the isolated rural existence of Stonefield and eventually moved away. Shortly after, Stonefield was destroyed by fire. Only the brick walls of Dewey's home and assorted pieces of millwork were spared. In 1887, the property was purchased for a vacation retreat by a Chicagoan, Walter Cass Newberry, who rebuilt the Dewey home in the Victorian style. The park now offers beautiful wooded campsites for individuals and groups, as well as a 10-acre restored prairie. Call the park office at (608) 725-5374 for campsite reservations.

Part of the park, but located across the road, is Stonefield Village, a reconstructed village of the late 1800s, operated by the State Historical Society of Wisconsin. The large stone building at the entrance to the historic site was once Dewey's horse barn. The other buildings are reproductions of a turn-

This ride begins with a two-mile downhill to the Mississippi River.

of-the-century bank, barbershop, millinery shop, blacksmith shop, and general store. Guides costumed as shopkeepers, merchants, and traders provide interpretive information. Also located within the village walls is the State Agricultural Museum, which includes historic farm equipment and traces the development of agriculture in Wisconsin from the 1840s to the 1950s.

Right onto County Highway VV from the parking area, continuing north.

37.2 *A detour on Duncan Road (unpaved) will take you to the Eagle Valley Nature Preserve, where migrating and wintering bald eagles congregate. About 1,000 eagles are spotted during an annual count held each January.*

39.0 *Left onto County Highway V toward Glen Haven.*

40.7 *Left onto Main Street.*

41.0 *Glen Haven Recreation Area Park. Here you can see the toe end of Lock and Dam #10; the visitors' area is across the river in Guttenberg, Iowa. There are rest rooms in the park. Backtrack into town from here.*

41.1 *Left onto First Street.*

41.2 *Stay left on Bluff Street.*

41.3 *Right onto Dugway Road (dirt surface). This 2.7-mile stretch of dirt road is worth the extra effort for an up-close view of the river and its adjacent sloughs and backwaters, a haven for wildlife.*

45.0 *Left onto County Highway A.*

47.3 *Right onto County Highway P.*

51.0 *Left onto County Highway X.*

53.9 *Right onto County Highway C. No road sign here; follow signs for Wyalusing Park.*

55.2 *You're back at the ranger station.*

Bicycle Repair Service

Spoke & Wheel (Shirley Panka's home)
1217 South Eleventh Street, Praire du Chien, WI
(608) 326-8787

RAILS-TO-TRAILS
SAMPLER

31
Favorite Railroad Bed Trails

Biking on railroad bed trails offers several advantages: you can ride two abreast and chat as you bike; you don't need to keep checking your map or directions; the terrain is nearly flat; and there's no traffic noise or worry. Trails also provide a fun, safe, do-able outing for small children who are beginning bikers.

Since a comprehensive, user-friendly guide to Wisconsin's State Park Trails is available from the Department of Transportation (see *Resources* in Introduction) and because all of the trails are easy to follow, point-to-point routes, we haven't detailed them in this book.

We think all of the trails are worth riding in their entirety, but a few stretches stand out as our favorites:

Military Ridge Trail

Verona to Riley, 14.2 miles round-trip

Start the tour at the trailhead on County Highway PB, just south of WI 18/151 in Verona. Take a Sunday morning spin along the watershed of the Sugar River, ending up at the itty-bitty burg of Riley, where in-the-know cyclists congregate for blueberry pancakes at the Riley Tavern. The tavern (restaurant would be more appropriate—this is a family-style event) occupies what was once a general store and post office, when "Riley's Station" was a water stop on the steam engine line between Madison and Lancaster. Stoke up on a stack of cakes, and reverse your course to the starting point.

Sugar River Trail

New Glarus to Albany, 32 miles round-trip

New Glarus is a picturesque small town founded in the 1840s by immigrants from the canton of Glarus, Switzerland. Swiss heritage remains strong, with a summer schedule chock-full of Swiss cultural events. Begin at the trail headquarters, a century-old Milwaukee Road depot, and follow the trail to Albany. If you don't have the energy for a round-trip, you can arrange for someone to drop you off along the trail and drive your car back to the start. The trail follows the Sugar River watershed, through pleasant farmland and prairie land. End the ride with dinner at the New Glarus Hotel—schnitzel, weissbeer, and old-world ambience.

Bicycle Repair Service
Dan Atkin's Bicycle Shoppe
517 Half Mile Road, Verona, WI
(608) 845-6644

Glacial Drumlin Trail

Cottage Grove to Lake Mills, 31.4 miles round-trip with optional extension to Aztalan State Park

Start at the trailhead, located on County Highway N, just south of Interstate 94 in Cottage Grove. The trail heads west to to Lake Mills, where several downtown cafés serve hearty stick-to-your-ribs food. If you want to divide the ride into a two-day trip, the Bayberry Inn, (414) 648-3654, offers bed-and-breakfast accommodations; more elegant lodging is available at the Fargo Mansion Inn, (414) 648-3645. Continue on the trail past Lake Mills to County Highway Q, turning left to Aztalan State Park. Aztalan, the most important archaeological site in Wisconsin, has been called "America's Stonehenge." You can climb giant mounds, built by Native Americans between 1100 and 1300 A.D., which served as a solar calendar. It's also possible to return to Cottage Grove on County Highway BB, which parallels the trail.

Crossing a plank bridge on a former rail bed

Bicycle Repair Service
Village Pedaler
5511 Monona Drive, Monona, WI
(608) 221-0311

Great River Trail

Trempealeau to northern end of trail, 17 miles round-trip

Park near the Trempealeau Hotel, a historic riverside restaurant/hostelry that serves both good vegetarian and nonvegetarian food in a serene setting overlooking the mighty Mississippi. There's often live music on an outdoor stage during the summer. The trail begins a few blocks away—ask at the hotel for directions. The highlight of this trip is Perrot State Park, where a short hike to Brady's Bluff provides a spectacular view of the converging Trempealeau and Mississippi Rivers. Beyond the park, the trail borders the Trempealeau National Wildlife Refuge, passing bottom lands where herons, egrets, and ospreys are frequently seen.

251

Author Scott Hall on the 32-mile Elroy–Sparta Trail

Bicycle Repair Services
Bikes LTD
1001 LaCrosse Street, LaCrosse, WI
(608) 785-2326

Vagabond Touring
539 Main Street, LaCrosse, WI
(608) 782-2453

Valley Ski & Bike
321 Main Street, LaCrosse, WI
(608) 782-5500

Red Cedar Trail

Menomonie to Downsville, 15 miles round-trip

Park at the trail headquarters, just off WI 25 in Menomonie. This scenery-packed trail clings to the course of the Red Cedar River with pleasant pull-offs along the way. Downsville thrived in the late 1800s when Knapp, Stout,

252

and Company was the largest white-pine milling company in the world. The company store still stands on the north side of Main Street; the original hotel is across the street. One block east of the store is the Empire in Pine Museum, which brings to life the colorful lumbering era. A little farther down Main Street is The Creamery Inn and Restaurant, a delightful place for a "civilized" lunch—fettucine with smoked salmon and herbal iced tea, for instance—served on a screened porch overlooking the river valley.

Bicycle Repair Services

Red Cedar Outfitters
910 Hudson Road, Menomonie, WI
(715) 235-5431

Spoke House Cyclery
632 South Broadway, Menomonie, WI
(715) 235-1440

Bearskin Trail

Minocqua to the South Blue Lake Rest Area, 20 miles round-trip

The trail begins on WI 51 in downtown Minocqua. The Bearskin Trail offers a true wilderness experience, passing through the Northern Highland/ American Legion State Forest and past dozens of pristine lakes. Because of the expense of shipping limestone screenings to northern Wisconsin, crushed granite was used as a trail surface on the Bearskin. Look for loons as you pass Baker Lake, and evidence of beavers at work farther along. The trail leaves the railroad grade and travels on old Baker Lake Road for a short stretch. Pick up the makings for a picnic in Hazelhurst, a short detour off the trail; enjoy your lunch on the shores of South Blue Lake, which has a park with a picnic area and rest rooms. On the return, work up an appetite for an all-you-can-eat family-style feast at Paul Bunyan's on WI 51 in Minocqua.

Bicycle Repair Service

BJ's Sport Shop
917 WI 51 North, Minocqua, WI
(715) 356-3900

Elroy–Sparta Trail

Elroy to Sparta, 32 miles

It's worth riding every mile of this trail. Developed in 1966, the Elroy–Sparta was the country's first rails-to-trails conversion. The trail offers a raised vantage point overlooking verdant farmland, along with three tunnels ranging from ¼-mile to ¾-mile in length. The tunnels are cool, moist, and very dark, so bring a jacket and a flashlight. If you stay at the Tunnel Trail Campground, (608) 435-6829, near the midpoint at Wilton, you can bike to opposite ends on two days. Wilton is also where you want to be when the Lions Club serves up a pancake breakfast in the municipal park every Sunday morning, June to September. If you wish to bike the entire trail in one day, a car shuttle service is available from the trail headquarters in Kendall.

Look for Bikin' Boyd, an old railroad man who hangs around the Summit Rest Area near Tunnel #3, hoping for a chance to spin some yarns about the days when locomotives, not cyclists, chugged along this line. The Elroy–Sparta trail draws over 60,000 visitors a year. There's plenty of camaraderie on weekends, but it's surprisingly peaceful during the week or slightly off-season.

Bicycle Repair Service
Speed's Bike Shop
1126 John Street, Sparta, WI
(608) 269-2315

More Biking Guides from Backcountry Publications

Backcountry Publications is well known for its books on biking, hiking, walking, fishing, and other outdoor recreational activities. Here's a sample of what we have to offer.

Biking

25 Bicycle Tours in Maryland:
From the Allegheny Mountains to the Atlantic Ocean, $12.00
25 Bicycle Tours on Delmarva:
Day Trips and Overnights on the Eastern Shore of the Chesapeake Bay, $12.00
The Bicyclist's Guide to the Southern Berkshires, $14.95
25 Bicycle Tours in Maine: Coastal & Inland Rides from Kittery to Caribou, $10.00
25 Mountain Bike Tours in Massachusetts:
From the Connecticut River to the Atlantic Coast, $11.00
25 Mountain Bike Tours in Vermont:
Scenic Tours Along Dirt Roads, Forest Trails, and Forgotten Byways, $11.00
30 Bicycle Tours in New Hampshire:
A Guide to Selected Backcountry Roads throughout the Granite State, $11.00
25 Bicycle Tours in Vermont:
950 Miles of Sights, Delights and Special Events, $10.00
25 Bicycle Tours in the Adirondacks: Road Adventures in the East's Largest Wilderness, $13.00
20 Bicycle Tours in and around New York City, $9.00
25 Bicycle Tours in the Hudson Valley:
Scenic Rides from Saratoga to West Point, $10.00
25 Bicycle Tours in Eastern Pennsylvania:
Day Trips and Overnights from Philadelphia to the Highlands, $12.00
25 Bicycle Tours in New Jersey:
Over 900 Miles of Scenic Pleasures and Historic Treasures, $12.00
25 Bicycle Tours in and around Washington, D.C., $10.00
25 Bicycle Tours in Ohio's Western Reserve: Historic Northeast Ohio from the Lake Erie Islands to the Pennsylvania Border, $12.00
25 Bicycle Tours in Southern Indiana:
Scenic and Historic Rides through Hoosier Country, $10.95
25 Bicycle Tours in Coastal Georgia and the Carolina Low Country: Savannah, Hilton Head, and Outlying Areas, $13.00
25 Bicycle Tours in the Texas Hill Country and West Texas: Adventure Rides for Road and Mountain Bikes, $14.00

We offer many more books on hiking, travel, biking, walking, fishing, and canoeing in the Midwest, New England, New York, and the Mid-Atlantic states—plus our mysteries, history, gardening, and how-to.

Our books are available through bookstores, or they may be ordered directly from the publisher. For shipping and handling costs, to order, or for a complete catalog, please contact:

The Countryman Press, Inc.
P.O. Box 175
Woodstock, VT 05091-0175
Our Toll-free number: (800) 245-4151

The LEGO® Christmas Ornaments Book

16 DESIGNS TO SPREAD HOLIDAY CHEER!

VOLUME
2

CHRIS MCVEIGH

No Starch Press

San Francisco

The LEGO® Christmas Ornaments Book, Volume 2.

Copyright © 2018 by Chris McVeigh.

Printed in China

First printing

22 21 20 19 18   1 2 3 4 5 6 7 8 9

ISBN-10: 1-59327-940-X
ISBN-13: 978-1-59327-940-0

Publisher: William Pollock
Production Editor: Serena Yang
Cover Design: Mimi Heft
Developmental Editor: Tyler Ortman
Compositor: Serena Yang
Proofreader: Emelie Burnette

For information on distribution, translations, or bulk sales, please contact No Starch Press, Inc. directly:

No Starch Press, Inc.
245 8th Street, San Francisco, CA 94103
phone: 1.415.863.9900; info@nostarch.com; www.nostarch.com

The Library of Congress has catalogued the first volume as follows:

Names: McVeigh, Chris (Artist) author.
Title: The LEGO Christmas ornaments book / by Chris McVeigh.
Description: San Francisco : No Starch Press, [2016]
Identifiers: LCCN 2016003449| ISBN 9781593277666 | ISBN 1593277660
Subjects: LCSH: Christmas tree ornaments. | LEGO toys.
Classification: LCC TT900.C4 M38 2016 | DDC 745.594/12--dc23
LC record available at http://lccn.loc.gov/2016003449

Production Date: 6/6/18
Plant & Location: Printed by Everbest Printing Co.
Job / Batch #: 82037

To Dad,
who found the strength
of ten Grinches, plus two!

Contents

Introduction

It gives me great joy to bring you and your family a second collection of LEGO Christmas Ornaments. I hope you have a wonderful time building these colorful creations and hanging them on your tree. Don't hesitate to swap colors, switch parts, and put your own spin on things—mixing it up is all part of the fun!

You can find more ornament designs at my site: *chrismcveigh.com.*

Santa

2x
6001609

1x
4159553

2x
302401

3x
6046922

1x
6115248

1x
403201

2x
4249563

2x
4114026

3x
6092587

4x
4113917

2x
302321

4x
245021

1x
4649049

3x
4179875

3x
4179874

1X
4114309

2X
366601

1X
6147792

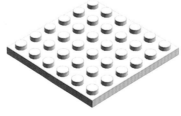

4X
4178429

1X
4144012

1x
6096955

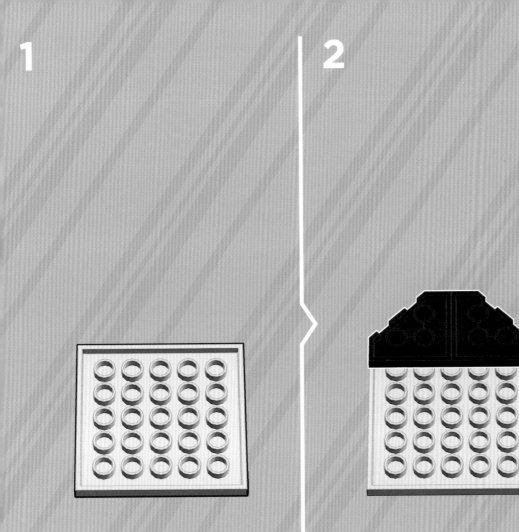

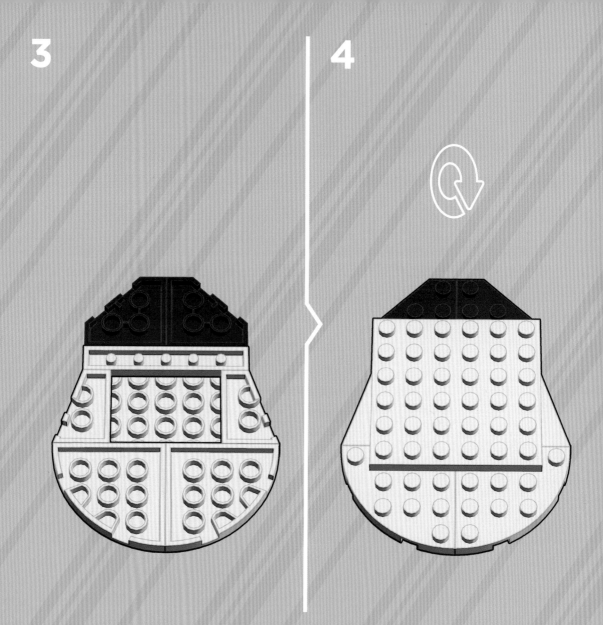

5

6

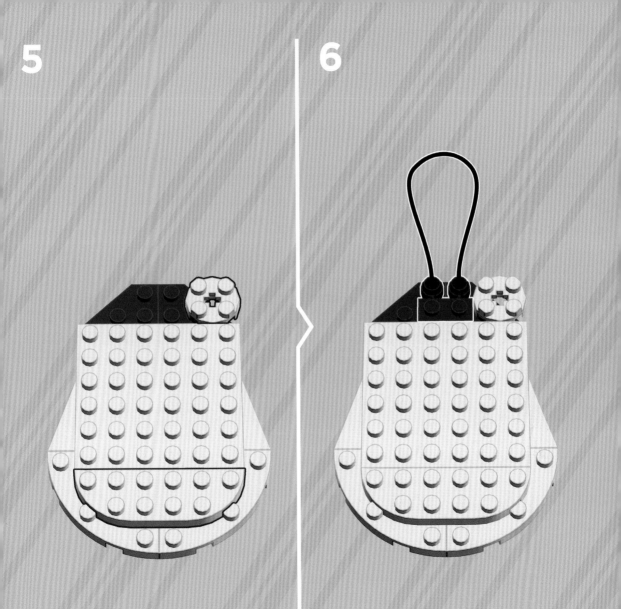

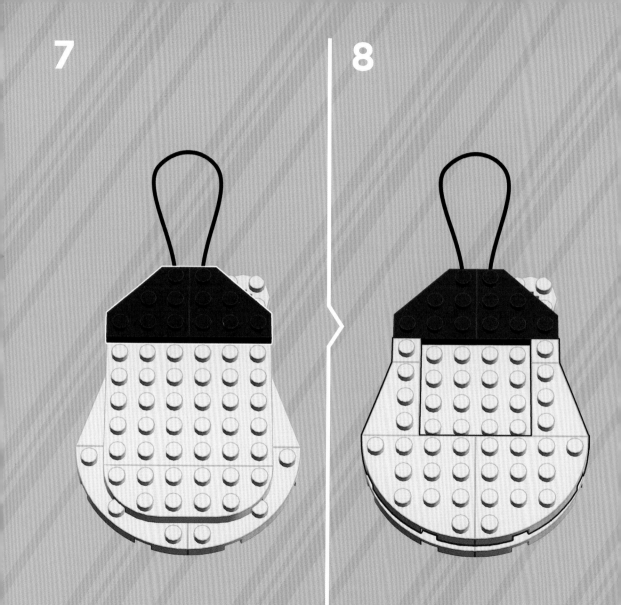

9

10

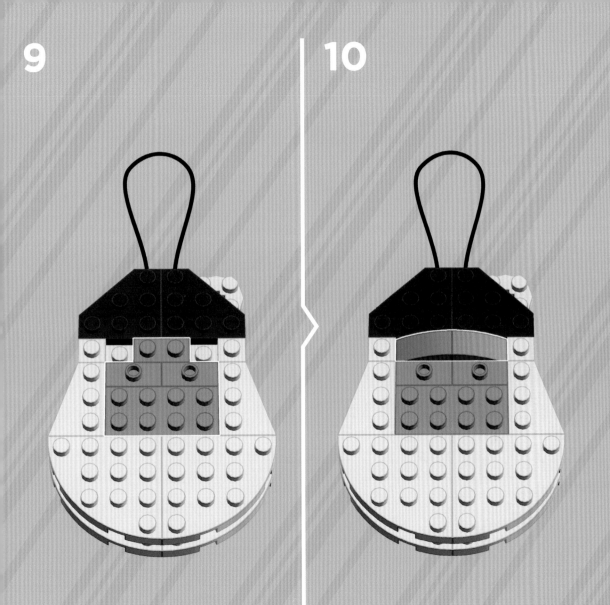

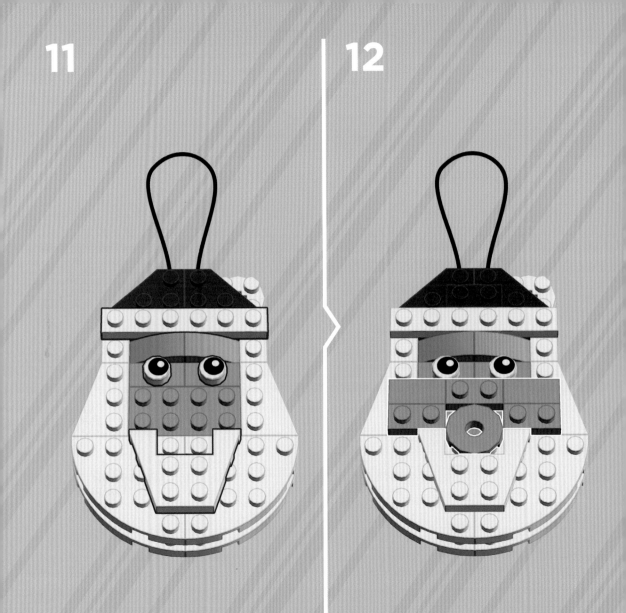

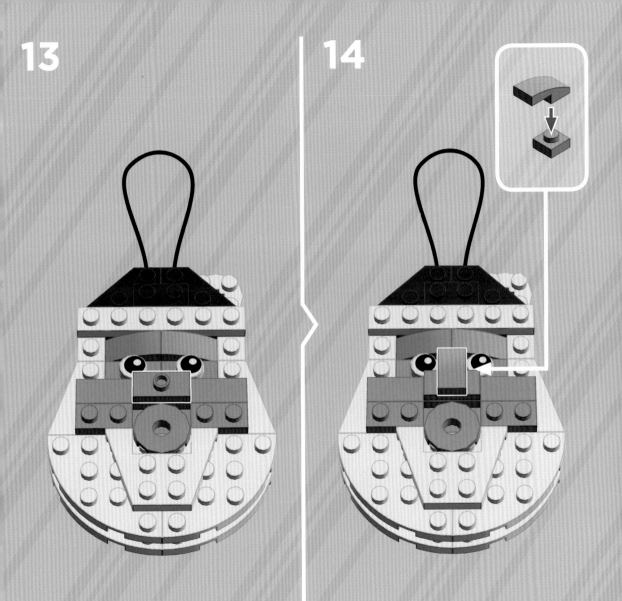

Reindeer

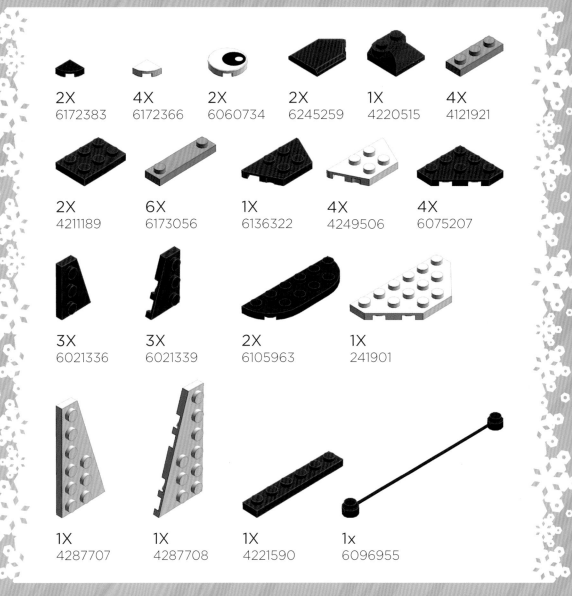

2X
6172383

4X
6172366

2X
6060734

2X
6245259

1X
4220515

4X
4121921

2X
4211189

6X
6173056

1X
6136322

4X
4249506

4X
6075207

3X
6021336

3X
6021339

2X
6105963

1X
241901

1X
4287707

1X
4287708

1X
4221590

1x
6096955

1

2

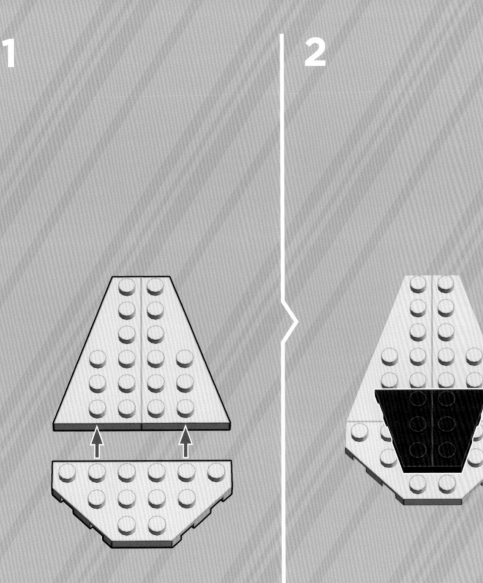

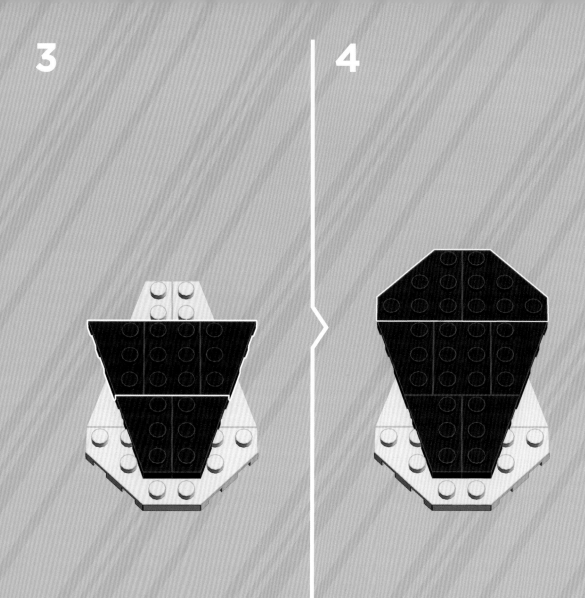

5

6

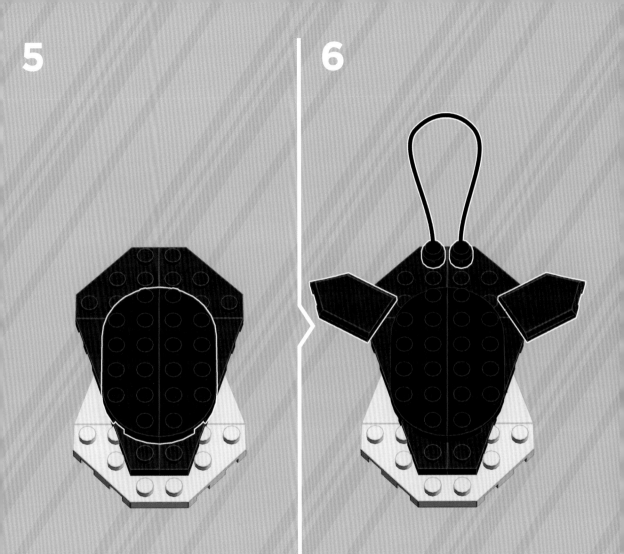

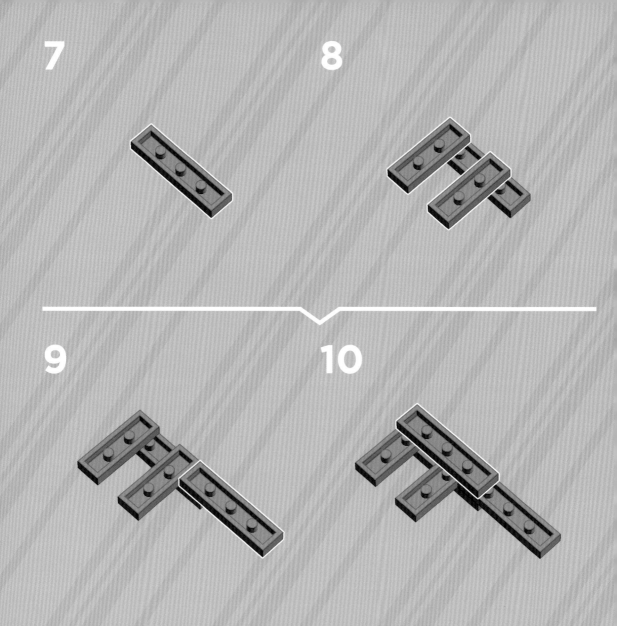

7

8

9

10

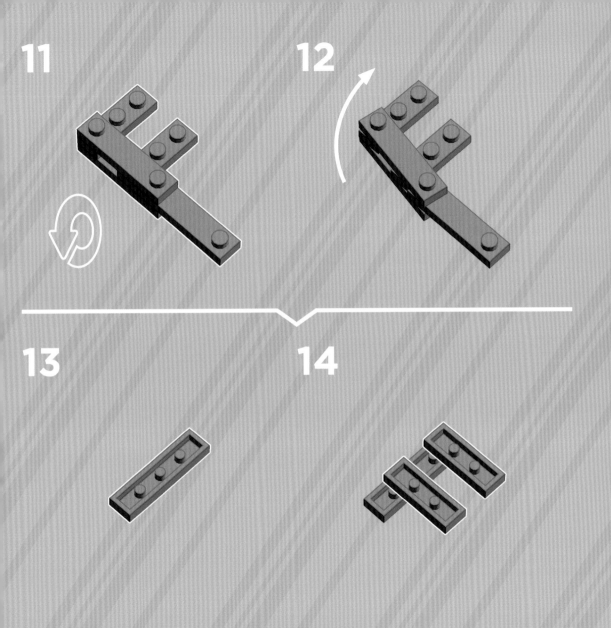

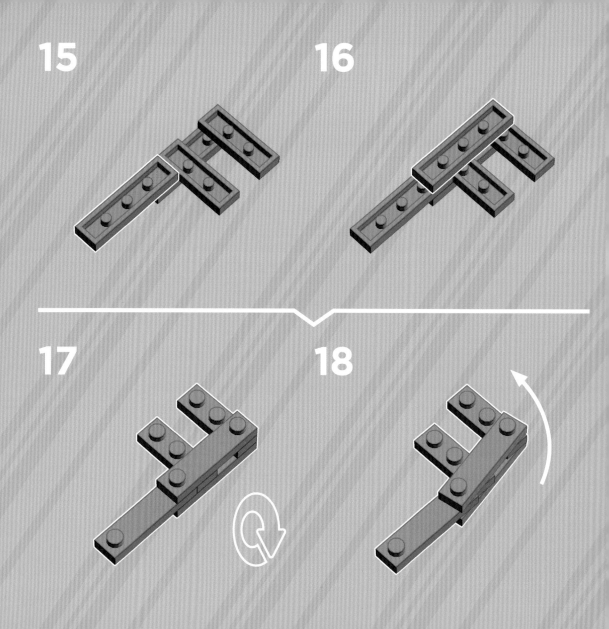

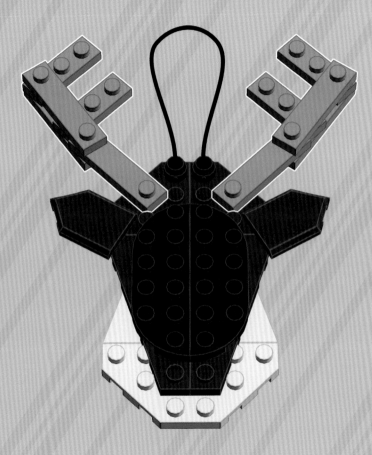

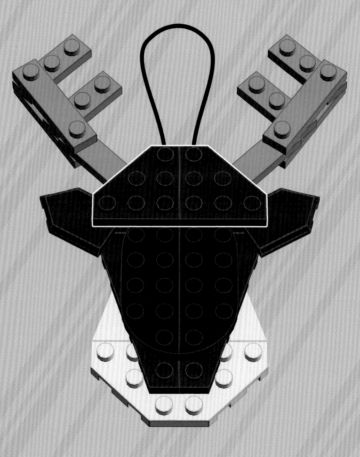

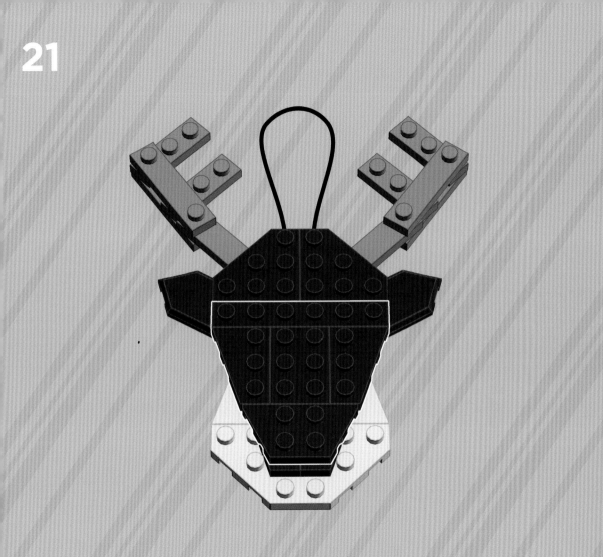

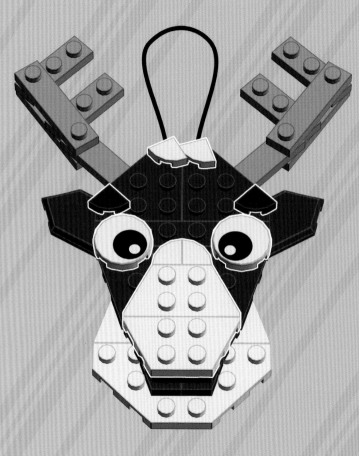

Mr. Snow

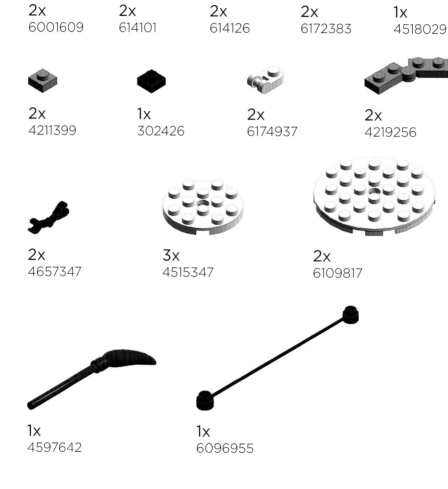

2x
6001609

2x
614101

2x
614126

2x
6172383

1x
4518029

2x
4211399

1x
302426

2x
6174937

2x
4219256

2x
4657347

3x
4515347

2x
6109817

1x
4597642

1x
6096955

1

2

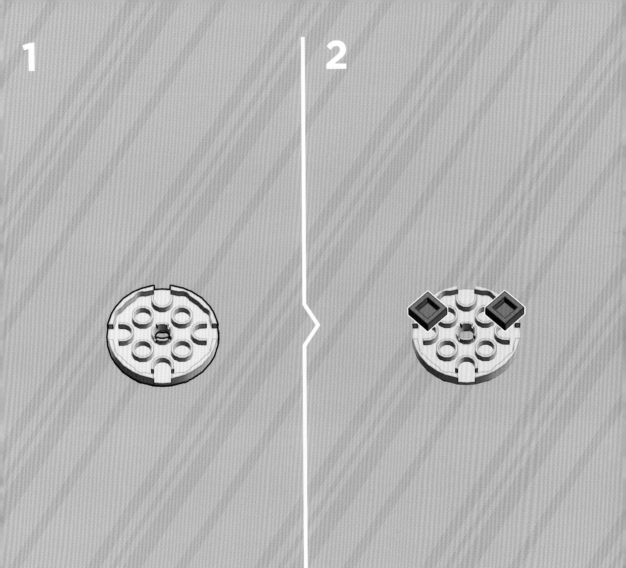

3

4

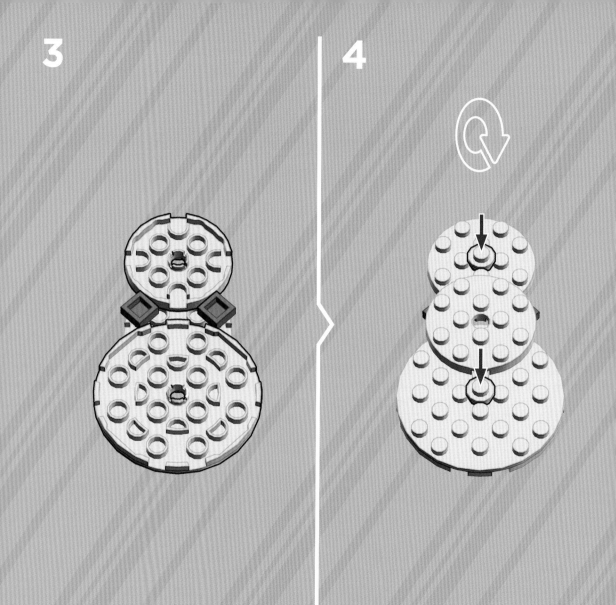

5

6

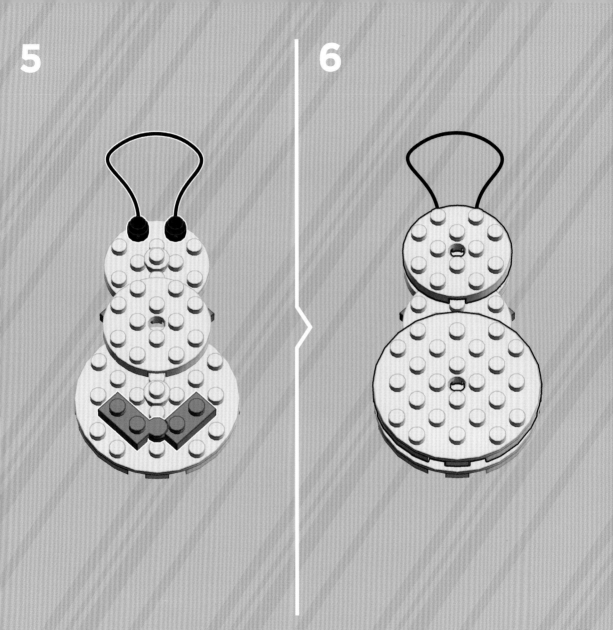

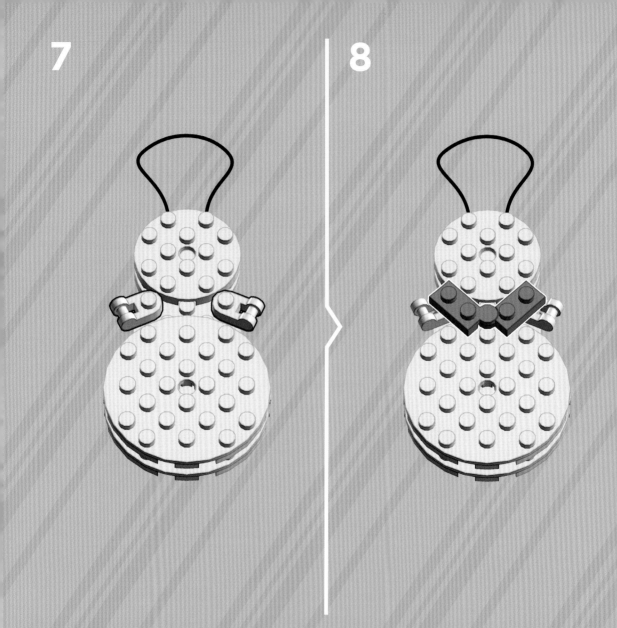

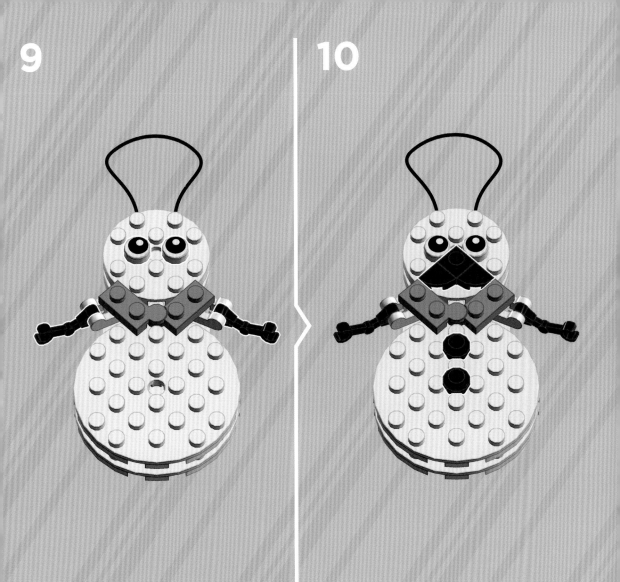

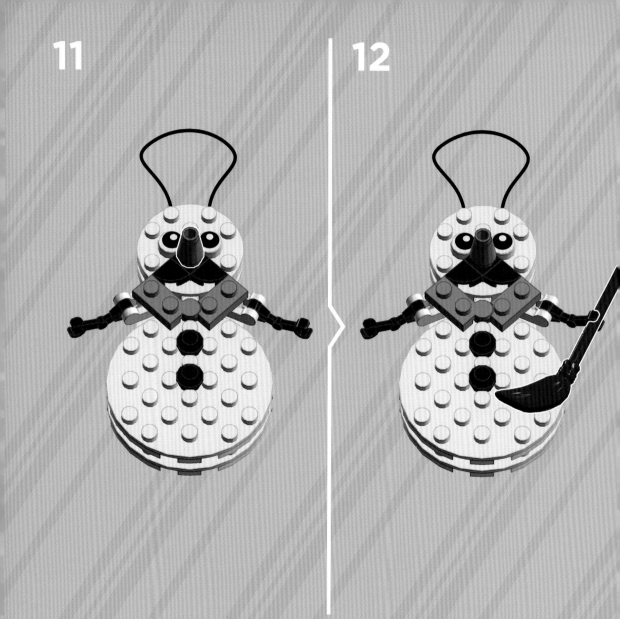

Mrs. Snow

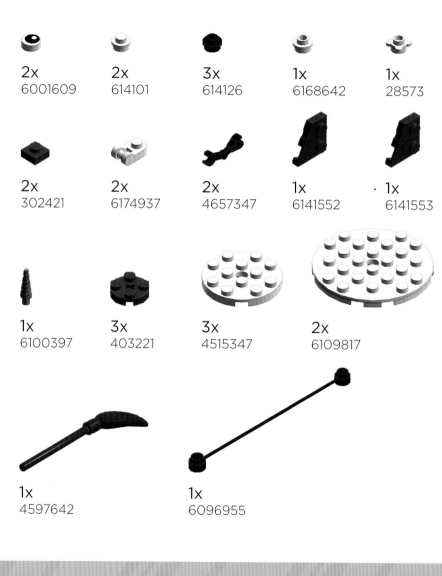

2x
6001609

2x
614101

3x
614126

1x
6168642

1x
28573

2x
302421

2x
6174937

2x
4657347

1x
6141552

· 1x
6141553

1x
6100397

3x
403221

3x
4515347

2x
6109817

1x
4597642

1x
6096955

1

2

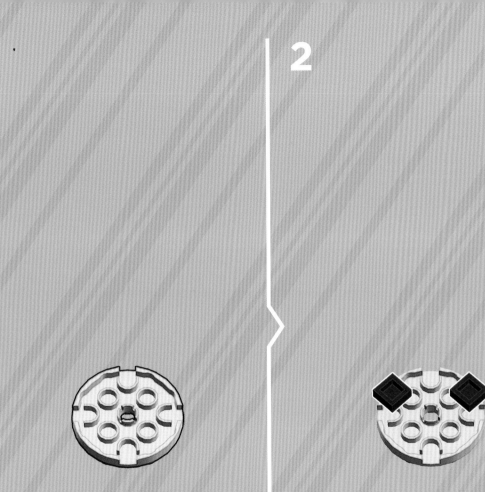

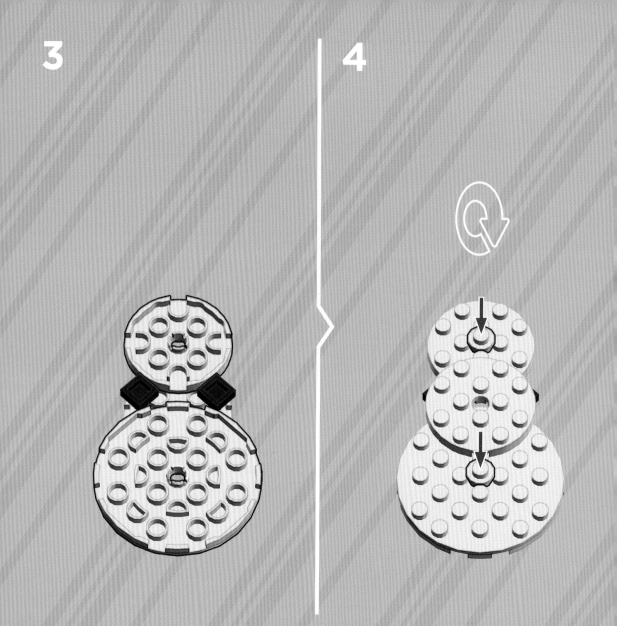

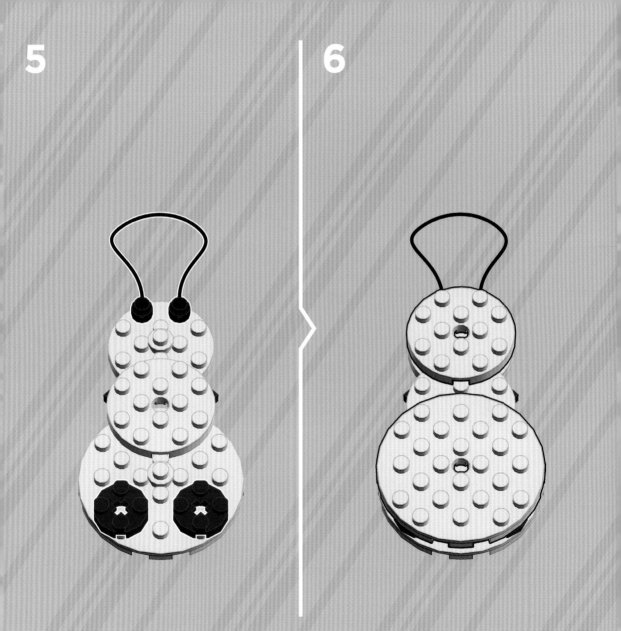

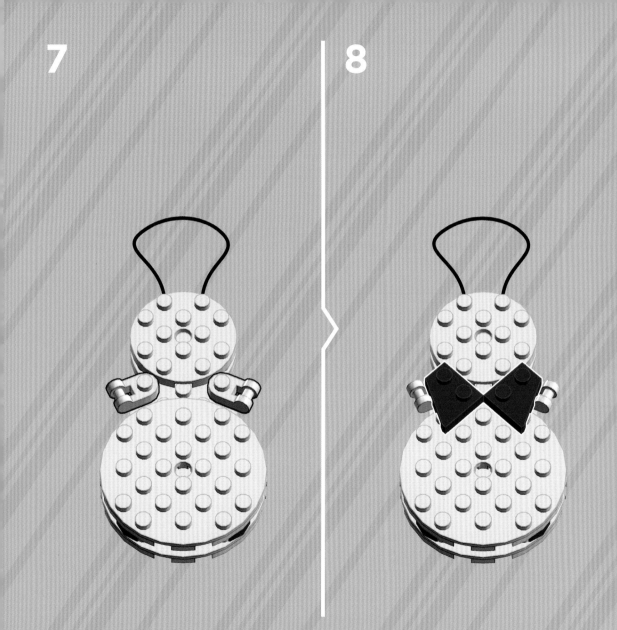

9

10

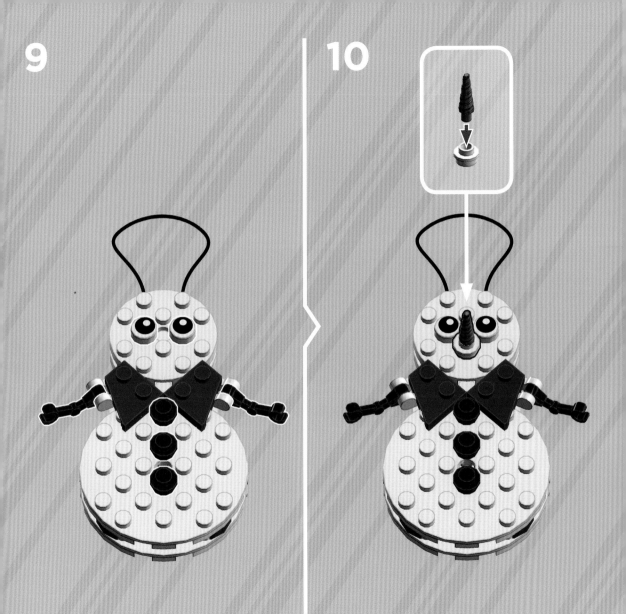

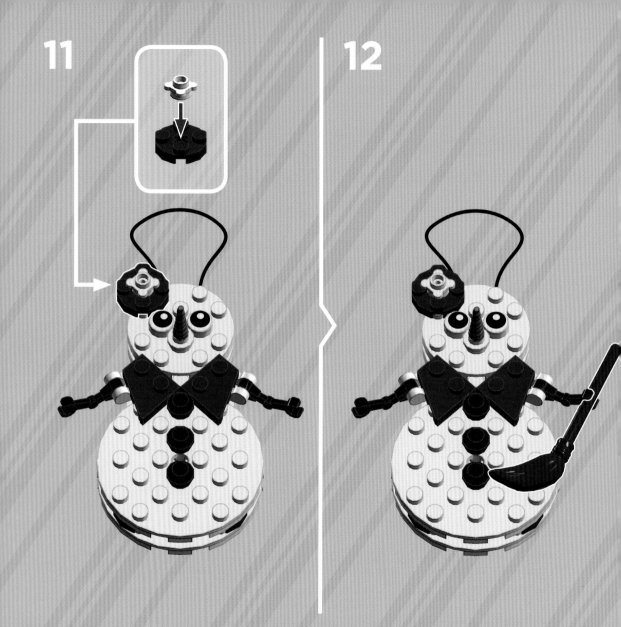

Gingerbread Man

8x
6172366

1x
6250591

2x
4646844

4x
6063445

1x
6167641

8x
6167690

2x
6021997

2x
4211150

4x
6174856

3x
6167643

1x
6168612

4x
6177535

2x
4211257

6x
6056383

2x
4211190

5x
6167647

1x
6096955

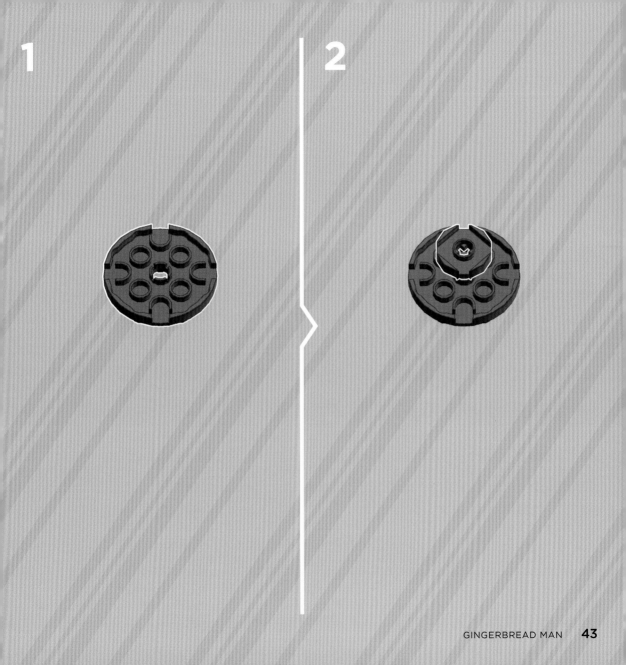

3

4

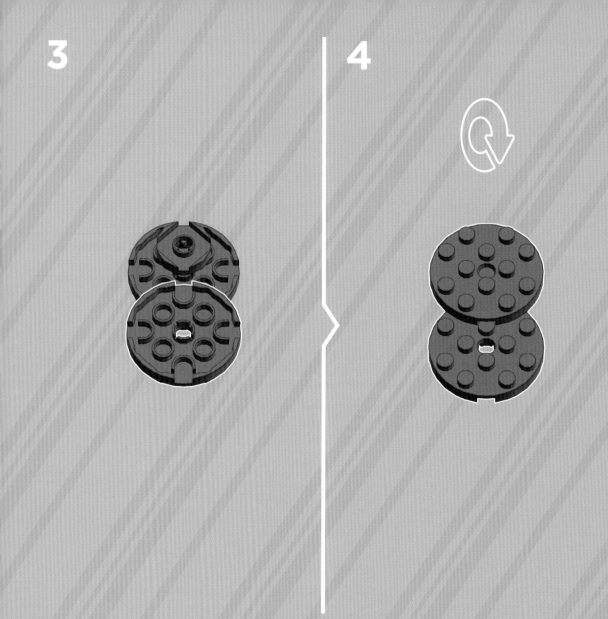

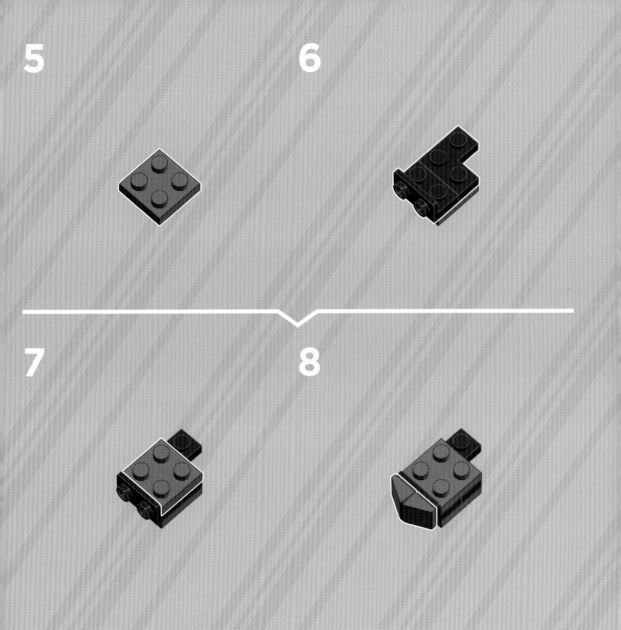

5

6

7

8

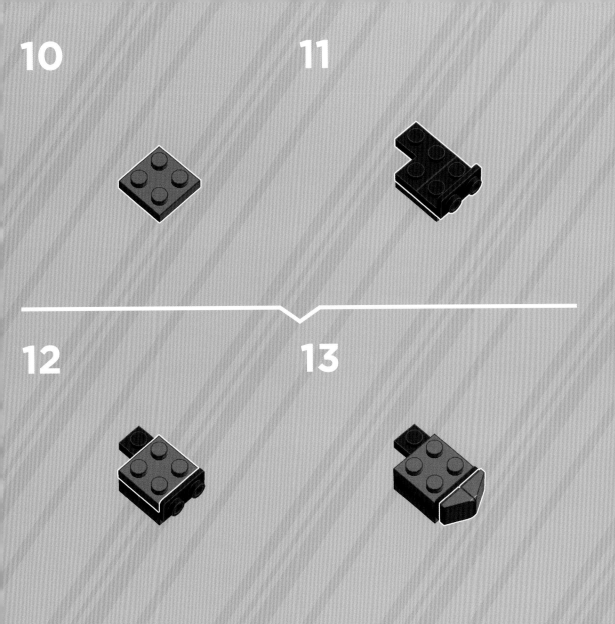

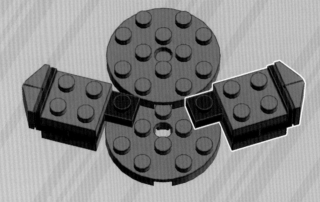

15

16

17

18

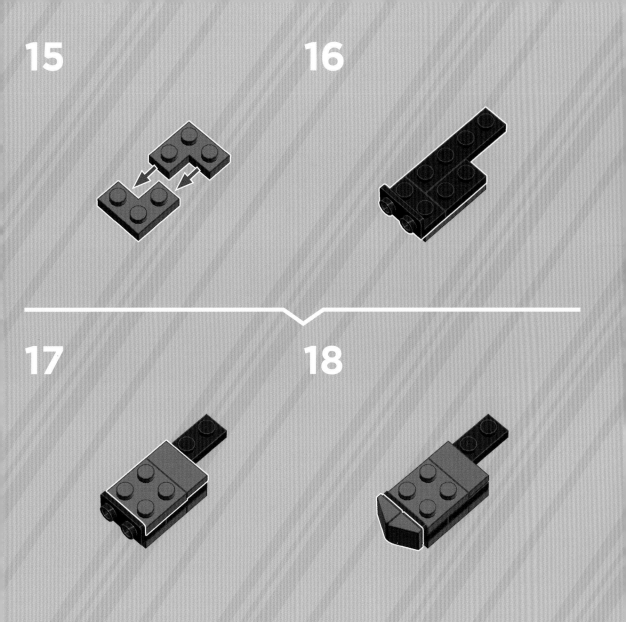

19

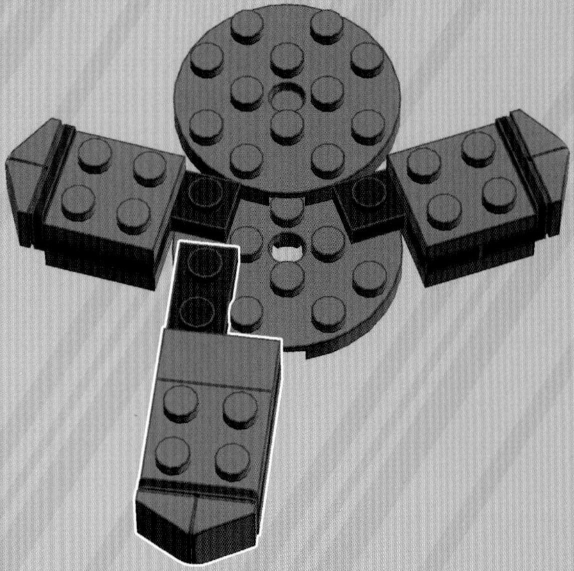

20

21

22

23

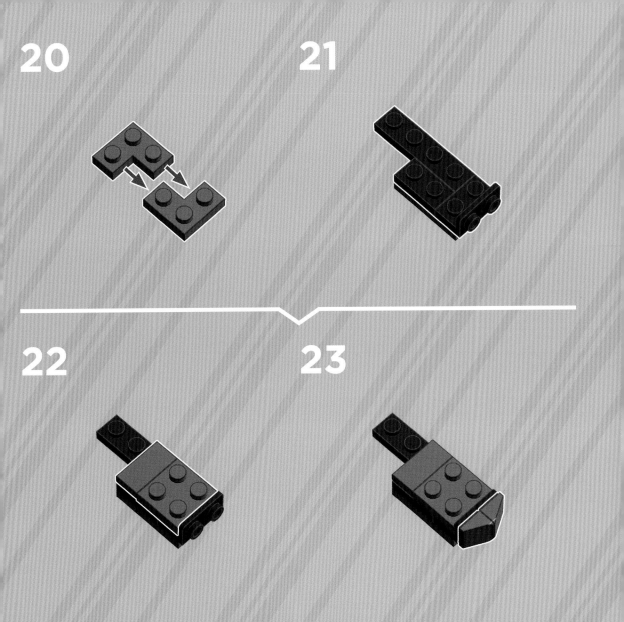

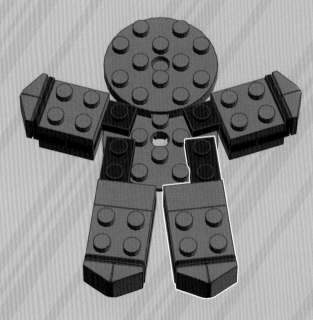

Gingerbread House

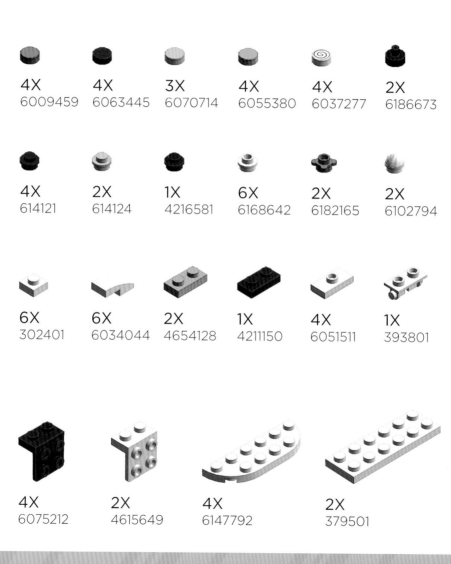

4X	4X	3X	4X	4X	2X
6009459	6063445	6070714	6055380	6037277	6186673
4X	2X	1X	6X	2X	2X
614121	614124	4216581	6168642	6182165	6102794
6X	6X	2X	1X	4X	1X
302401	6034044	4654128	4211150	6051511	393801

4X
6075212

2X
4615649

4X
6147792

2X
379501

1X
6147052

2X
4612342

1X
6102990

1X
306801

1X
368001

4X
6167643

1X
6035291

3X
6186045

4X
6058135

4X
4211199

1X
6029774

1X
6089696

1X
4211210

2X
4560178

2X
6055309

1X
4144012

1X
6096955

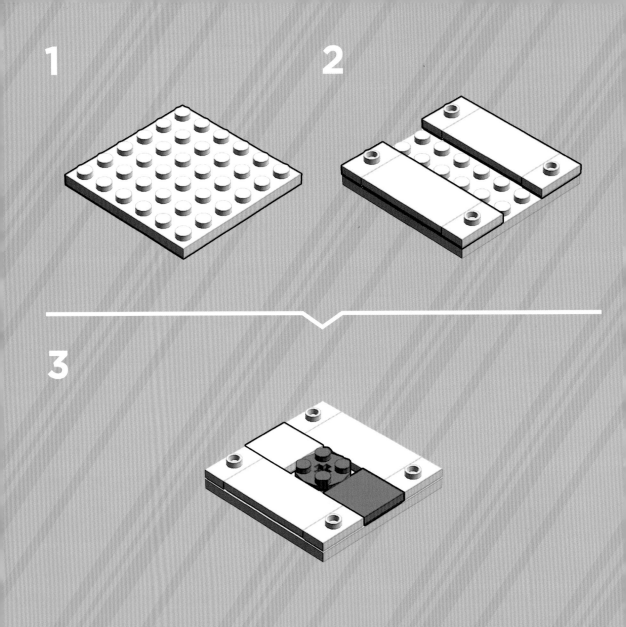

4

5

6

x2

7

x2

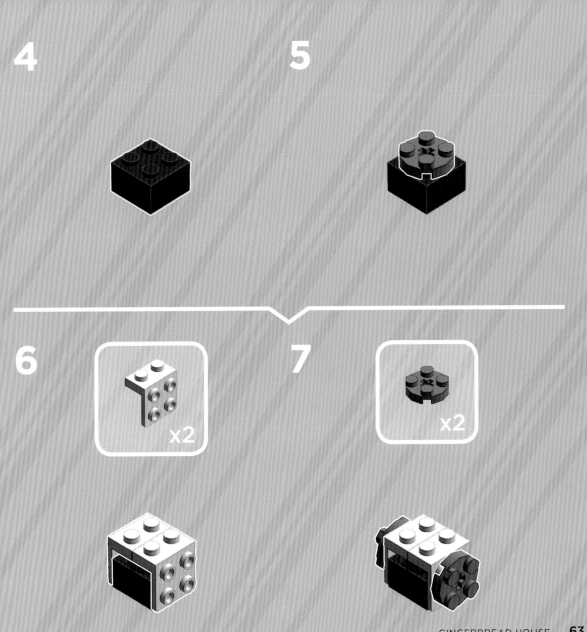

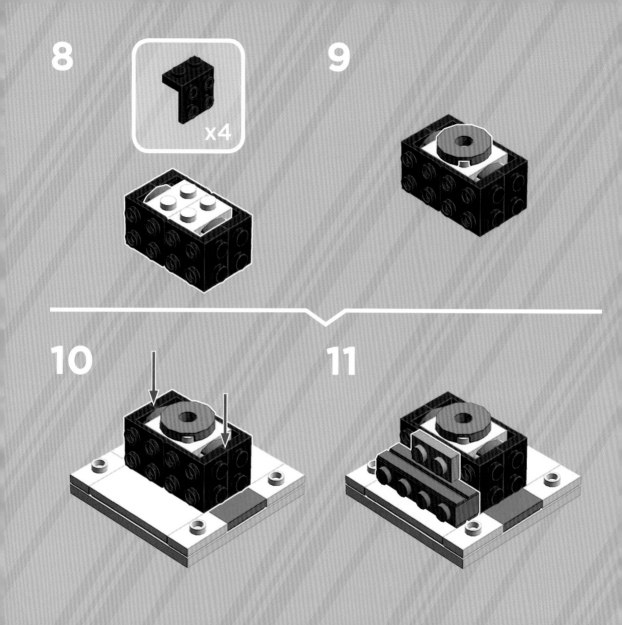

8

x4

9

10

11

12

13

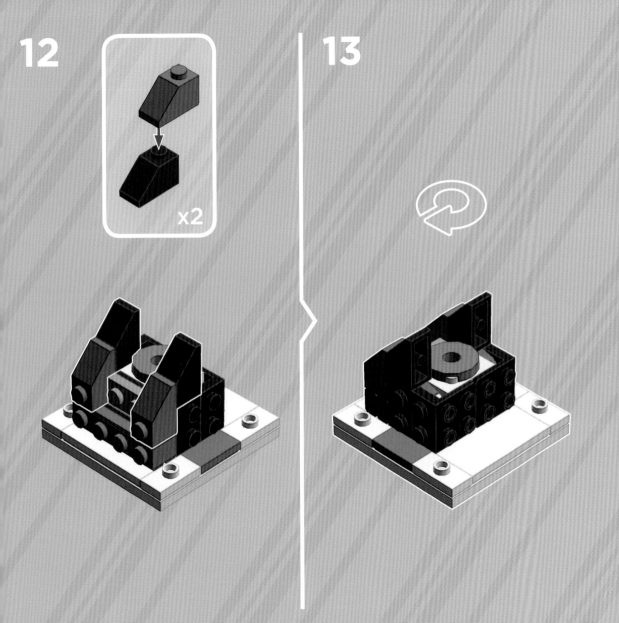

14

15

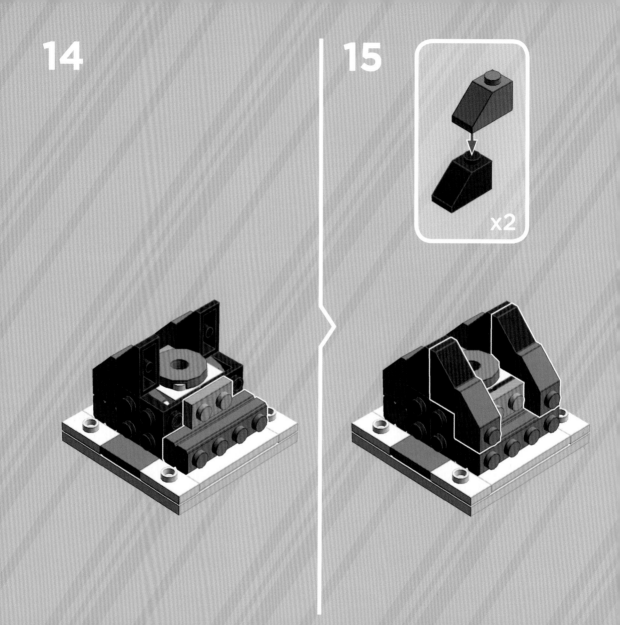

16

17

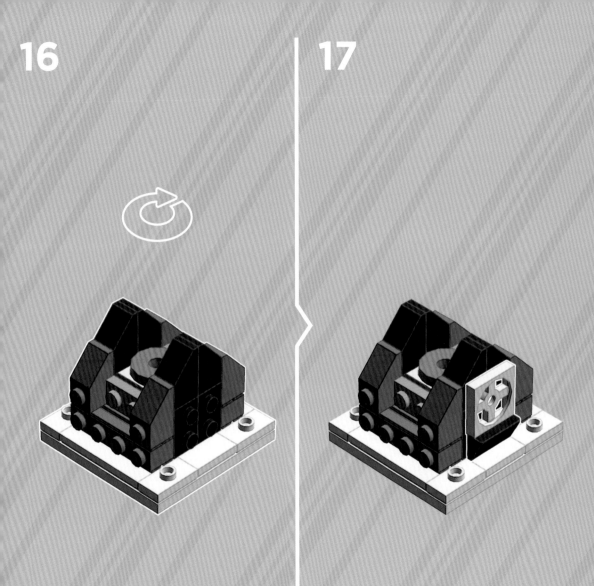

18

19

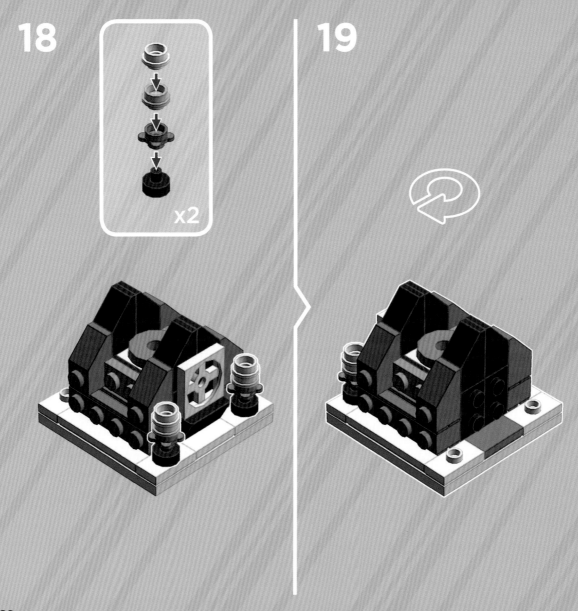

20

21

x2

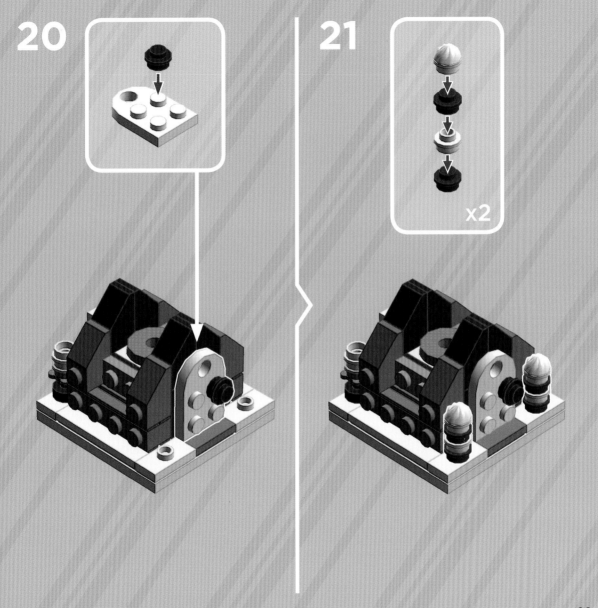

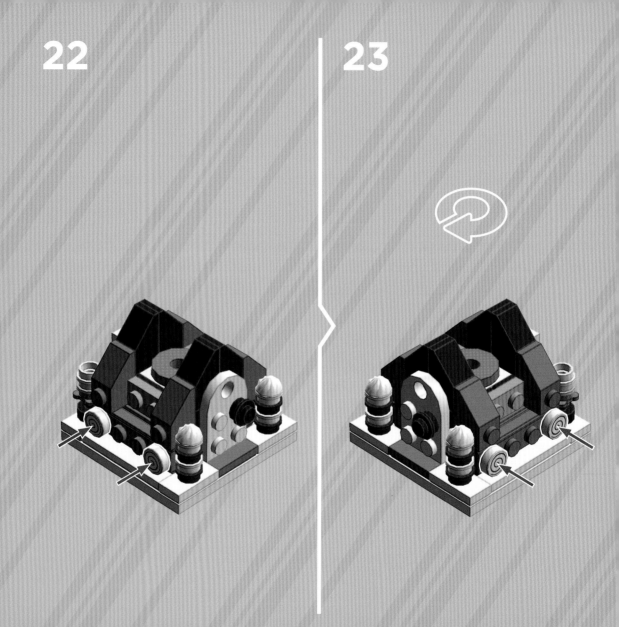

24

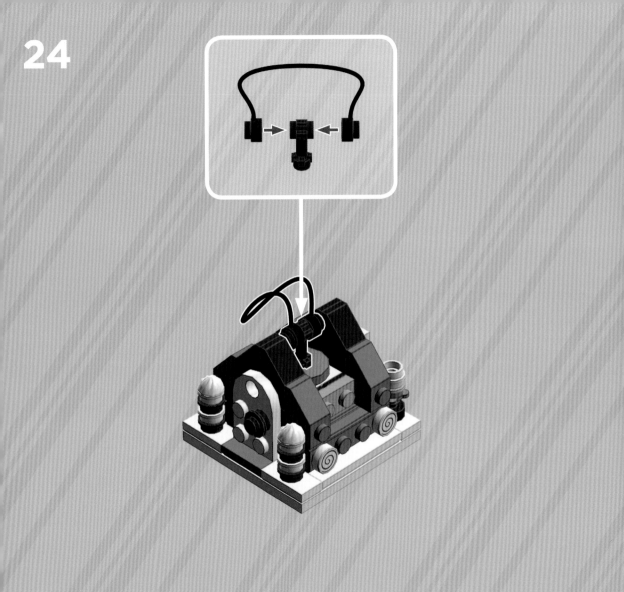

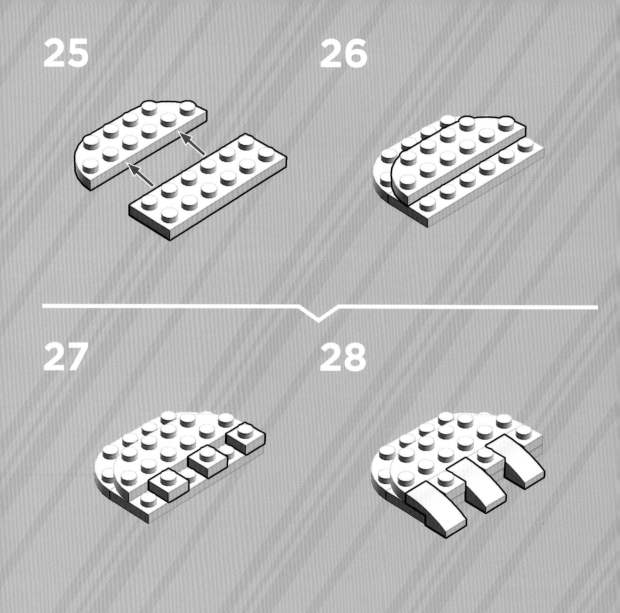

29

30

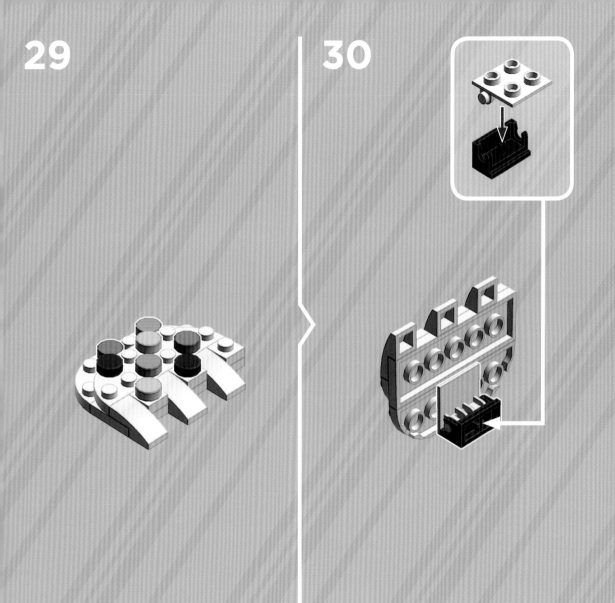

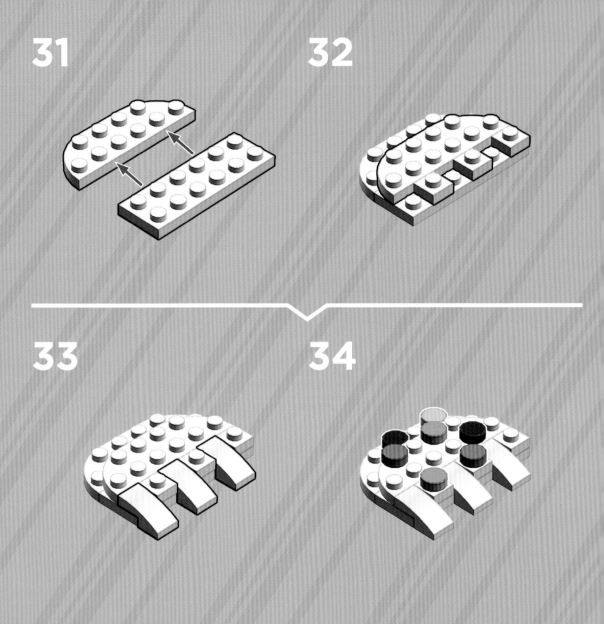

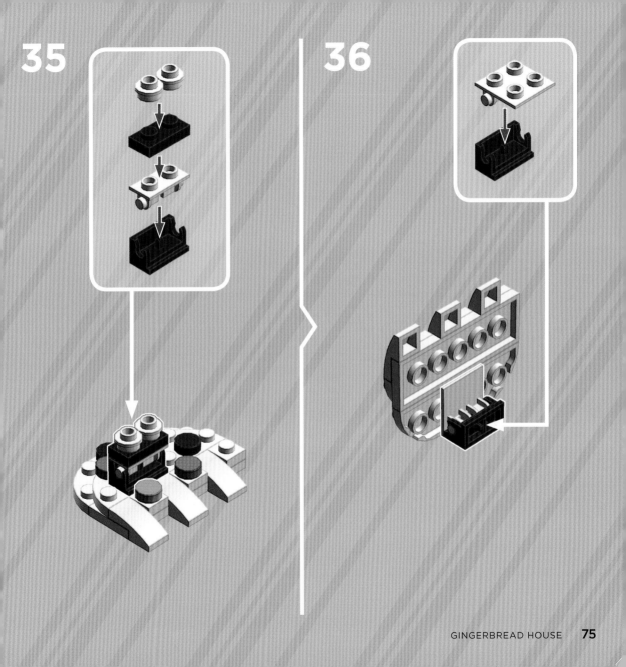

35

36

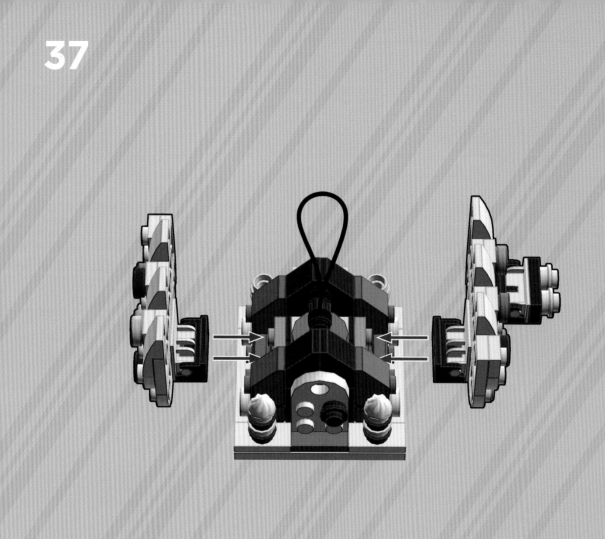

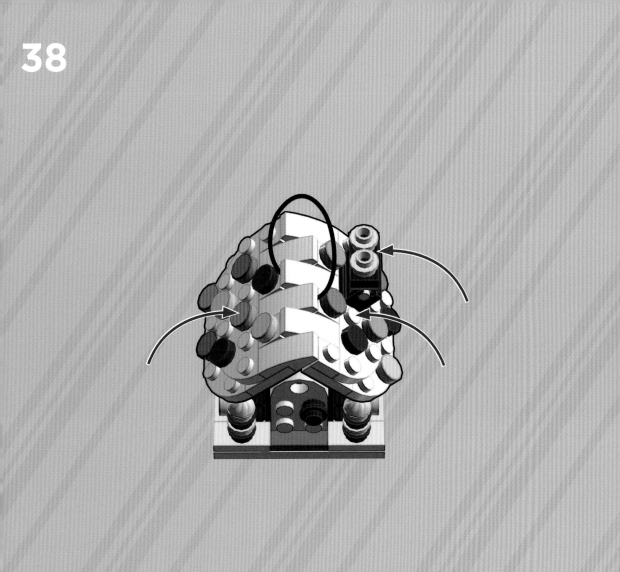

Confetti Tree

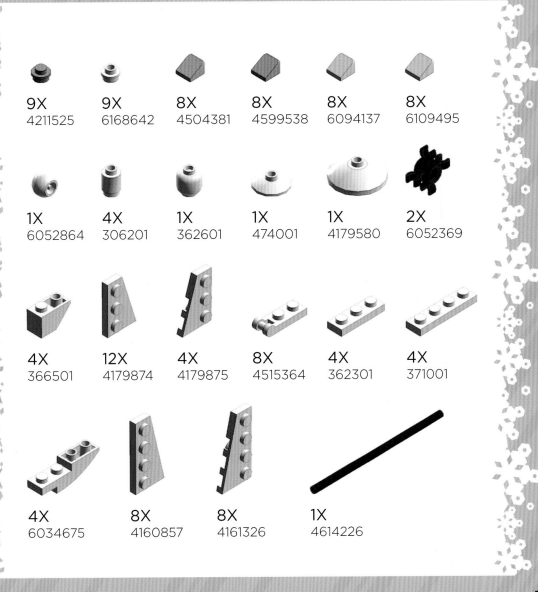

9X
4211525

9X
6168642

8X
4504381

8X
4599538

8X
6094137

8X
6109495

1X
6052864

4X
306201

1X
362601

1X
474001

1X
4179580

2X
6052369

4X
366501

12X
4179874

4X
4179875

8X
4515364

4X
362301

4X
371001

4X
6034675

8X
4160857

8X
4161326

1X
4614226

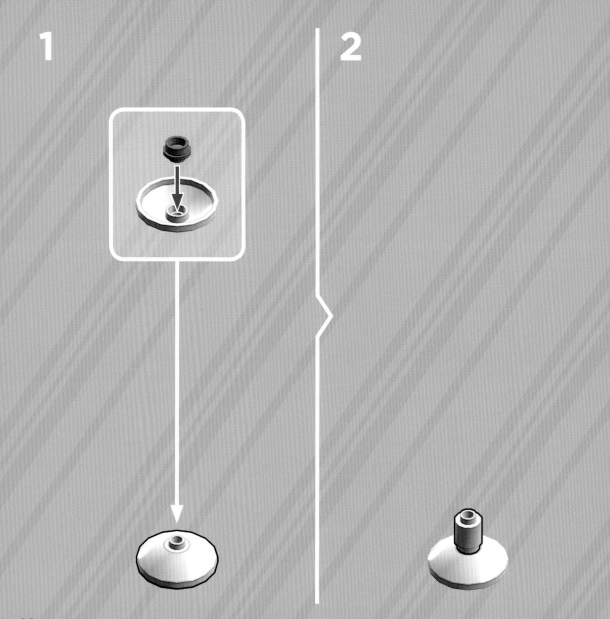

1

2

CONFETTI TREE

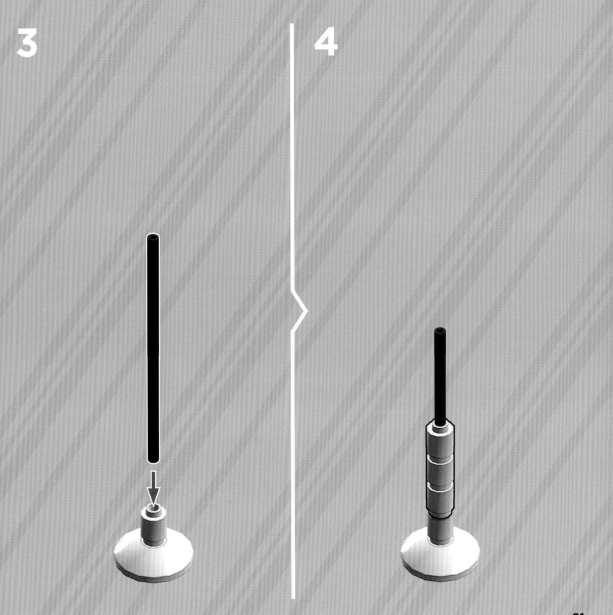

3

4

5

6

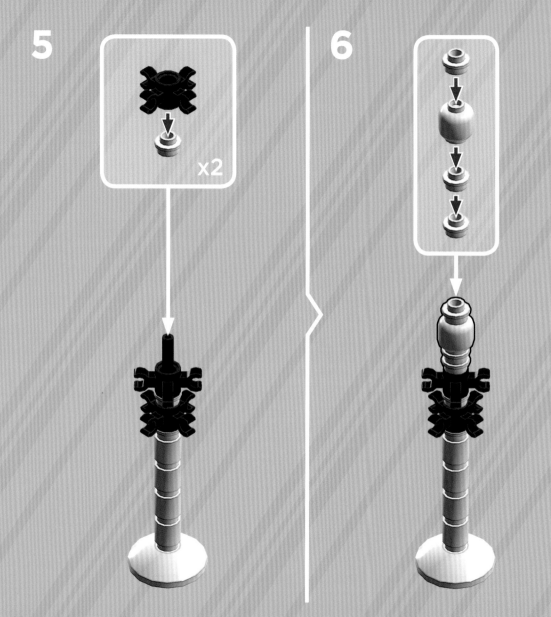

x2

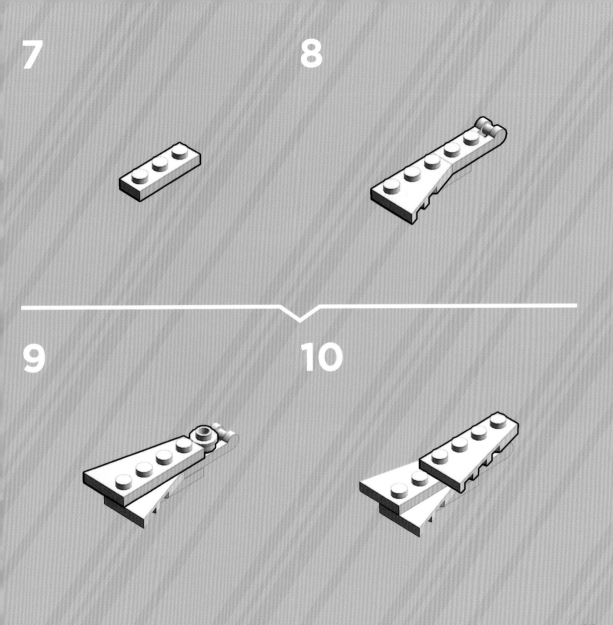

7

8

9

10

11

12

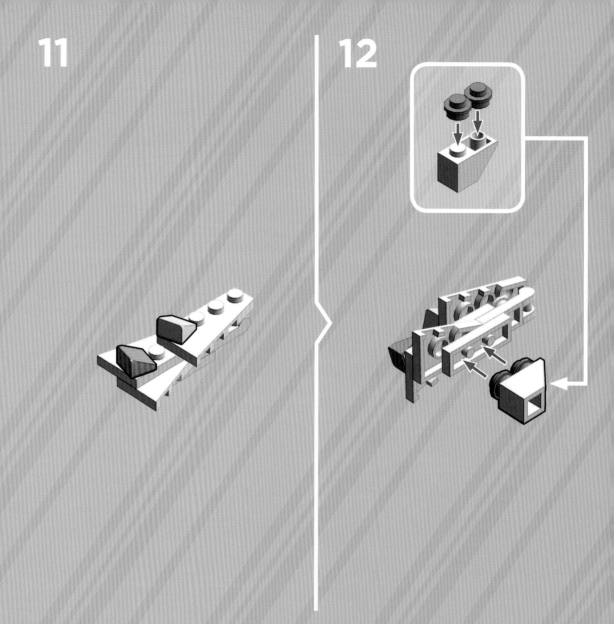

13

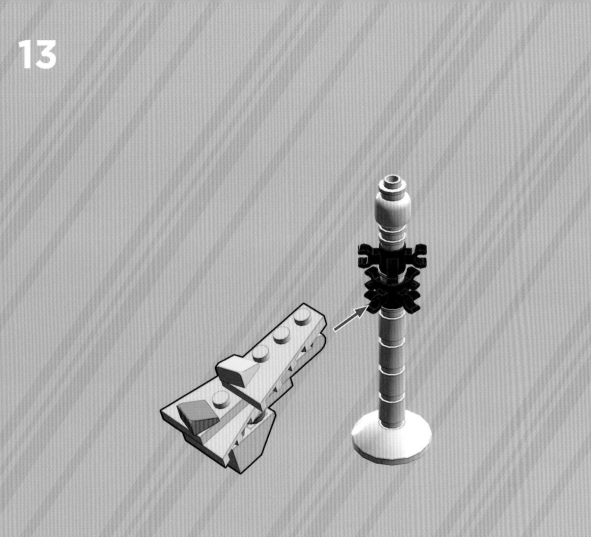

14

x4

15

16

17

18

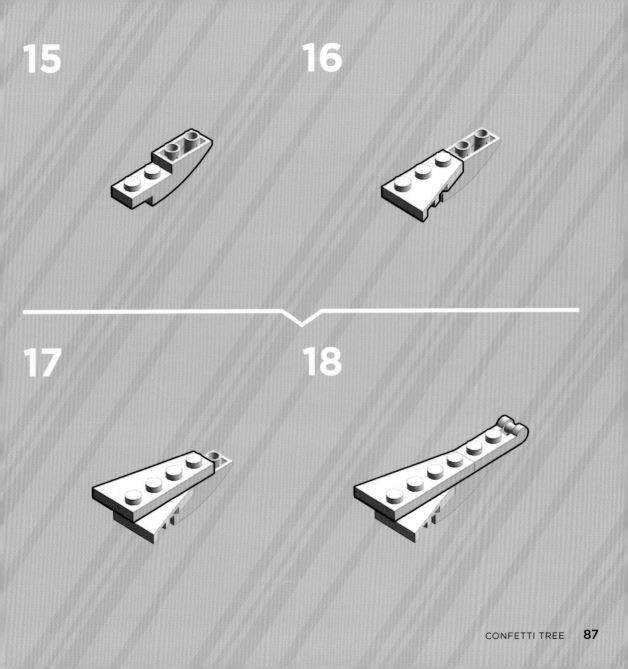

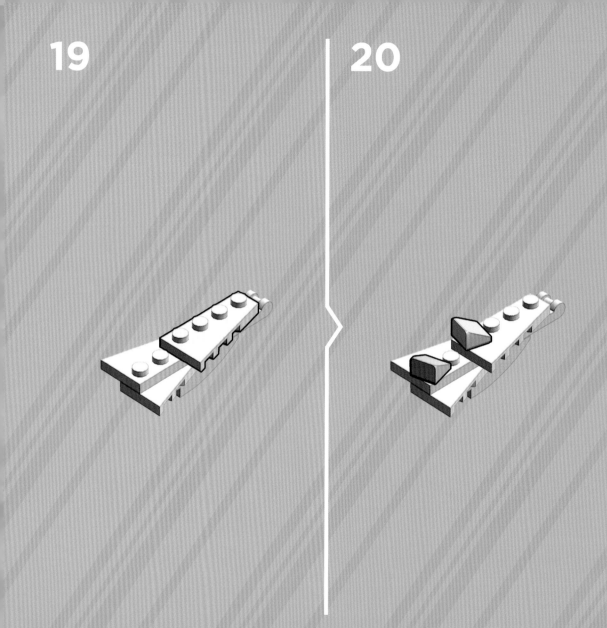

21

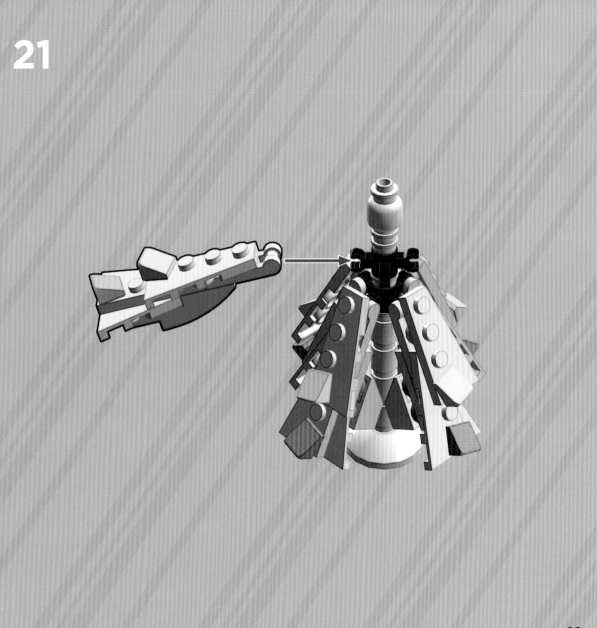

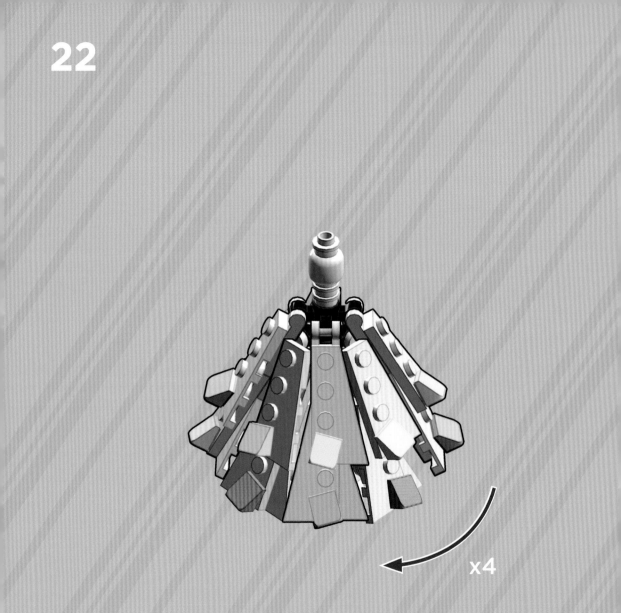

x4

23

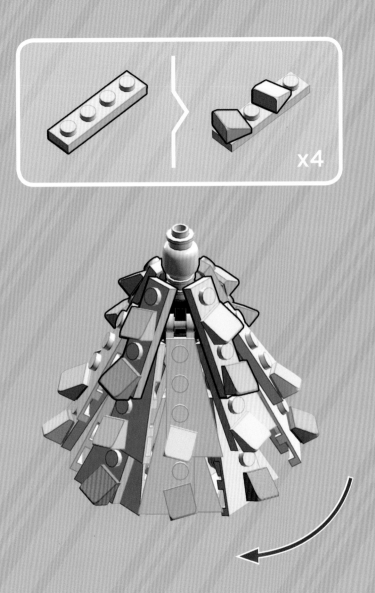

24

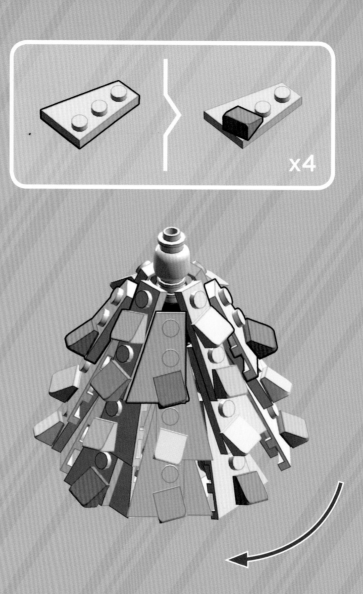

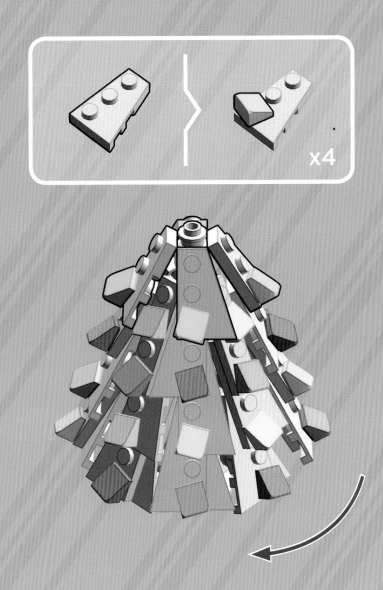

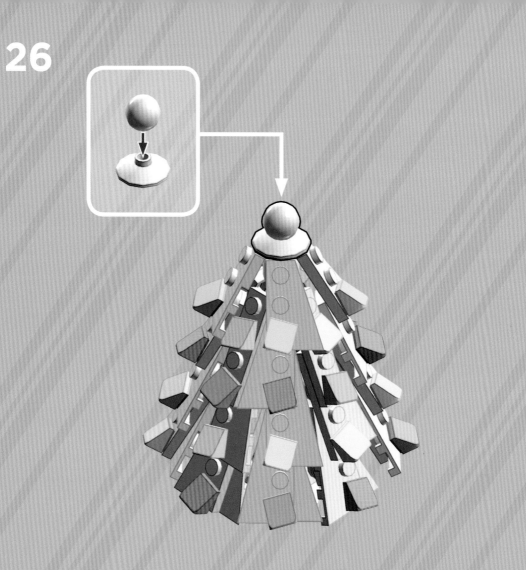

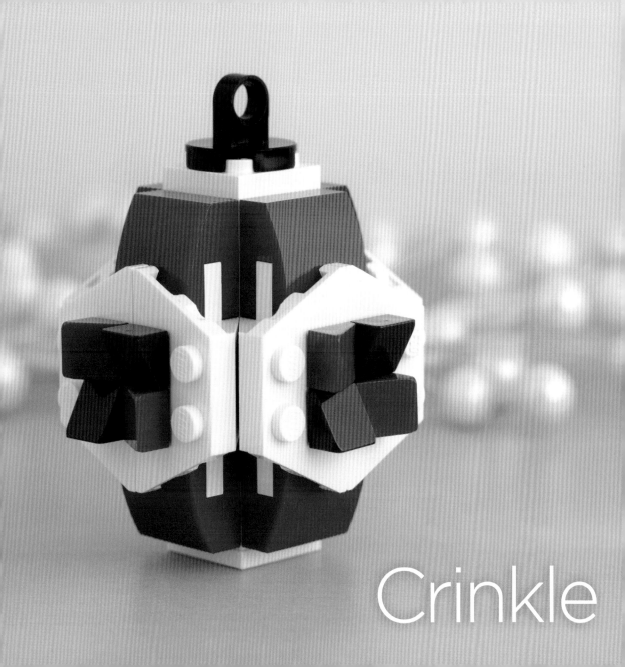

Crinkle

8X
4504379

8X
4531415

8X
6175968

1X
6010831

8X
6105976

2X
302201

12X
302221

3X
300301

8X
4249506

4X
302001

4X
4173943

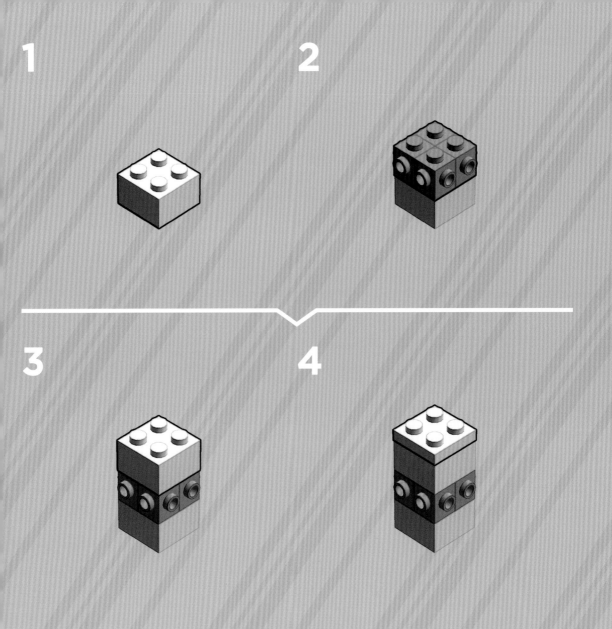

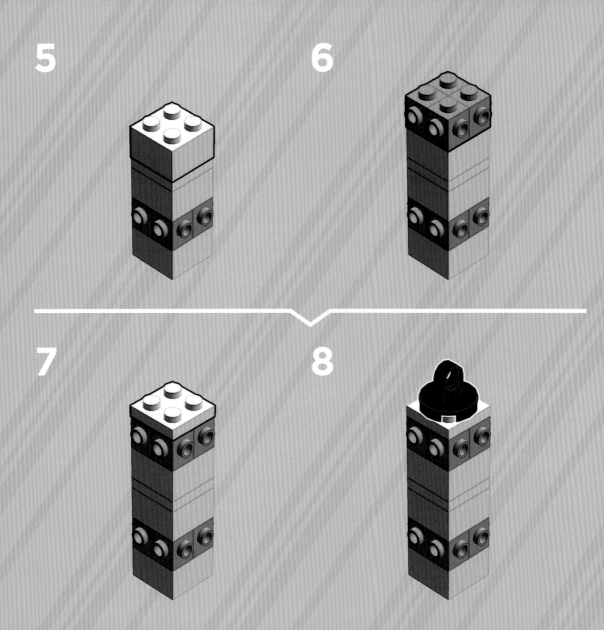

5

6

7

8

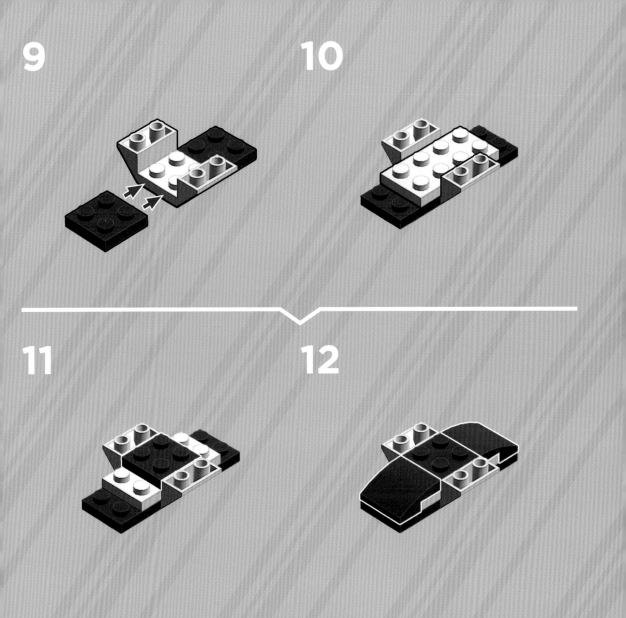

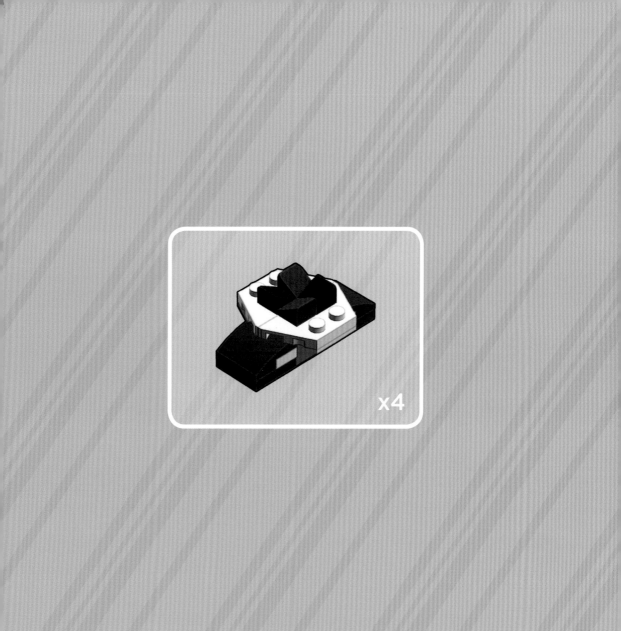

x4

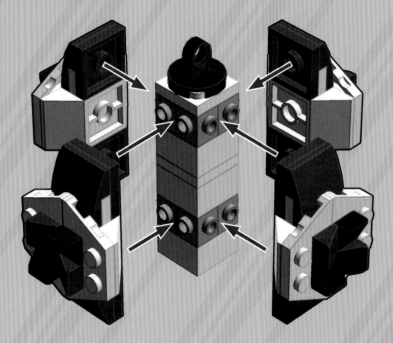

15

Chime

4X
6168642

2X
4211483

1X
4526981

8X
6097095

2X
4211475

2X
6003007

1X
6103444

2X
6116608

4X
4179580

2X
6058118

8X
4615649

4X
6037658

2X
4514791

2X
6109817

1

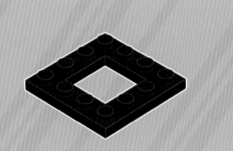

2

3

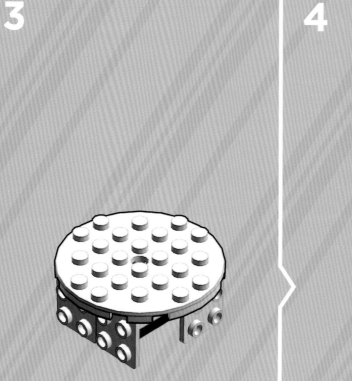

4

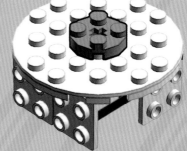

5

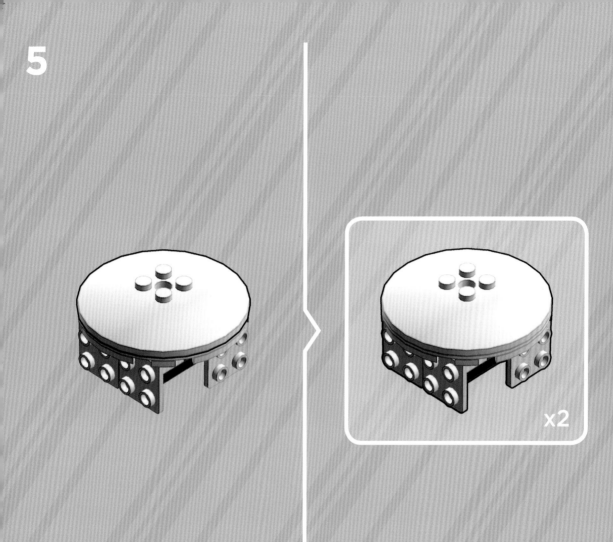

x2

6

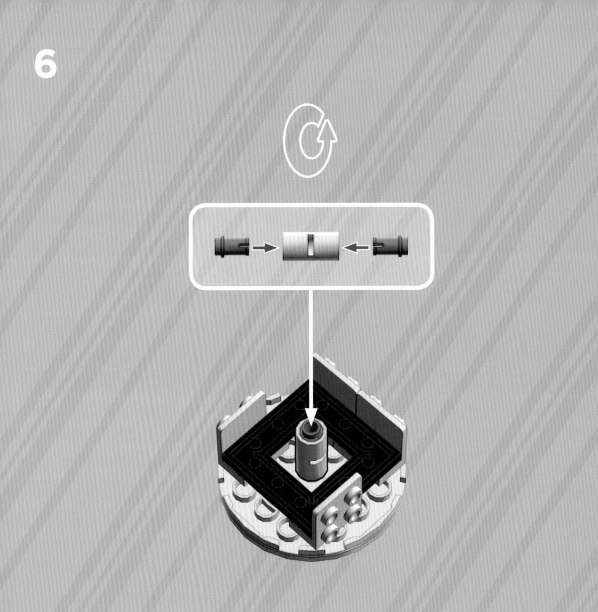

7

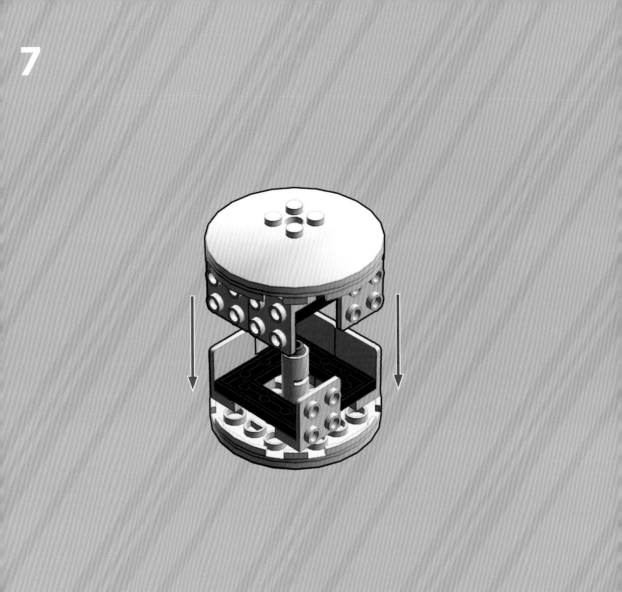

8

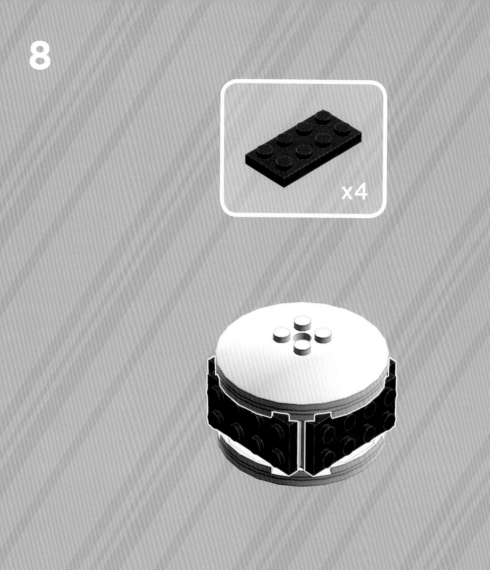

x4

9

x8

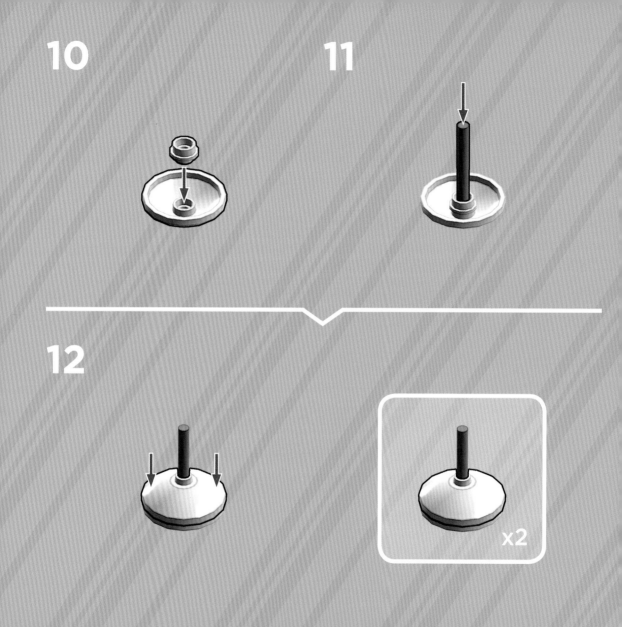

13

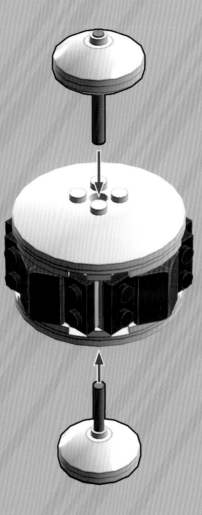

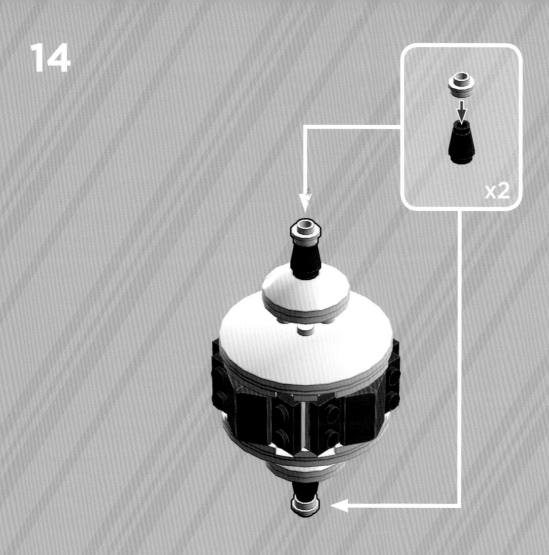

x2

15

Blizzard

24X
6172366

1X
4211622

12X
4518400

2X
403201

1X
6010831

2X
396001

4X
4502595

6X
6101858

1X
4211805

1

2

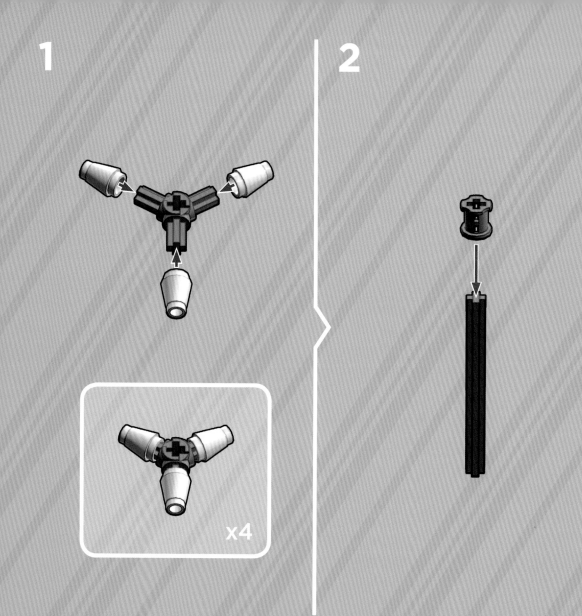

x4

3

4

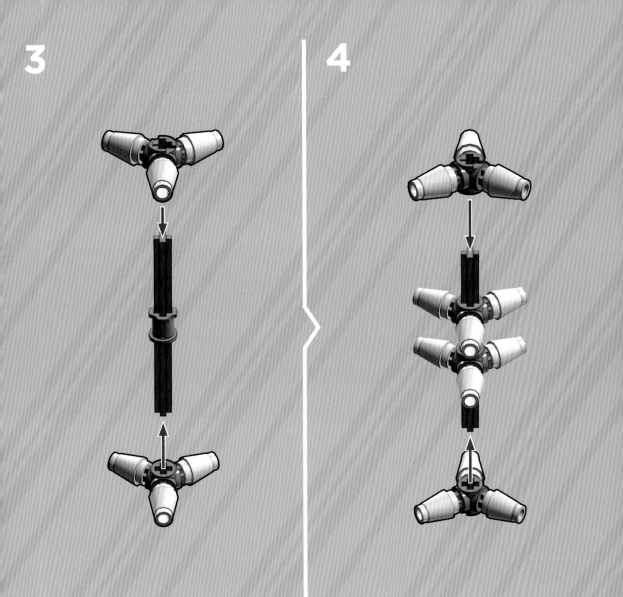

5

6

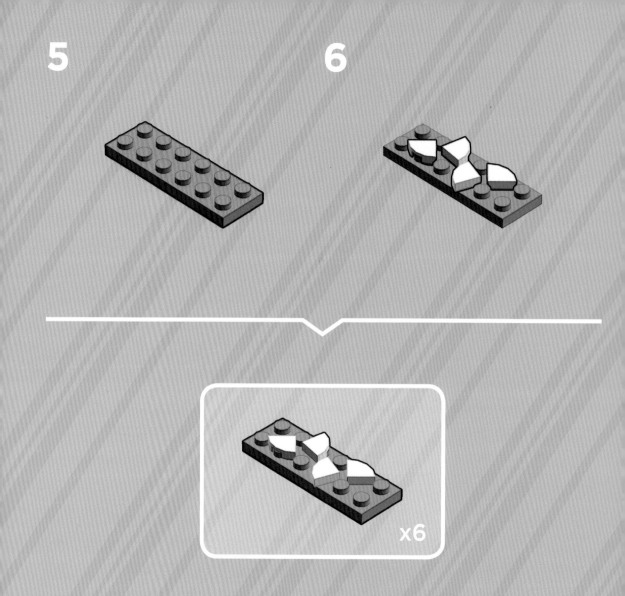

x6

7

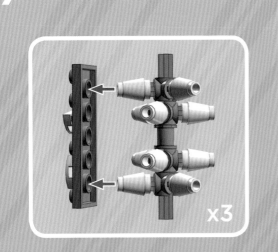

x3

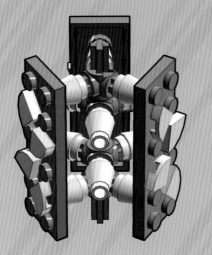

8

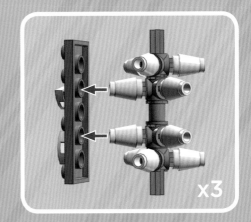

x3

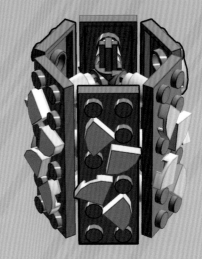

9

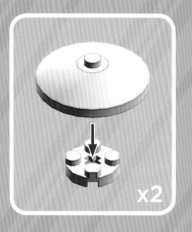

x2

10

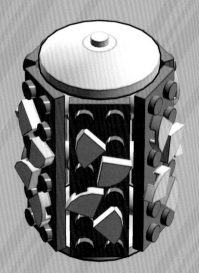

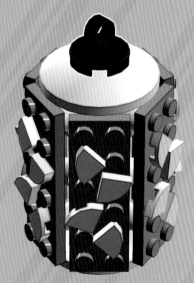

Pendant

2X
6168642

16X
6172366

4X
6164329

8X
6175968

1X
6103444

2X
6093053

2X
6245307

2X
4179580

8X
6133728

8X
6097093

2X
4514791

4X
302201

8X
6126046

4X
4658973

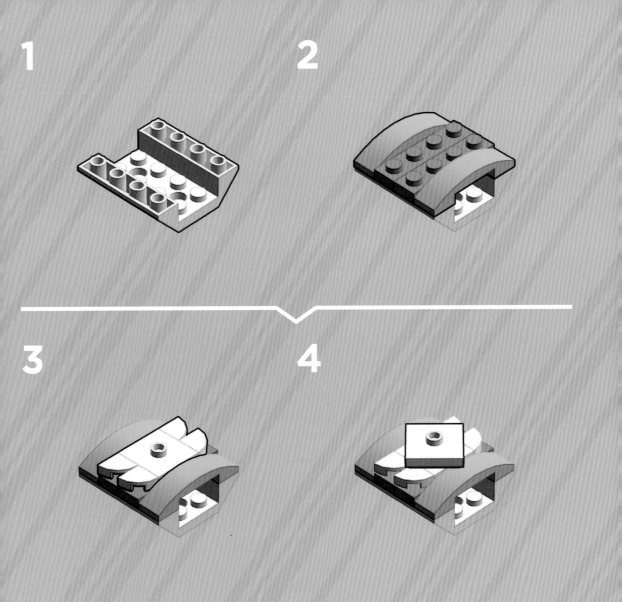

5

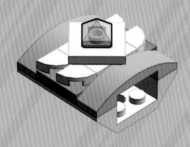

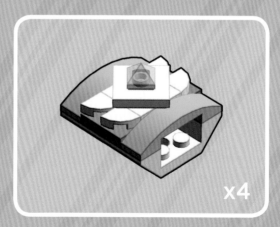

x4

6

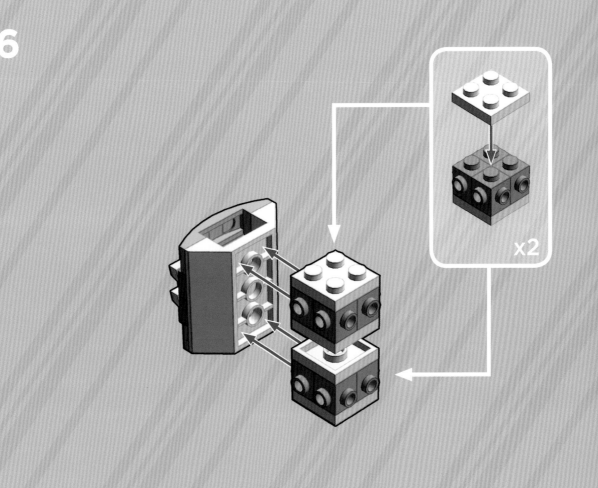

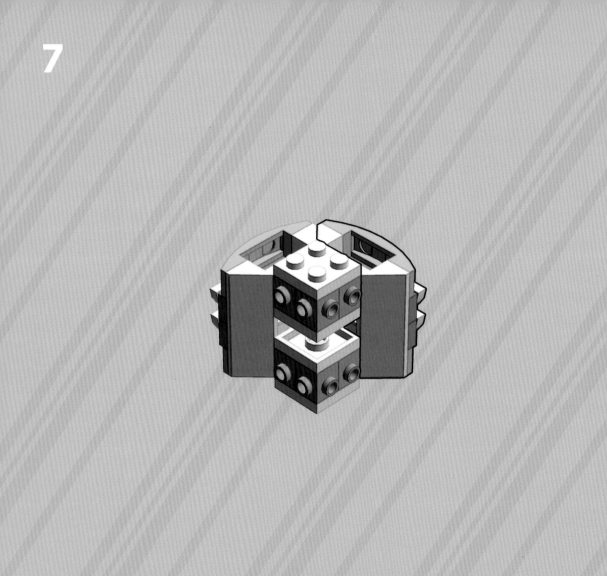

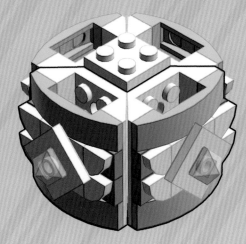

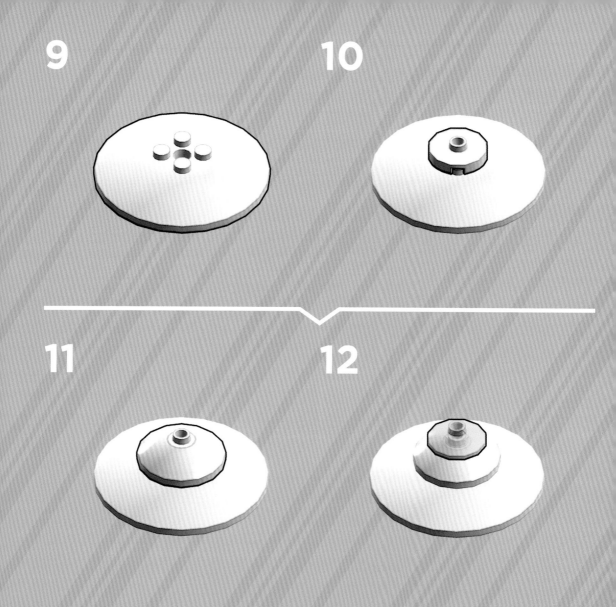

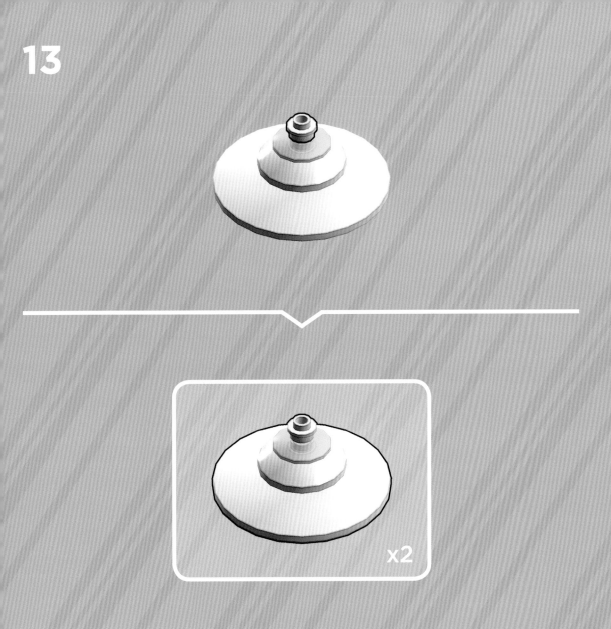

x2

14

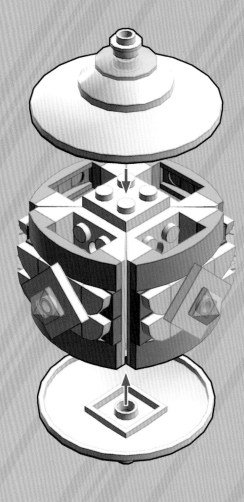

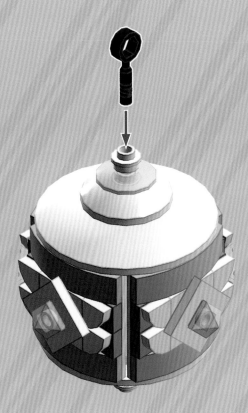

Swirl

1X
6168646

2X
4143005

2X
4206482

2X
4526981

2X
4649167

6X
6069006

6X
302301

6X
4164037

6X
4518992

6X
4537927

1X
6030875

6X
609101

12X
4212446

1X
4502595

1X
6116602

3X
4527839

3X
4243812

3X
4527947

1

2

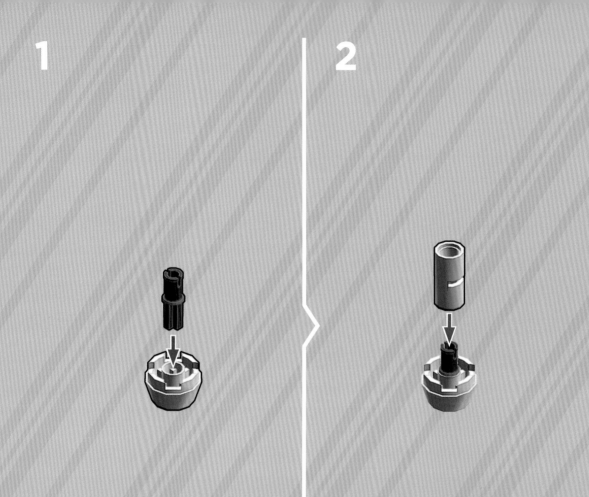

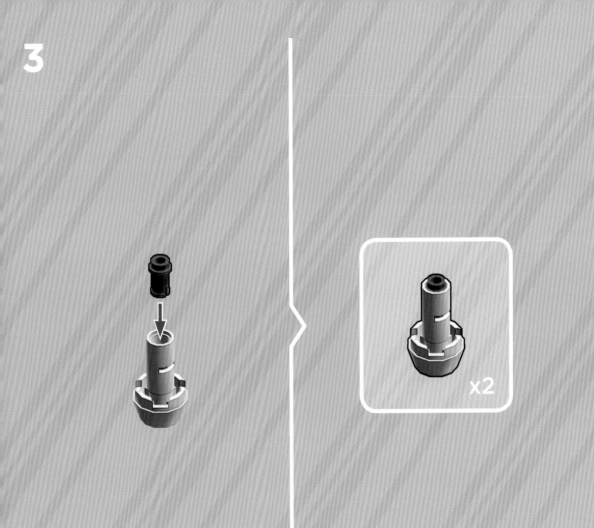

x2

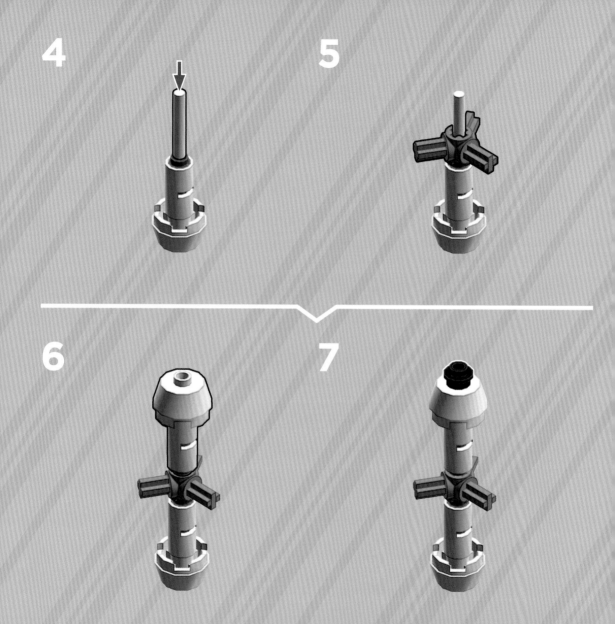

8

9

10

11

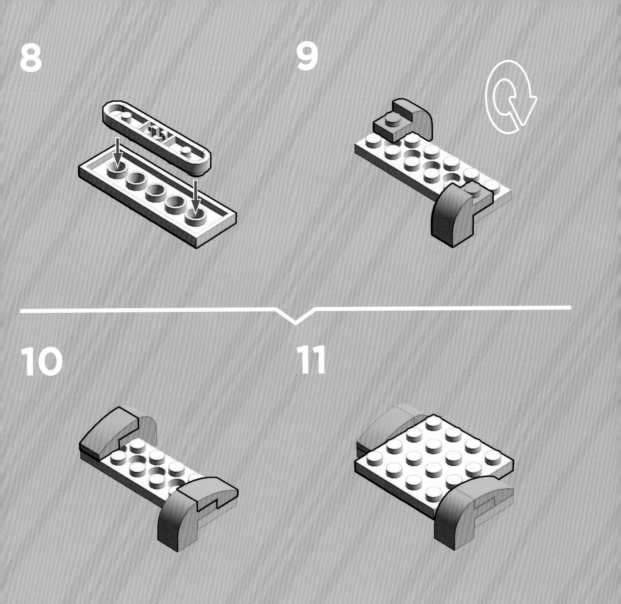

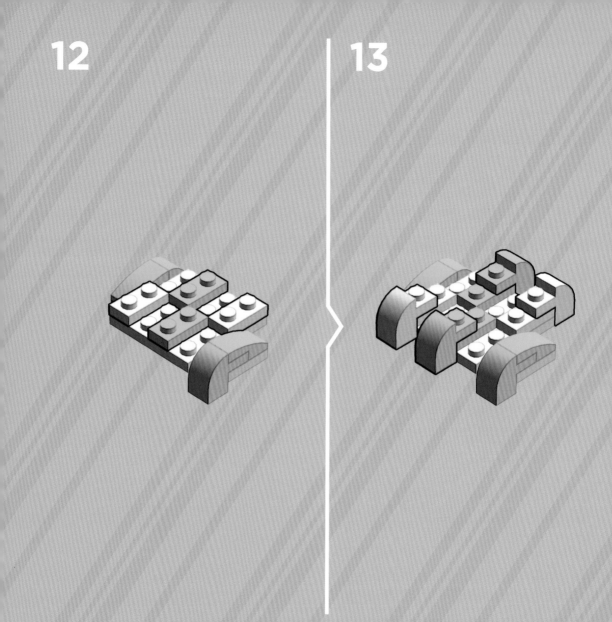

14

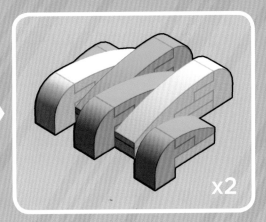

x2

15

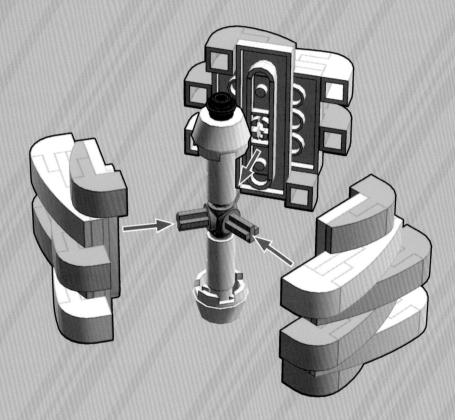

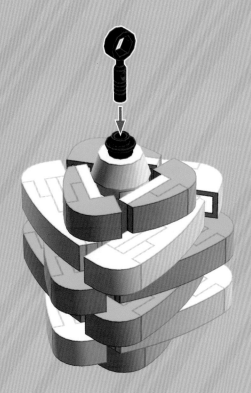

Twist

2X
6168642

2X
403201

8X
6058329

8X
4528778

1X
6030875

8X
6069257

8X
371001

4X
6100234

2X
370901

2X
6056297

4X
4515347

4X
4560179

8X
4633693

4X
366601

1X
4535768

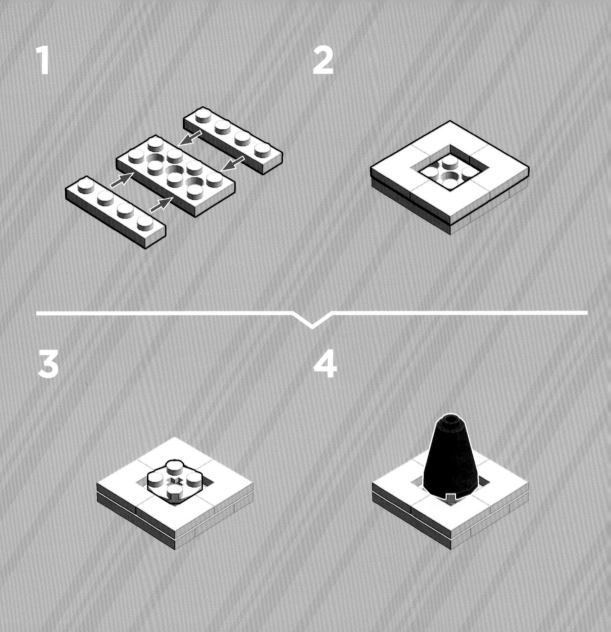

5

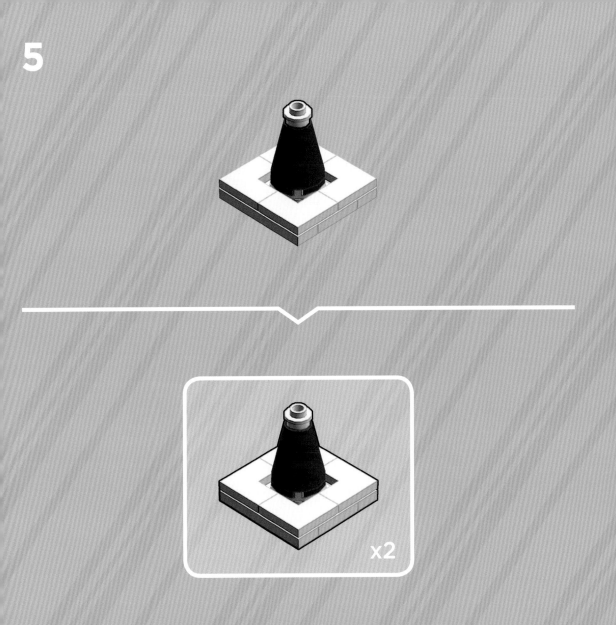

x2

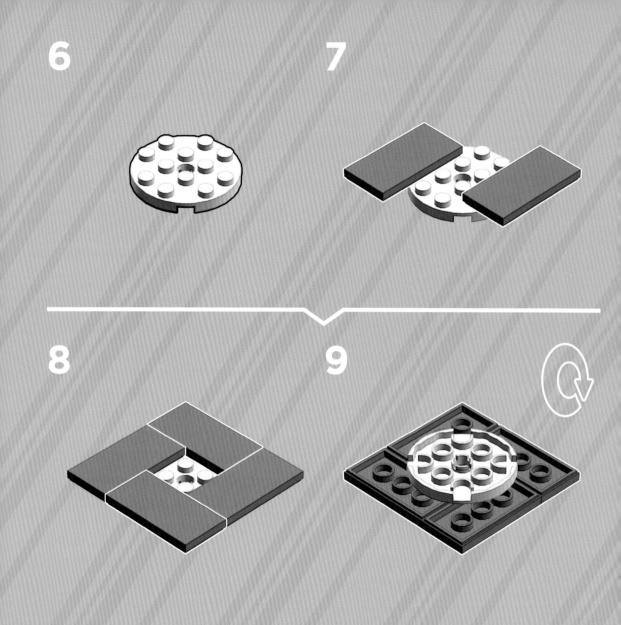

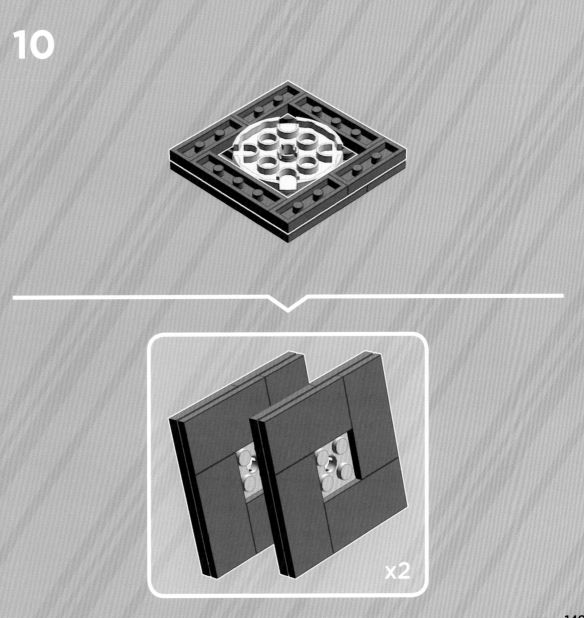

x2

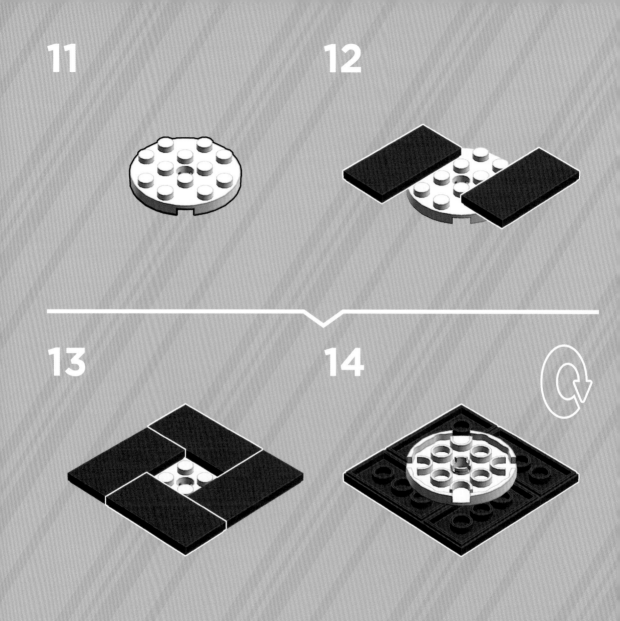

15

16

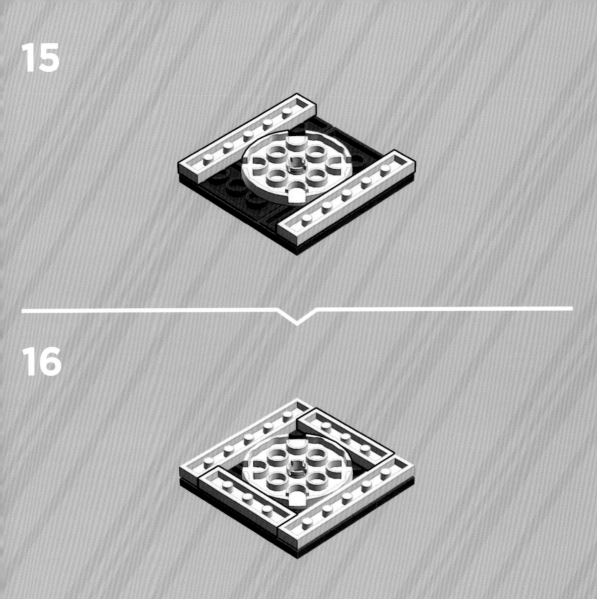

17

18

19

20

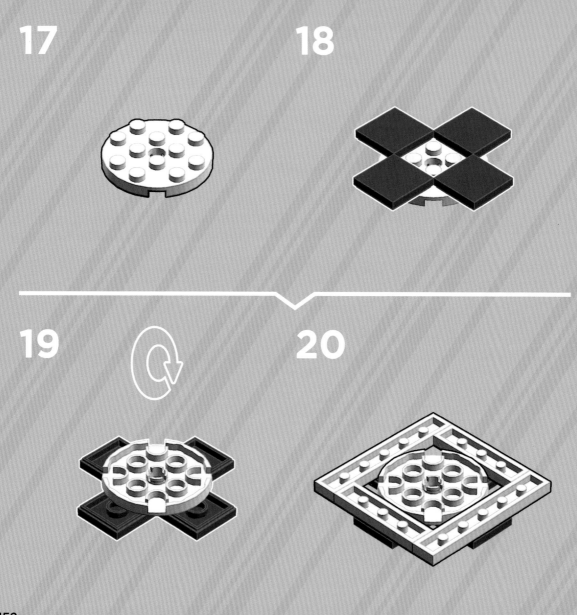

21

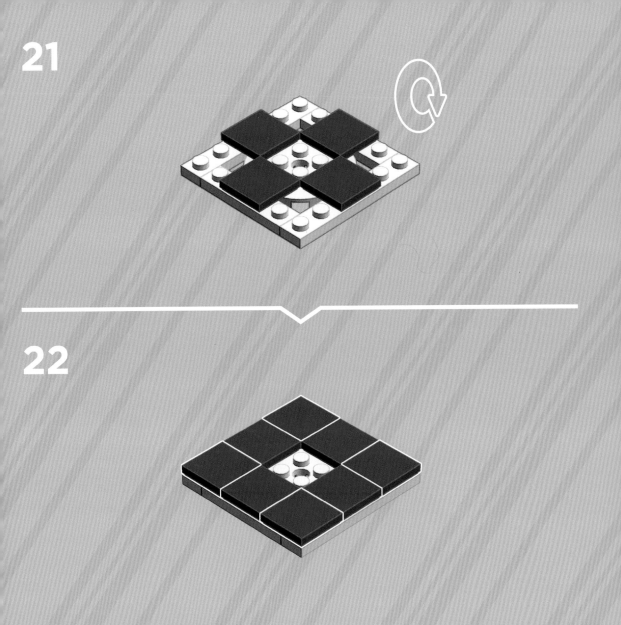

22

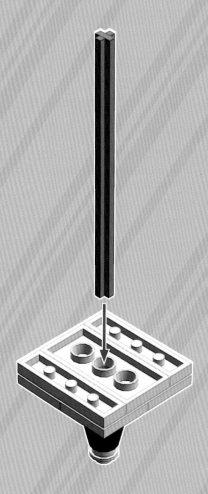

24

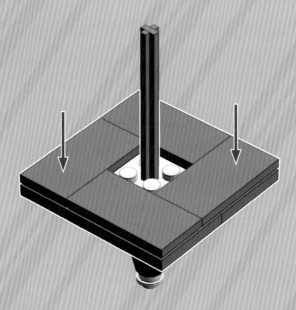

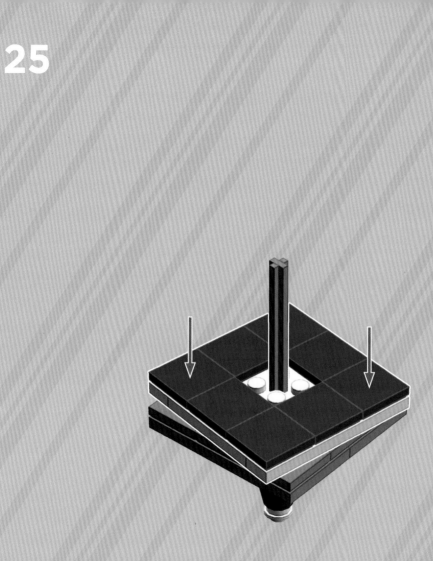

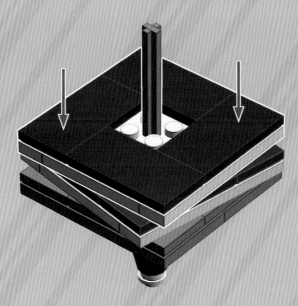

27

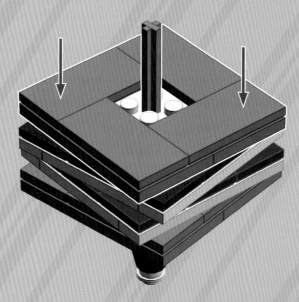

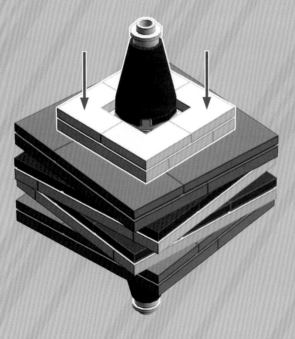

29

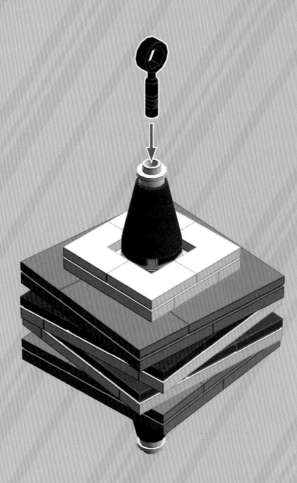

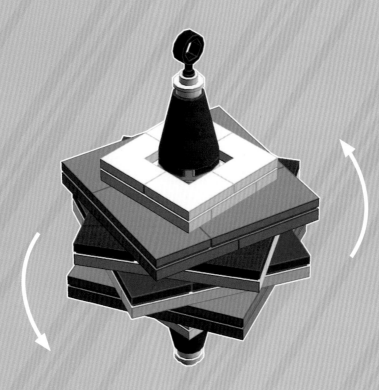

Crane Game

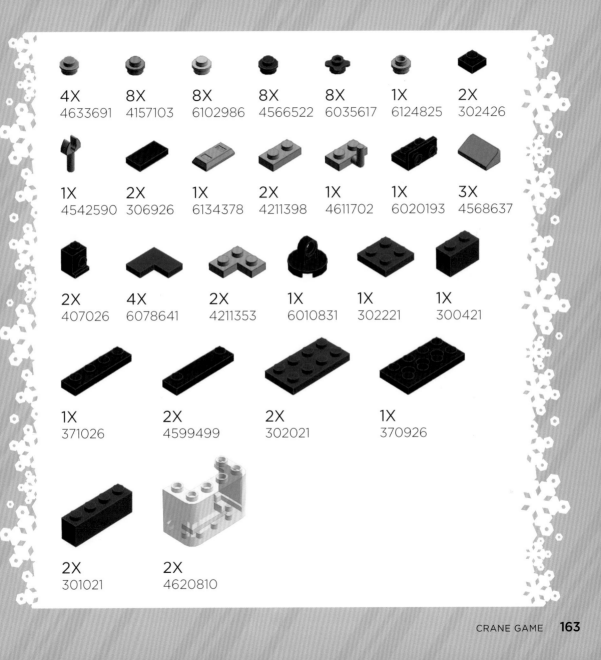

4X
4633691

8X
4157103

8X
6102986

8X
4566522

8X
6035617

1X
6124825

2X
302426

1X
4542590

2X
306926

1X
6134378

2X
4211398

1X
4611702

1X
6020193

3X
4568637

2X
407026

4X
6078641

2X
4211353

1X
6010831

1X
302221

1X
300421

1X
371026

2X
4599499

2X
302021

1X
370926

2X
301021

2X
4620810

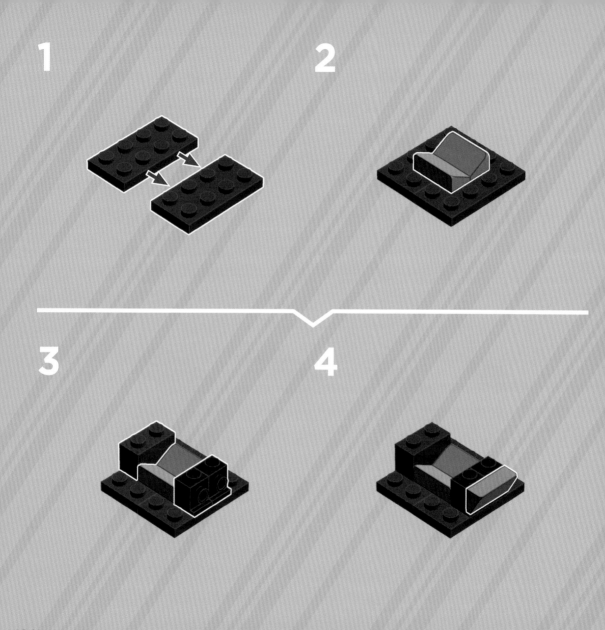

5

6

7

8

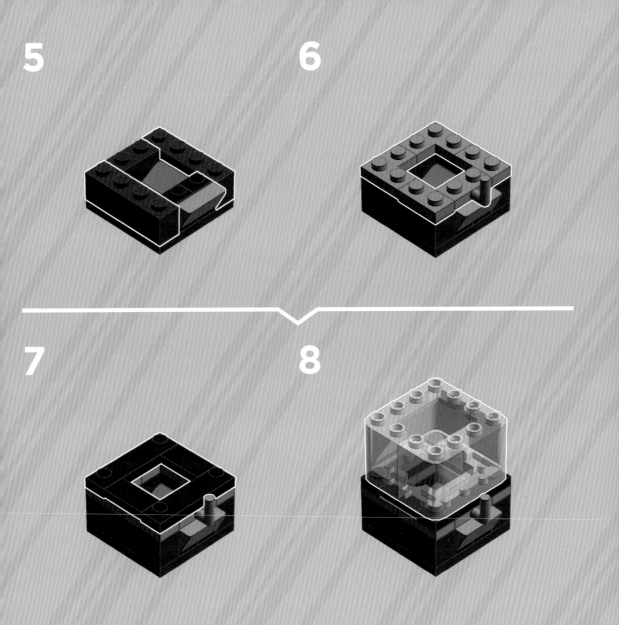

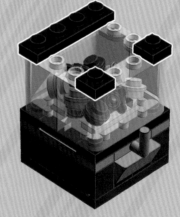

11

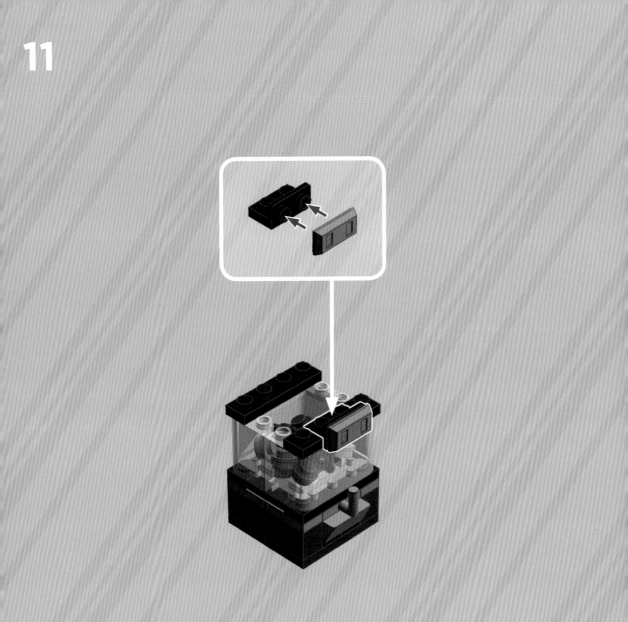

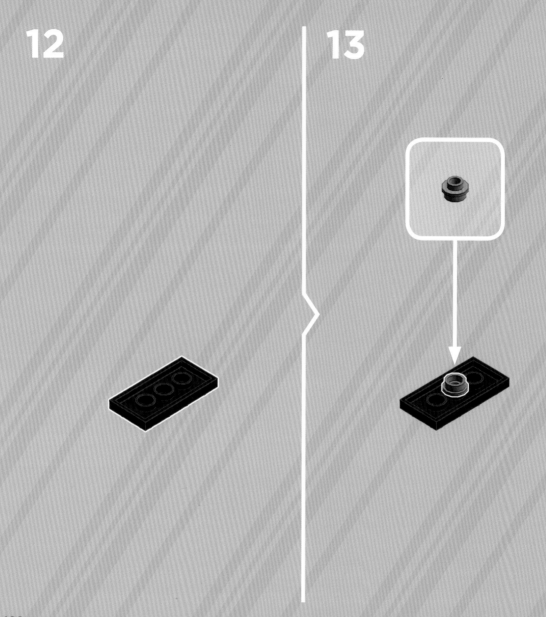

14

15

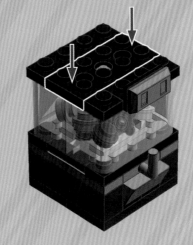

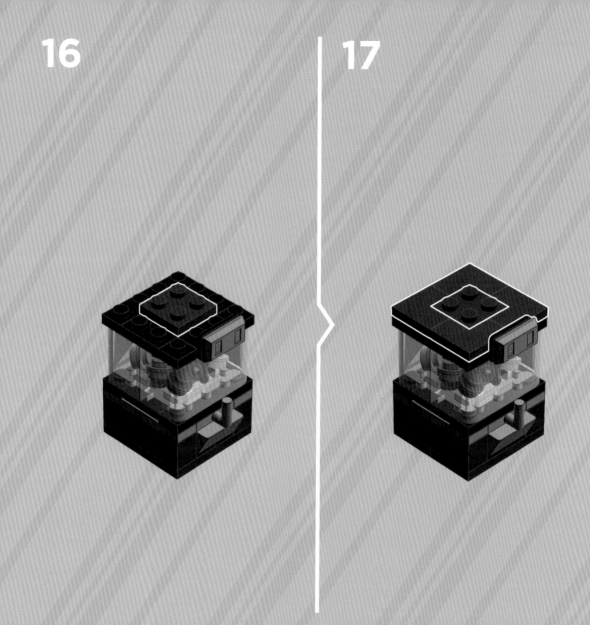

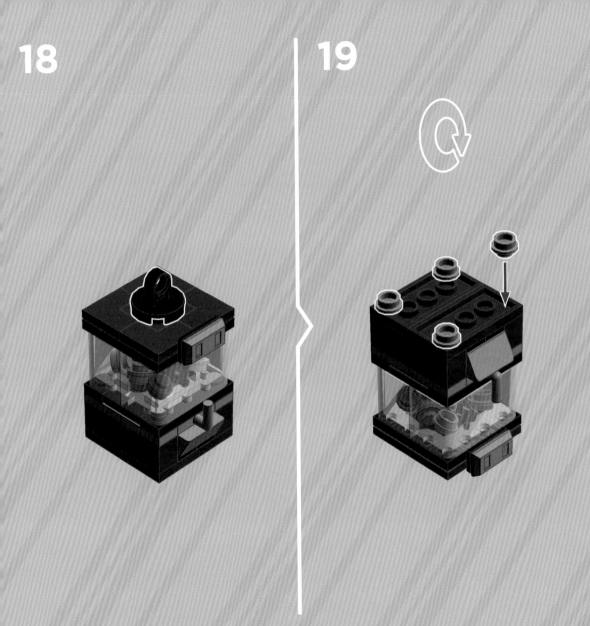

'90s PC

2X
6145570

1X
307001

2X
302401

2X
4159553

2X
4114026

3X
6092587

1X
6134378

2X
4211398

4X
4113917

2X
6070698

2X
4654582

2X
6144138

1X
6179186

1X
4211469

1X
6015344

1X
4655900

1X
4253815

2X
4273526

2X
242001

2X
4114077

1X
4185177

1X
4565387

5X
4114084

4X
4624088

3X
4211881

4X
4654577

1X
4114306

2X
6048857

2X
6131896

2X
362301

1X
6089696

1X
6132423

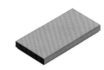

2X
6014615

2X
4211445

3X
4113233

1X
4550324

1X
243101

6X
6122047

1X
4666611

3X
6133057

1X
4243831

1X
4157277

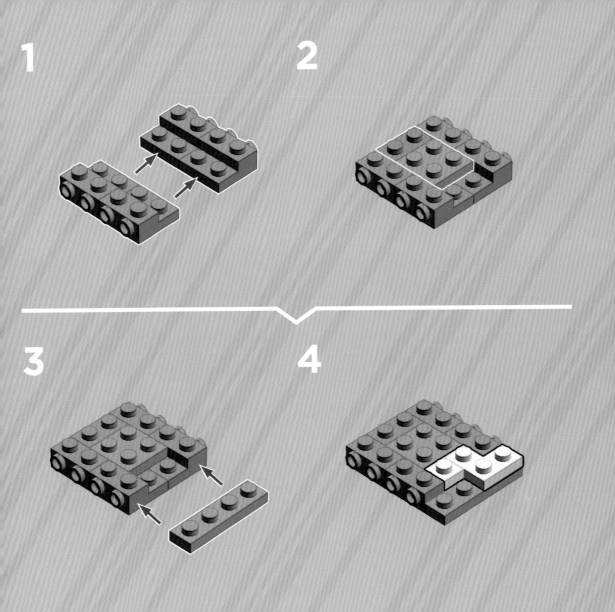

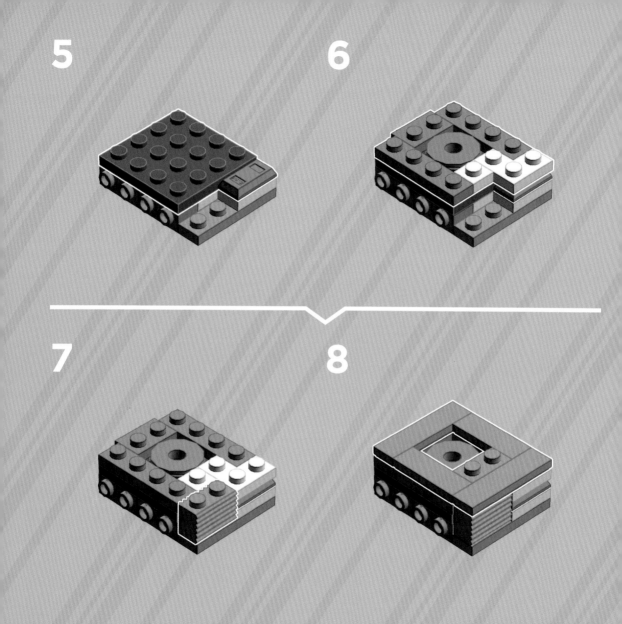

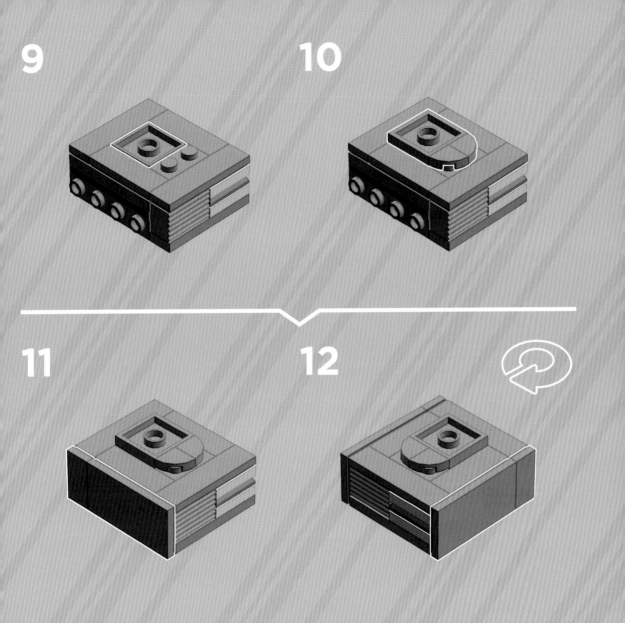

13

14

15

16

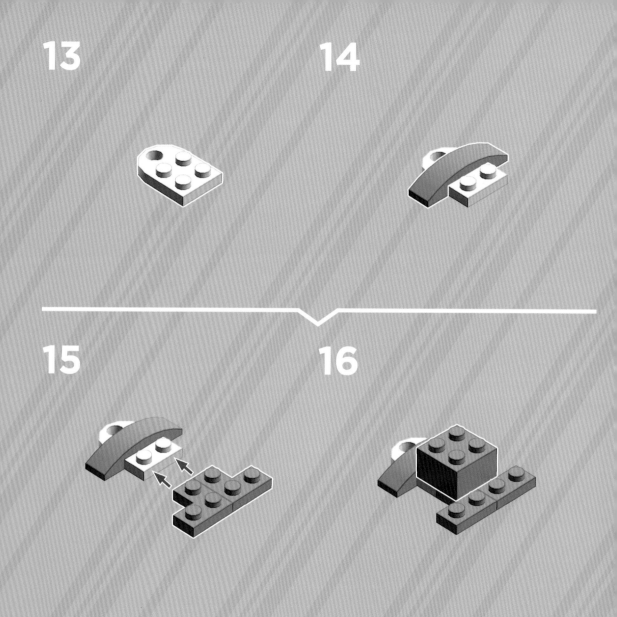

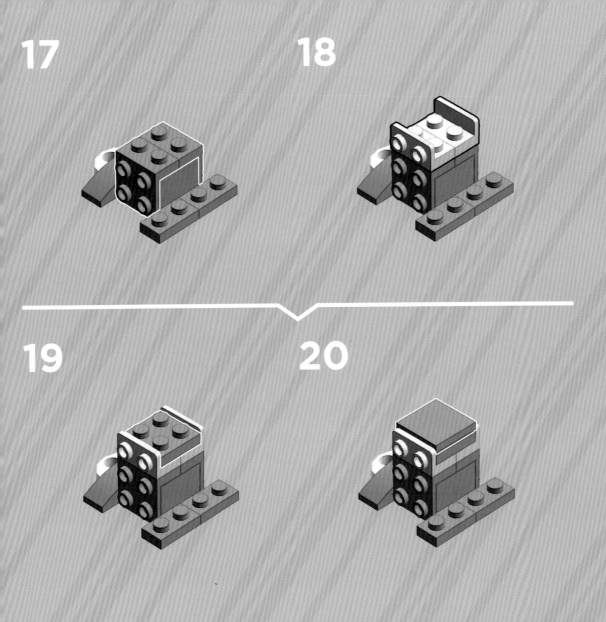

21

22

23

24

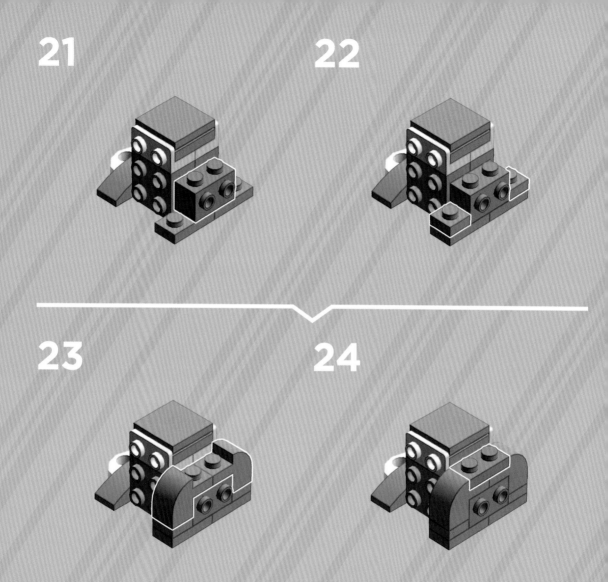

25

26

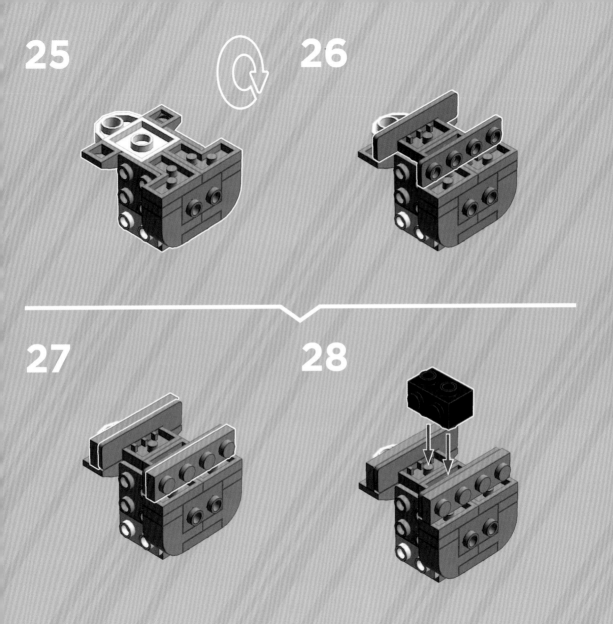

27

28

29

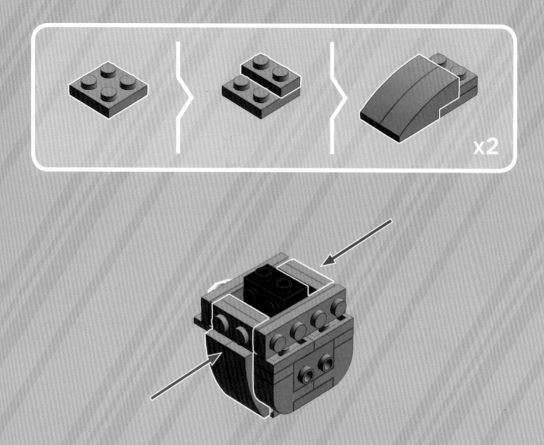

x2

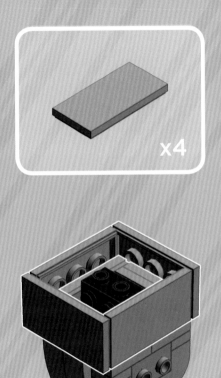

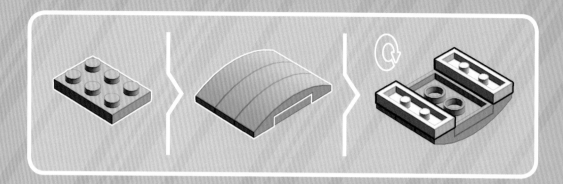

32

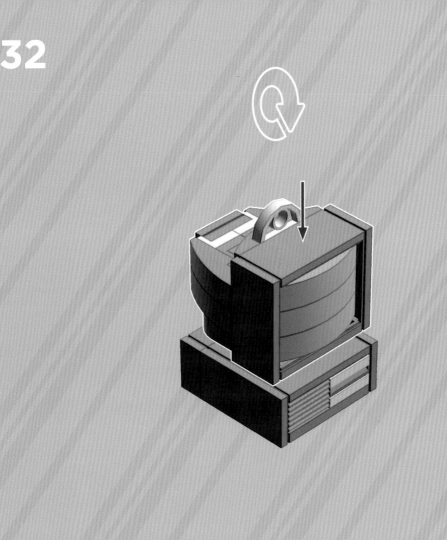

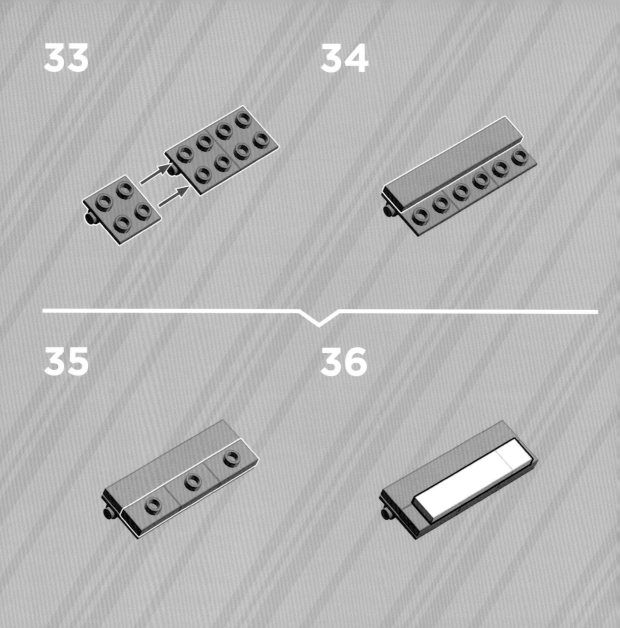

33 **34**

35 **36**

37

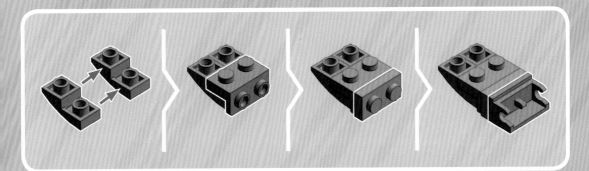

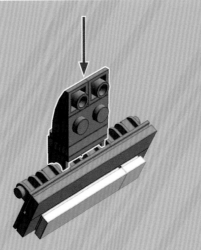

Fries

4X
6172366

5X
4216581

3X
307024

1X
302424

2X
4159553

2X
4540203

4X
6078641

2X
4211469

2X
4612342

2X
6058177

3X
243124

1X
243121

4X
371024

2X
4113233

2X
6141553

2X
6141552

2X
4160866

2X
4161329

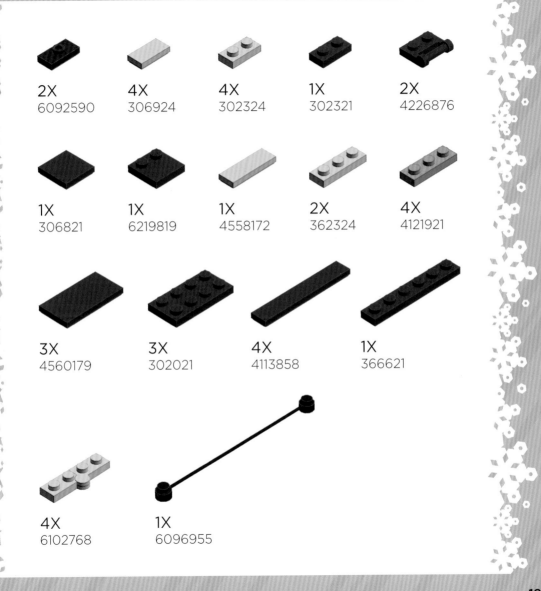

2X
6092590

4X
306924

4X
302324

1X
302321

2X
4226876

1X
306821

1X
6219819

1X
4558172

2X
362324

4X
4121921

3X
4560179

3X
302021

4X
4113858

1X
366621

4X
6102768

1X
6096955

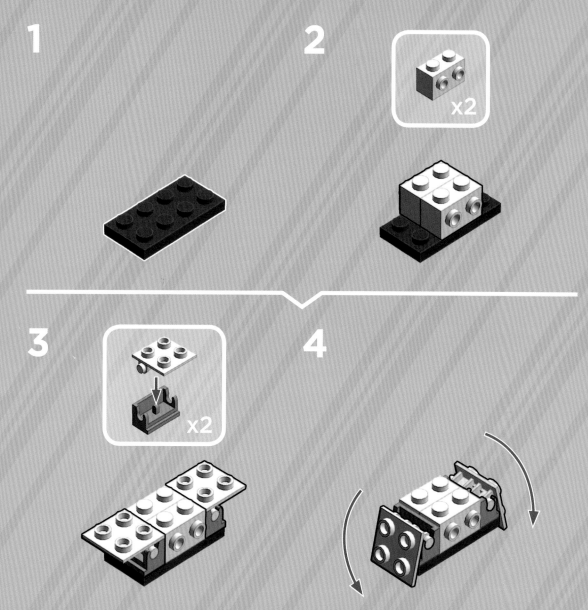

5

6

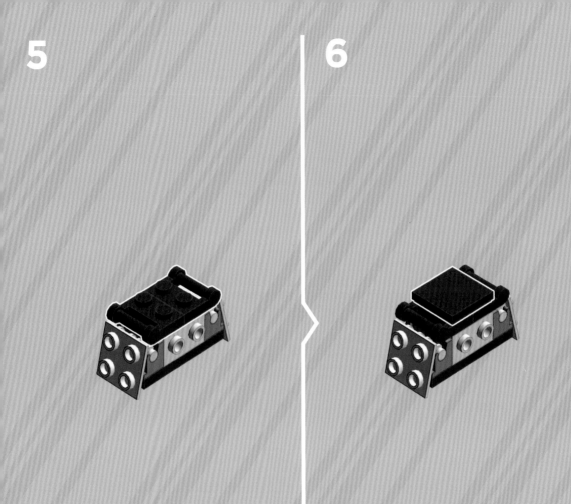

7

8

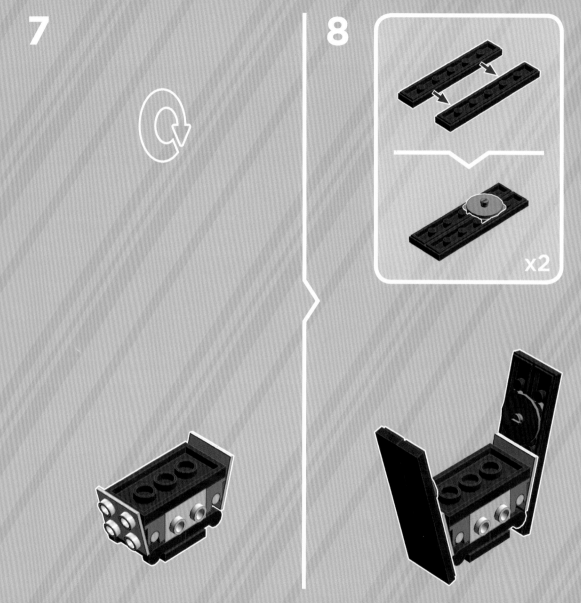

x2

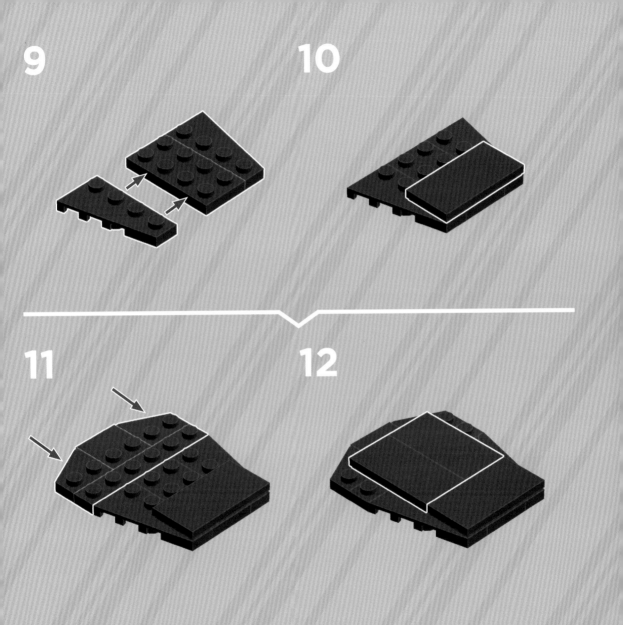

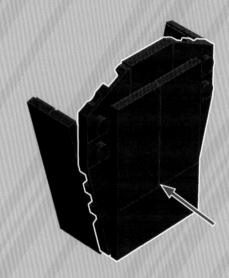

14

15

16

17

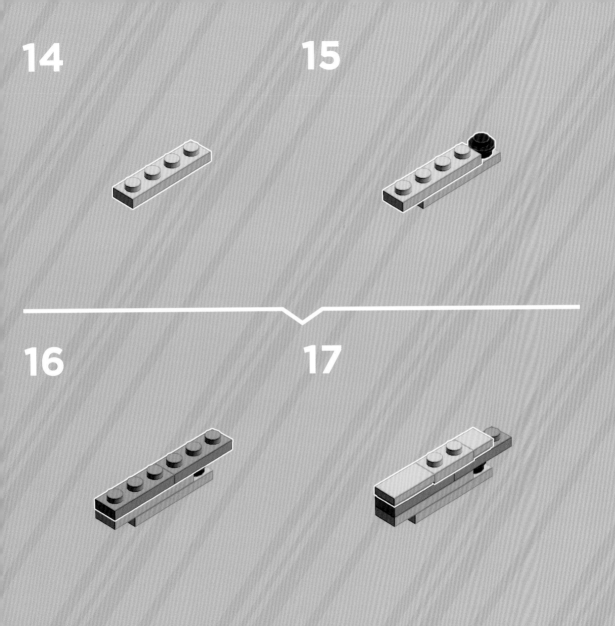

18

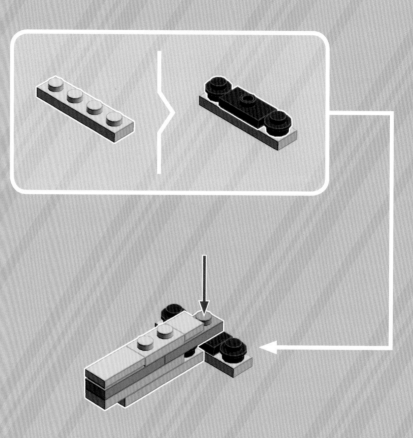

19 **20**

21 **22**

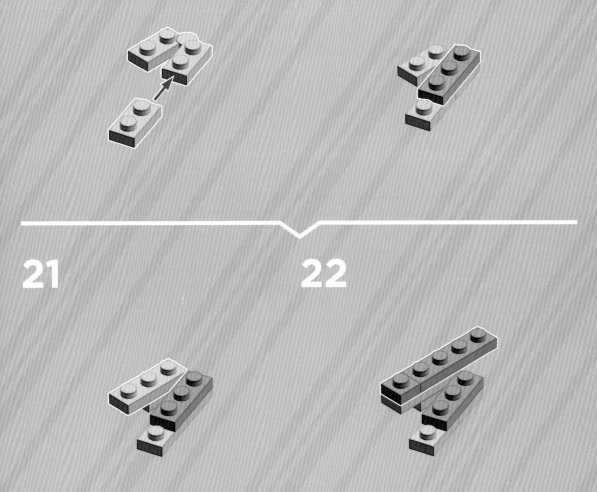

23

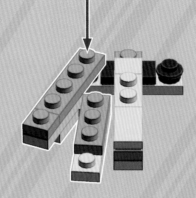

24

25

26

27

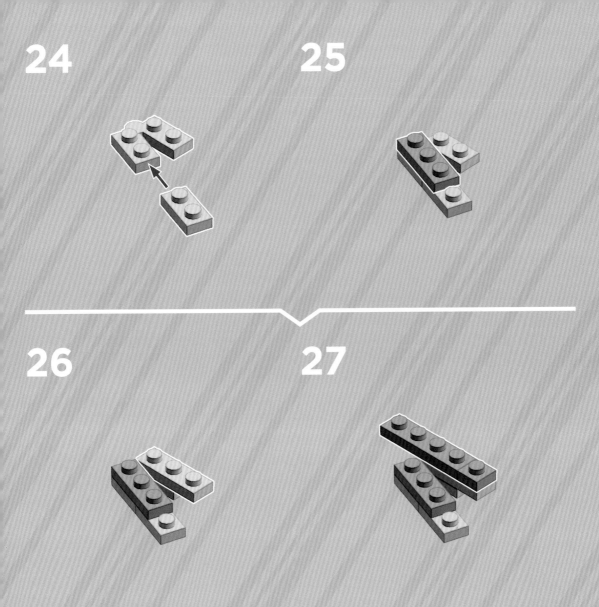

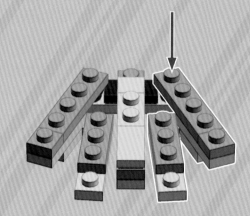

29

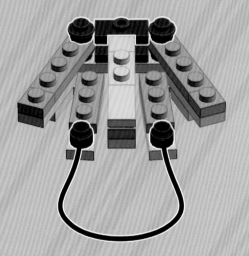

30

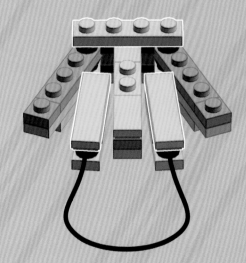

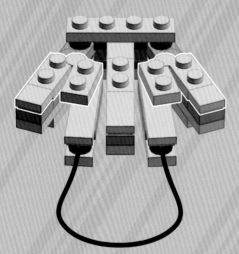

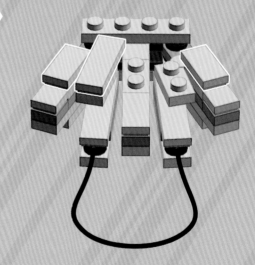

33

34

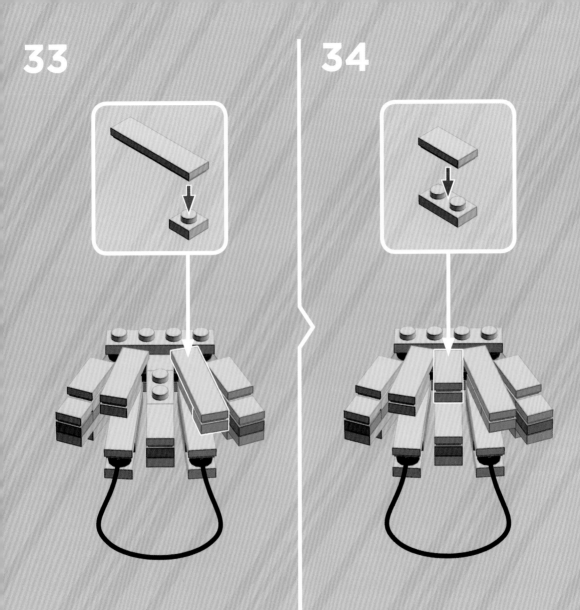

35

36

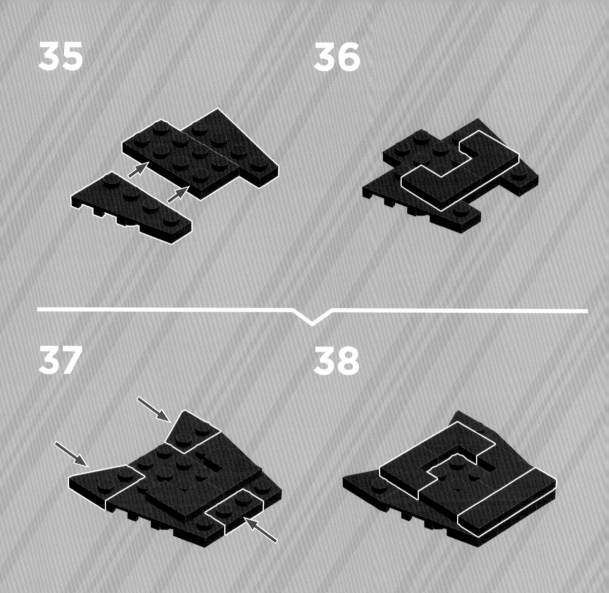

37

38

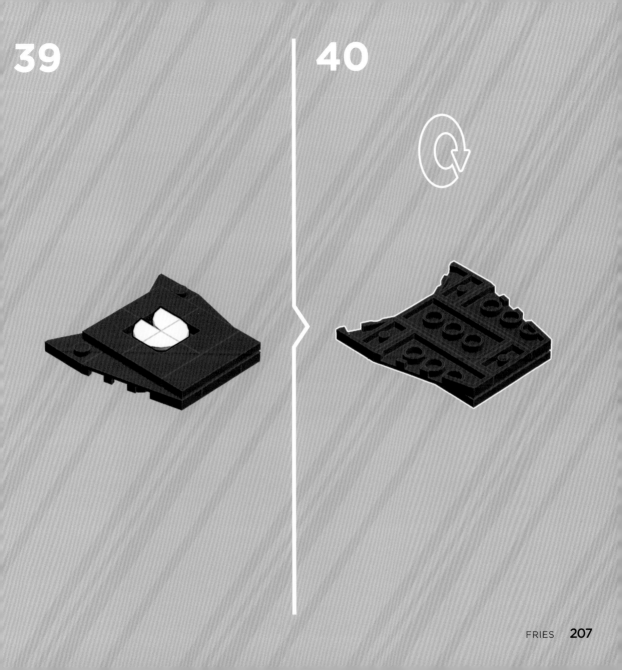

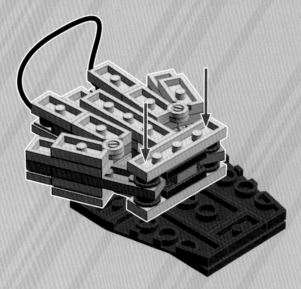

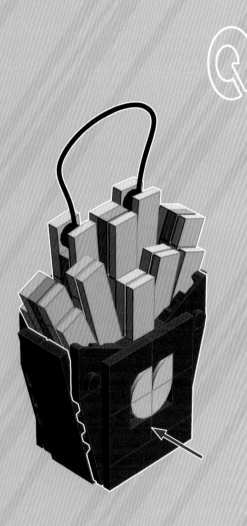